from
Plagues
to
Miracles

from Plagues to Miracles

The Transformational Journey of Exodus, from the Slavery of Ego to the Promised Land of Spirit

ROBERT ROSENTHAL, M.D.

HAY HOUSE, INC.

Carlsbad, California • New York City
London • Sydney • Johannesburg
Vancouver • Hong Kong • New Delhi

Published and distributed in the United States by: Hay House, Inc.

Project editor: Patrick Gabrysiak
Cover & interior design: Tricia Breidenthal

ISBN: 978-1-4019-3130-8

Printed in the United States of America

FOR BILL THETFORD, PH.D.,
WHO ALWAYS SAID I'D
WRITE A BOOK ONE DAY.

AND FOR AL ROSENTHAL, M.D.,
MY FATHER, WHO SADLY DID NOT
LIVE TO SEE THIS BOOK COMPLETED.

Contents

————— •◆• —————

Preface

The Exodus Journey

---•◦•---

The idea that life is a journey is an old and familiar one. Just as the sun travels its course across the sky from dawn to dusk, so do we set out at birth upon an unknown road, following its twists and turns through childhood and adolescence, adulthood and old age, until at last death steps forth, calling an end to our adventure. The sun's path is unswerving, its purpose and destination never in doubt. Not so with the journey we make.

For within life's journey, there are many side trips that call to us. We travel down byways of relationship, career, and family. We eagerly explore those trails that promise happiness and success. We seek the fair maiden, the handsome prince, the dragon to be slain, the pot of gold at the rainbow's end. We pursue our own versions of Ahab's white whale, Kurtz in the jungle's heart of darkness, and Shangri-La.

Behind all these journeys, however, there lies another, more fundamental journey, one that enfolds all the others in its scope and purpose. This is the spiritual journey—to discover, and to recover, our innate spiritual essence and the absolute freedom that comes with it. The spiritual journey is by its nature transformational, for it takes us from a limited, ego-bound sense of who we are and how we fit into the world to the recognition of our true Self: timeless, boundless, and extending well beyond the realm of the five senses.

Somewhere along life's path, this spiritual journey awaits each of us. We undertake it in our own unique way, in our own time, and at our own pace. I have been both traveler and guide on this journey. As traveler, many's the time I've found myself stumbling, lost, uncertain of my progress, or even of the destination itself. Am I headed in the right direction? Are the landmarks along the route—the people and events that show up in my life—true and trustworthy? Or are they false decoys bound to lead me astray? Am I moving forward, or traveling in circles? And how will I know for sure when I've finally reached my destination?

The spiritual journey is arduous enough as it is. If we lose our way chasing after diversions, it becomes almost impossible. So how do we stay on track? How do we keep our bearings? If only there were a map of some kind to pinpoint our location and steer us through this unfamiliar terrain. Such a map would indicate the stage of the journey that we're currently passing through, as well as what's necessary to successfully navigate it. It would also warn us of what obstacles lie ahead, in the next stage, so we can be prepared to meet them.

There are, of course, many road maps available to the spiritual seeker, some helpful, none perfect. Some come from esoteric religious traditions that are closed off to the average aspirant. Others are rooted in Buddhist or Hindu concepts that can be hard for the Western mind to grasp. But there is one map that's grounded in the Judeo-Christian heritage: the book of Exodus from the Hebrew Bible. In fact, it's so well-known that few people ever recognize it for what it is. Yet read and understood correctly, Exodus turns out to be a profound guide to the spiritual journey. It marks the path out of bondage. It makes clear what we must do to reach God directly. And it demonstrates by example those patterns of thought and behavior that stand in the way of transformation and detour us into years of fruitless wandering.

Exodus tells the tale of the Hebrews' escape from slavery in Egypt. It chronicles their transition from a people suffering without hope and seemingly cut off from God to a free people led by God Himself in a very direct and personal way through his representative, Moses. Over the centuries, Exodus has inspired many renowned seekers of freedom, including Benjamin Franklin, Thomas Jefferson, and Dr. Martin Luther King, Jr. This alone would make it one of the greatest teaching tales of all time. But as we shall see, there is more to Exodus . . . much more.

❧

I am neither a biblical scholar nor a clergyman. I am a psychiatrist—a psychotherapist—and my knowledge of scripture is limited. But when I come upon an extraordinary tale (such as Exodus)—whether from a patient's lips or the pages of a book—I am trained to seek out its deeper layers of meaning. I can't help myself. I need to delve beneath the words, to find and grasp the story's essence. What is it that makes this particular story so meaningful? How does it speak to us? Well, when I read Exodus in this way, what I find there is a handbook for transformational change.

What do I mean by transformational change? Any change that completely alters our sense of self and our place in the universe. We emerge truly a different person. To others we may look the same, but something fundamental within us has shifted. The familiar old worries and preoccupations, the desires and hopes that once held us captive and that still grip those around us, no longer apply. It's as though we've been reborn into a new world . . . and there's no going back. Not that we would ever want to.

In my psychotherapy practice, I've been privileged to help many people make such changes. They've come to me enslaved by their own personal versions of Pharaoh and Egypt. They've suffered plagues aplenty and run smack up against impossible obstacles like the Red Sea. They've wandered lost in the wilderness, confused and unable to find their way. Some have experienced miracles. In a few instances, they've made it to the Promised Land or something akin to it—a state of mind so transformed from where they started that they truly are a different person. The issue with which they once struggled is no more. It's gone, as if it had never existed.

Their journeys have begun in all manner of bondage: horrific childhood abuse; irrational anxiety and paralyzing phobias; depressions that descend like suffocating clouds to blot out all light and hope; abusive relationships with seemingly no way out;

crippling fears about money and survival; and tyrannical, all-consuming addictions to alcohol, drugs, sex, and spending.

These individuals are not "crazy." They are your sister, your father-in-law, your co-worker, the bank teller, the pizza-delivery girl. Their fears are really no different than yours or mine, except that these individuals reached the point where they had no choice but to turn and face them. To go on living, such fears must be faced.

I will share their journeys in the pages ahead to illustrate the larger journey that Exodus portrays, the one we must all eventually make: escaping from the limited, fear-bound ego-mind and reclaiming our true, expansive, spiritual nature. This is the ultimate transformational journey, the one to which all the others are leading. It's the only journey worth the effort, because it's the only one truly capable of fulfilling us.

Not all of us, however, are ready or even interested in making such a journey. We're less concerned with reaching the Promised Land than with paying the bills, getting along with our partners, raising our kids to be decent human beings, and in general contending with all of the stress and anxiety that go with life in the 21st century. Exodus speaks to these concerns as well, because growth in *any* area of our lives that's truly transformational—that takes us from bondage to freedom—will follow the pattern set forth in Exodus.

Furthermore, if you genuinely and meaningfully change any one area of your life, then you've changed everything. Extricate yourself from a thankless relationship or a punishing job . . . and your life will change. Quit drinking, smoking, or overeating . . . and your sense of self will change. The people with whom you associate will change. The way others see you and respond to you will change. So even though we may not think of ourselves as spiritual seekers en route to the Promised Land, the simple fact that we want to be freer, happier, and more fulfilled sets our feet upon that path.

The journey is never straightforward, however. We encounter obstacles. We find ways to overcome them. We celebrate breakthroughs. We feel like we're almost there, almost where we want to be—only to discover that we've barely begun. Like the lines at the most popular rides at Disney World, we advance slowly, thinking we're finally getting close, just around the corner . . . only to discover that we're at the back of another very long line. These stretches of hardship wear us down until we start to feel that we'll never make it, that it's just too difficult. Our wounds go too deep. And then—surprise! An old conflict comes up to ambush us, only this time it doesn't really, at least not like it used to. We shake it off, because the truth is, we've transformed. And we keep on walking.

Wherever you find yourself in life, whatever challenges you may be facing, the transformational journey of Moses and the Hebrews is your journey, too. The path to freedom calls out. Why wait? And what better time to begin than now?

Introduction

The Parable of Exodus

———•◦•———

*"[It is] our obligation to tell the story of the
Exodus from Egypt. Moreover, whoever searches
deeply into its meaning is considered praiseworthy."*[1]

— A Passover Haggadah

The story of Exodus has been preserved and handed down for nearly 3,000 years. Not very many stories can make that claim. Whether or not we accept its historical accuracy, this must be a remarkable tale indeed to survive for so long across so many different eras. It must speak to us in some very powerful ways. It must address the human condition in a manner so fundamental that it rings true for people of all different backgrounds down through the ages.

In the New Testament, much of the wisdom taught by Jesus comes in the form of parables—tales that appear rather simple and straightforward on the surface, but which, when explored more deeply, open up to reveal profound spiritual insights. The beauty of the parable as a teaching device is that it engages us at our current level of understanding, yet beckons us to go deeper. It doesn't offer pat answers and easy explanations. It tickles our curiosity. It entices us to think and then think some more about the story we've just heard. In this way, parables encourage us to become seekers of a deeper, hidden truth.

I believe that the story of Exodus is a parable on a grand scale. Therefore, whether you're barely familiar with the book of Exodus or can cite it chapter and verse, it will prove well worth your while to revisit Moses, Pharaoh, and the Hebrews and live their journey again. Exodus holds secret wisdom that can be yours. It can transform you at the deepest levels of your being—if you understand how and where to look.

The Parable of Exodus

In Dan Brown's best-selling novel *The Lost Symbol,* one of the main characters states, "When you start to understand the cryptic parables in the Bible . . . you realize it's a study of the human mind."[2] Exodus is indeed all about the human mind. You may well ask how a story that is so obviously about slavery and redemption could also be about the mind. After all, how do we get from bondage in Egypt to the inner workings of the mind? The story must be written in some kind of code, for which we need the key to unlock its secret meaning.

Fortunately, we have such a key. It's been available all along, hidden in plain sight. The story of Exodus reveals itself as "a study of the human mind" the moment we realize that its two central characters—Pharaoh and Moses—are not just historical figures, not just characters in a biblical drama. They are archetypes that portray opposing aspects of the human mind in its relationship to Spirit.

Pharaoh represents the part of the mind that sees itself as separate from God and Spirit: the limited ego-mind. Moses represents the part of the mind that is and has always been in full, direct connection with God and Spirit—what I call the Moses-mind. Both are present within us. The plagues brought on by Pharaoh's stubborn resistance to freeing the Hebrews are *our* plagues. They afflict us whenever we bow to the Pharaoh-like ego—when we identify with it and accept its goals and worldview as our own. Likewise, the miracles performed by Moses are *our* miracles. They arrive the moment we make the decision, consciously or unconsciously, to be free from ego and follow instead the guidance of Spirit that comes to us through the Moses-mind.

The Hebrews of Exodus are tossed back and forth between these two powerful, opposing forces. As we will see, they toil in slavery under Pharaoh with no hope of release. When Moses first appears, they reject his help. After the devastation of the tenth plague, he leads them out of Egypt and across the seemingly impassable barrier of the Red Sea. Despite these miracles, however, when confronted with the forbidding desolation of the wilderness, they question his guidance. Yet at Mount Sinai, they cling to Moses, refusing to let him go, retreating from a direct encounter with God, because He seems too fearful.

In their vacillation, the Hebrews offer a compelling portrait of our own spiritual dilemma—a mirror of our own confused wanderings as we seek the Promised Land of inner peace and freedom. To whom do we listen, Moses or Pharaoh? Which voice is stronger in us? Which is the more trustworthy? Their agendas for us are starkly opposite. So which do we choose to follow?

We are the Hebrews—all of us, regardless of our religious affiliation—and the journey of Exodus reflects our ongoing struggle as we're pulled between these two dueling aspects of the mind: ego and Spirit, Pharaoh and Moses. This makes Exodus as relevant today as it was 3,000 years ago, for the human mind has not changed.

In the pages ahead, I will retrace the journey of the Hebrews exactly as it appears in the book of Exodus. I will look at each significant step along the way, both for what it meant to the Hebrews and, more importantly, how it relates to our own spiritual progress. I'll also use frequent examples from real life to make this as clear as possible.

My hope is that the Hebrews' journey, with its triumphs and failures, will cast a light to help guide you on your own path. For, like the Hebrews of Exodus, we have not yet reached the Promised Land. We are still en route, still in the process of making that journey. Perhaps now, in the pages that follow, and with the help of Spirit, you and I can complete the journey together.

The Origins of This Book

People often ask how I came to write this book. Where did the ideas come from? In a strange way—or perhaps not so strange after all—they arose from my own spiritual journey. When I look back, of course, the trajectory of people and events that led me to the story of Moses and the Hebrews seems perfectly obvious. But up until a few years ago, the thought of writing a book such as this was the furthest thing from my mind. So how did it come to be? By way of an answer, let me offer an overview of my own journey, focusing specifically on those individuals and events that turned out to be instrumental in giving birth to what you're now reading.

I was raised Jewish. I attended Sunday school and dutifully completed my *bar mitzvah* (the Jewish initiation into manhood) at age 13. Although I'd learned the stories of Noah, Lot, Abraham, Sarah, Jacob, Rachel, Joseph, and Moses, I cannot say they really moved me. Attending synagogue was a chore—not as bad as the dentist, but certainly nothing I looked forward to. When I became an adult, I dropped all pretense of being an observant Jew and attended services only for the sake of my grandparents, whom I loved very much. After their deaths, I saw no reason to enter a synagogue ever again for the purpose of worship.

As a college freshman, my interest in spirituality began to blossom, so I signed up for an introductory course on religion that covered all the world's major faiths. The professor, Theodor H. Gaster, was a scholar of the "old school" variety. Sharp, witty, and often irascible, he would stand at the front of the room, leaning hard on his cane, and lecture us without the benefit of notes, sharing from his considerable fund of knowledge. Gaster's command of folklore and mythology was breathtaking, unequalled except by a rare few (Joseph Campbell comes to mind). He was also a master linguist. Fluent in Hebrew, Ancient Greek, Latin, and a host of modern languages, he could track the words of the Bible as it passed from century to century and tongue to tongue, highlighting the all-too-frequent errors in translation that resulted in significant changes of meaning.

But for me, Professor Gaster's greatest contribution was his understanding of the Jewish festival of Passover: the celebration of the events described in the book of Exodus. Gaster saw that the rituals performed on this holiday drew upon roots that ran in many directions and across different cultures. Passover had all the elements of a seasonal festival of renewal. It is celebrated in the springtime (the start of the new year for many cultures) when the Nile River floods to irrigate the surrounding fields. Thus, according to Gaster, Passover was most likely co-opted by the Hebrews from some earlier Egyptian festival. Yet the Hebrews imprinted their own history upon it, taking this universal celebration of spring and making it uniquely their own. Passover commemorates not just the seasonal renewal of nature, but the seminal event in the history of the Jewish people—their release from bondage by God and the renewal of His covenant with them.

After taking Gaster's class, Passover was never the same for me. It became my favorite holiday and the one aspect of Jewish life I cherished. And so, the first seeds of this book were planted.

❦

About two years later, during my junior year of college, I was introduced to *A Course in Miracles*. This was formative to my spiritual worldview, and so provides the foundation not only for this book, but for much else that followed in my life.

In May 1975, a woman named Judy Skutch met with two Columbia University psychologists, Helen Schucman and Bill Thetford. Through a process of inner dictation (a form of psychic channeling), Helen and Bill had brought into being a monumental work, now known all over the world, titled *A Course in Miracles*. Judy instantly recognized that it was a spiritual masterpiece and devoted herself to getting it published. As it so happens, Judy was also the mother of my college roommate and best friend. Knowing of my interest in spirituality, she was eager to share her find with me, which she finally did over the Christmas holiday in 1975.

My initial response to the *Course* was lukewarm. It felt restrictive, and its language was too Christian for me. But I persevered with it nonetheless, inspired by a number of unusual occurrences (explained in the pages ahead) that I could only interpret as miracles: signposts pointing me forward on the journey.

I spent the first months of the summer of 1976 living at Judy's West Side Manhattan condo, taking premed physics at Columbia University. It was not a good summer for me. I disliked the city, and I hated physics. But I had by then become a dedicated student of the *Course.* Helen and Bill were around a great deal that summer, as Judy was spearheading the first publication of the book. Bill and I formed an instant connection. It was as though we'd known each other for years. Despite my youth, he treated me as an equal and a serious student of the *Course,* and our friendship continued up until his death in 1988.

Although not directly involved in the goings-on, I had a front-row seat to the many miracles that eventuated in the *Course*'s publication. When the first copies arrived, Judy held a dinner to honor Helen and Bill and celebrate the newly published volumes. She invited me to join in the festivities. My presence at the book's coming-out party struck me as somehow significant, yet at the time it all felt rather overwhelming, strange, and a bit surreal.

In 1992, I joined the board of the Foundation for Inner Peace, the publisher of the *Course,* and I continue to use its workbook lessons daily. I believe that, had *A Course in Miracles* not entered my life when it did, my path would have been very different, and this book would never have been written (at least not by me).

⚕

In 1985, I completed my psychiatric residency at Hahnemann University Hospital in Philadelphia and joined the staff there, working in liaison with the department of neurosurgery in their chronic pain clinic. The salary was paltry, yet I recall remarking to friends that I could not have created a more perfect job for myself—not if I'd been handed a magic wand and told to wave away. It took advantage of all my skills and interests: pharmacology, psychotherapy, hypnosis, and the complex interactions between mind and body. Besides, the position just fell in my lap, without any planning or effort on my part. And best of all, it was part-time, leaving me with enough free hours to begin building my private practice.

The first year was wonderful, just as I'd anticipated. Not so the second. The intellectual stimulation, the camaraderie, even the immense rewards of helping people learn to manage their pain all fell hostage to a depressed division chief and the infighting so common to departmental politics in academia. Soon I grew disheartened. I felt trapped. Entering the hospital each morning seemed increasingly like returning to prison. I was enslaved, toiling long hours with nothing to show for it in a job I'd come to despise.

In February, amidst the gloomy slush of a Philadelphia winter, my wife and I decided to get away to Mexico. We signed up for a weeklong workshop with two Huichol Indian shamans. The accommodations were meager (and that's being generous). Nonetheless, it was an immensely healing interlude during which I reconnected with my spiritual nature. More important, I remembered how to laugh, and did so loudly and often.

That first morning back at work—knotting my tie, weaving through the angry rush-hour traffic, trudging the hospital corridors with their dull, waxy pallor, nodding greetings to my dour-faced colleagues—I knew I wanted out. In fact, it wasn't even a choice anymore. *I had to leave.* But how? I had neither the gumption nor the financial resources to simply quit. And there was one further obstacle.

My division chief—a man I greatly admired—had a reputation for fiercely protecting his own. Unfortunately, that fierceness had a darker side to it as well. If someone left the division to pursue a career elsewhere, instead of wishing him or her well, he'd feel betrayed. He'd become angry, even vindictive—fully capable of sabotaging one's career. I knew this well, because he'd just done it to a friend of mine, and I had no intention of adding my name to the chief's blacklist. So how could I move on without putting my professional reputation in danger? I had no answer. But with the glow from the Huichols' fire still warm within me, I trusted that somehow an answer would come.

When the time came to renegotiate my contract, the chief called me into his office. In somber tones, he informed me that budgetary constraints had forced him to eliminate my current position. I could still remain on staff; however, I would have to manage not just the chronic pain clinic, but the vast oncology service as well. This was a monumental task—impossible to fulfill within the constraints of a part-time position. I told the chief I'd need to think about it, but I already knew my answer. He'd made me an offer I couldn't *not* refuse. He'd handed me my exit strategy. I would leave the department, but it wouldn't be of my own doing; it would be in reaction to his offer. How could he feel betrayed by my leaving, when it was *he* who'd forced *me* out? And so it came to pass. The chief attended my good-bye party with a gracious smile. He shook my hand and wished me well in private practice.

It was shortly before the Passover holiday when I turned down that offer. Sitting with my family at the Seder (the ritual Passover dinner), I couldn't fail to appreciate how easily God had orchestrated my own release from bondage. I felt immense gratitude for my freedom. Previously, I'd appreciated Passover in a purely intellectual way. I'd never before experienced how profoundly it could apply to my own life.

From that year forward, I used Passover as an opportunity to review my life's journey. Where was I still enslaved? Who were my Pharaohs? More important, where was *my mind* still trapped in bondage? What roles, beliefs, and relationships held it fast? And how could I help set it free? Looking back, this marked the true beginning of the ideas that led to this book.

※

My release from bondage to academia had another consequence as well, however, one of even greater significance to the inception of this book. Ever since high school, inspired by an outstanding English teacher, I'd wanted to be a writer. In college I signed up for a creative-writing class that demanded I produce a page a day. Sadly, I found I couldn't do it. I'd agonize for hours over a simple character description. I spent so much time trying to compose perfect sentences that I neglected my other studies. After a few weeks of this, I dropped the course, concluding that I just wasn't cut out to be a writer after all. My interest in writing never faded, though, and I went on to major in English.

When I resigned from my position at the teaching hospital and settled into private practice, I discovered something remarkable: I had free time—time to do the things that *I* wanted to do. I began taking long walks along a deserted stretch of abandoned highway near my house (known as "the Blue Route.") And while I walked, my mind, seemingly of its own accord, began to write: poetry, pithy observations, philosophical insights, and story ideas. I carried a small notepad in my shirt pocket to jot everything down.

So without ever making a conscious decision to do so, I took up writing again. This time around, it was no chore. I joined a weekly writer's workshop devoted to science fiction. I was an avid participant, and with good reason: I had a lot to learn. I wrote a dozen short stories, one of which was published in an anthology. And five years after parting ways with my division chief, I'd finished a novel. My escape from bondage had given me the freedom to reclaim an important part of my life's journey. I wasn't only a psychiatrist. I was a writer.

֍

My life has taken many twists and turns since then, each of which has propelled me forward on my journey—a divorce, a move to the West Coast, remarriage, two great children, relocating back to the East Coast. But the final event in the evolution of this book took place in 2008, once again at Passover. Some friends hosted a Seder service at which I briefly shared my insights into the holiday. I received an enthusiastic response, and as a result my wife urged me to put my ideas down in a book. I'd just ended a ten-year flirtation with Hollywood and screenwriting, my hopes for success dying the slow death of repeated rejections, empty promises, and lack of funding. So for the first time in ages, I had no project on the horizon. I was a writer with nothing to write. Perhaps my wife had a point.

I decided I'd write a short book, 50 pages at most, with large print, to share my thoughts on Passover. I doubted anyone would read it, much less publish it, but at least I'd have the satisfaction of getting it all down for the record.

I started by reading the book of Exodus for the very first time. I read it again. I looked at different translations. And the more familiar I became with the story, the more I saw in it. The Hebrews' journey out of bondage was a perfect metaphor for the spiritual journey, especially with regard to the battle between Pharaoh and Moses—the ego and God.

And so I began writing. A year later, with 200 pages under my belt, I stepped back to look it over. I farmed the manuscript out to friends—in particular, two writers whose opinions I value—and they helped me see how much more it could be. So, I started over.

The present book is the result of four years' effort. But looking back, I see it is so much more than that. It reflects the way that Exodus and Passover have shown up in my life again and again, insistently, until I finally paid attention. It's also a reflection of my own spiritual journey—my own learning curve—helping me make sense of where I went astray and why, and how to get back on track. It's a demonstration, for me at least, that with God, all things are possible. Miracles do happen. The Red Sea really does part when we're on the road to freedom.

A Few Words about God

Obviously, God is central to the spiritual journey, both in Exodus and in our own lives. Indeed, without God there *is* no journey. He is the force that sets us seeking, and He is the destination that awaits us at the end of all our searching. God is freedom's means as well as its end. But who or what is God?

People often ask, "Do you believe in God?" The answer divides the world into believers, nonbelievers, and the fence-sitters who either aren't sure or lack the conviction to commit one way or the other. To my mind, however, the question itself is misguided.

God is not a "thing" to be believed in. God is not an entity out there, separate from us, to which we can accord faith or not as we see fit. Nor is God a concept (sorry, John Lennon). God is within us, and, therefore, He is everywhere.

If you *know* God—if you've encountered His Presence, either directly or through miracles—then you know it's not really a question of belief. Belief is the fallback option, the consolation prize, for those who cannot yet say that they know.

God is pure Consciousness. Infinite Being. Purest Love. Behind all experience, infused through all things and events, He has no form and no gender; He isn't female, male, or neuter. I use masculine pronouns to refer to God only because of convention (and because they match the Bible from which I'll be quoting). To think of God as "He," however, is a cultural artifact that says a great deal about us, but nothing about God. It certainly does not reflect my understanding of Him. To my female readers, I can only offer an apology and beg your forbearance.

The God of the Hebrew Bible is highly anthropomorphized. His motives and emotions come across as all too human. But that's our projection as humans onto Him. Our minds try to remake Him in our image—to compress the Incomprehensible All into a concrete, finite, and therefore graspable form.

The Bible was written by humans and intended for humans. It contains a great deal of truth and, as we shall see, can point us to God when read correctly. It does not, however, paint a complete and accurate portrait of Him, for that is beyond what's possible. The ancient Hebrews were correct when they rendered the Name of God as unspeakable, and not because we are unworthy to utter so holy a Name, or to any implied sacrilege or desecration. They understood the simple fact that words can never communicate the nature of the Infinite All.

For lack of a better term, then, I will be referring to God as *God*. However, when I refer to our *connection* to God—the way that God enters our own lives through guidance and miracles—I prefer the word *Spirit*. Think of Spirit as a particular facet of God: the refraction of His Infinite Being into the limited world of form experienced by the ego-mind. And when I speak of God's Love, I choose to capitalize *Love* in order to emphasize that God and Love are indeed one and the same. Love is His essence: the very nature of His Being.

The goal of the Exodus journey is not to bolster a *belief* in God, but to come to *know* Him firsthand, to approach Him with open minds and open arms, to encounter Him and experience His Love, and to engage Him in a direct dialogue through Spirit. When we achieve this, we will find that the Promised Land is indeed ours.

ॐ ॐ

Chapter 1

SLAVES IN EGYPT:
THE ORIGINS OF EGO

In Buddhism, the first of the Four Noble Truths—the Buddha's key insights into the human condition—states that all of life is suffering. It is impossible to escape this. Illness, aging, and death are unavoidable. We may appear to dodge them for a time, taking shelter on islands of contentment and even joy, but eventually they catch up to afflict us all. Our moments of happiness and triumph do not endure. To simply be alive is to suffer.

According to Buddhism, the root of this suffering is *thirst*. When we desire a thing or an experience—when we thirst for it—we become attached. We believe we cannot live without that special person, treasured object, or cherished outcome. Our attachments give rise to suffering. We suffer because of what we want and lack, but also because of what we have and fear to lose, ultimately knowing that indeed we *must* lose it, since our lives are finite.

This duo of suffering and thirst in Buddhism is very much akin to the idea of slavery in Exodus. Our attachments bind us like unseen chains from which there is no hope of escape, thus giving rise to endless suffering.

In the parable of Exodus, suffering is portrayed through the metaphor of slavery. The Hebrews suffer because they are in bondage in Egypt, a land that is not their own. They seek deliverance. But for both Buddhism and Exodus, the goal is the same: To escape suffering. To be free.

Here lies the start of the spiritual journey.

Suffering and Slavery

For most people, the word *slavery* connotes physical bondage. We picture exhausted, battered bodies bound in chains, hauling heavy loads or working in fields under the eye of pitiless, whip-cracking overseers. If this is the extent of our view of slavery, however, then of course we won't see ourselves in it, and Exodus will have no bearing on our lives. We need to think more broadly.

Slavery results from a combination of two conditions: suffering and lack of freedom. Slaves are not free. Their lives are restricted. They have no choice about what happens to them, no options. They serve at their master's whim, toiling to meet his agenda with no benefit to themselves. They're treated poorly, as subhumans. As a result, slaves suffer.

Throughout history, tyrants like the Pharaohs of Exodus have confiscated freedom and brought about great pain. Whippings, beatings, and torture all leave the body wracked with pain. Suffering, however, is not merely a matter of physical pain inflicted on us by some external oppressor. Suffering goes beyond pain. It resides in the mind. It results from how we *interpret* what happens to us, not from the situation itself. It's subjective and, to some extent, under our control. We tend to think of suffering and pain as equivalent, but they are not. Bodies feel pain; only the mind can suffer. Indeed, it's possible to be in pain and yet not suffer at all.

A classic study by Harvard anesthesiologist H.K. Beecher helps illustrate this distinction.[1] While serving in World War II, Beecher noted that the wounded soldiers he cared for required very little morphine for their pain despite the severity of their injuries. When he returned to Boston after the war, he monitored morphine use in a group of civilians with similar injuries of equal severity resulting from car accidents. He found that these patients required significantly more morphine than the soldiers had. The reason? The civilians *suffered* more from their injuries. This was not because the soldiers were tougher or braver than their counterparts, but simply because their interpretation of pain was different.

For the soldiers, being injured meant the end of active combat duty. Their participation in the war was over. They'd made it out alive, and no amount of pain could sour that good news. For the civilians, just the opposite was true. Their injuries had disrupted their lives. They were trapped in the hospital, unable to work or be with their loved ones. Their pain was a constant reminder of these disruptions. As a consequence, they suffered more.

For both groups, the degree of suffering depended not on the actual physical pain itself, but on how it was perceived. We could say that the civilians were enslaved by their injuries. Their freedom was restricted, and so they suffered, unable to cope or escape. For the soldiers, pain meant freedom. The difference lay in the interpretation. As Eckhart Tolle writes, "The primary cause of unhappiness is never the [external] situation but your thoughts about it."[2] Slavery or freedom—it's all in the mind.

A Pharaoh Who Does Not Know Joseph

At the start of Exodus, the Hebrews are not yet slaves. They've prospered in Egypt under Joseph and their numbers have greatly increased. "Now a new king arose over Egypt, who did not know Joseph" (Exod. 1:8). This new Pharaoh enslaves the Hebrews. But why does the Bible go out of its way to tell us that this Pharaoh "did not know Joseph"? This is an important detail, and it's worth a closer look.

The story of Joseph appears in the book of Genesis. Joseph is the favorite of his father, Jacob (or Israel). Joseph's brothers are jealous of him and sell him into slavery, which makes him the first of the Hebrews to find himself enslaved in Egypt. But Joseph manages to surmount this oppression and become the right-hand man of the Pharaoh of his era. He accomplishes this through his connection to Spirit.

Joseph's early life is marked by two prophetic dreams. He also proves to be a gifted interpreter of dreams. Through them, Joseph is given a direct channel to God. When he correctly interprets the dreams of the Pharaoh of his era (see Genesis 41), he is appointed second in command over all Egypt and saves the people from the ravages of a seven-year famine.

Therefore, when Exodus says that this new Pharaoh "did not know Joseph," we must ask: How this could be? How could *any* Pharaoh not know of the man who saved the entire kingdom from ruin? Even assuming that many generations have passed, as the Bible suggests, Joseph's deeds should still be remembered or recorded somewhere. Given all he did for Egypt, it's just not plausible that this new Pharaoh would be ignorant of him.

But Exodus is a parable, and in a parable small details such as these can have great significance. What this detail tells us is that at the very outset of the spiritual journey, in some unexplained manner, our minds lose their freedom. They become enslaved to a tyrannical new Pharaoh, an entity that, unlike Joseph, has no connection to God. This ruler's own willful ignorance has cut him off from all possibility of direct guidance from Spirit. This new ruler of the mind is the ego, and we will trace its path to power later in the chapter.

Unjustifiable Fear

After Joseph saves Egypt from famine, his family follows him there, and for many generations they prosper. Then this new Pharaoh, insecure, uncertain, and cut off from divine guidance, decides he must enslave the Hebrews. Why? On the off chance that they might side with Egypt's enemies.

He said to his people, "Behold, the people of the sons of Israel are more and mightier than we. Come, let us deal wisely with them, or else they will multiply and in the event of war, they will also join themselves to those who hate us, and fight against us and depart from the land" (Exod. 1:9–10).

His fear has no basis in fact. Why would the Hebrews betray him when they've prospered? If Egypt came under attack, wouldn't they be more likely to fight side by side with the Egyptians to protect their land? But Pharaoh's irrational fears drive him to irrational measures.

Accordingly they put slave-drivers over the Israelites to wear them down under heavy loads. . . . The Egyptians forced the sons of Israel into slavery, and made their lives unbearable with hard labor . . . (The Jerusalem Bible, Exod. 1:11–14).

Unfounded fear is hardly unique to Pharaoh. We've all experienced it at one time or another: What if there's an accident? What if he turns out to be a jerk? What if she leaves me? What if we get lost? As we'll see, fear is a fundamental trait—perhaps *the* fundamental trait—of the ego-mind. And when we're afraid, we make poor decisions. These decisions can be impulsive and extreme, and they're prone to backfire.

🕉

Lori, a college junior, is convinced that she'll never get a good grade in organic chemistry, a requirement for her cherished goal of medical school. She fears that if she doesn't spend every waking hour studying, she'll fail the final. The week before the exam, her anxiety is so great that she stays up every night until 4 A.M. reviewing the material over and over again. By the morning of the test, she's totally exhausted and no less anxious. She has trouble remembering all she studied and ends up getting a bad grade. The actions she took to quell her fear backfired, and instead created a self-fulfilling prophecy.

James distrusts his wife, Pam. He's never really believed that a woman so beautiful could be happy with a plain, vanilla guy like him. Convinced that Pam must be cheating on him, he looks at her cell-phone record for calls to unknown numbers. He checks the odometer of her car to see if she's driven unaccounted-for miles to rendezvous with secret lovers. The fact that James finds nothing suspicious doesn't allay his fears; on the contrary, it fuels them. *Pam must suspect that he's checking up on her. She's being clever,* he reasons. He just needs to look harder.

He begins to stalk her. He follows her home from work, to the market, wherever he can. One day Pam happens to spot him. She confronts him and asks what on earth he's doing there. When she realizes the extent of his suspicions, she's understandably furious. The outcome? She leaves him, validating his belief that he wasn't good enough for her.

Both Lori and James illustrate the ego-mind in action—our "inner Pharaoh." Its intentions may seem noble—getting into medical school, refusing to be cuckolded—but they're driven by irrational fear and a sense of distrust that borders on the paranoid. As a result, their actions lead to disaster.

۞

Does Pharaoh's treatment of the Hebrews result in any better of an outcome? By enslaving them, does he in fact protect his kingdom?

One generation later, all of Egypt has been laid to waste by ten devastating plagues, and its firstborn children lie dead. Pharaoh's own successor—his son, we presume—drowns when the waters of the Red Sea flood down upon him and his armies. By enslaving the Hebrews, Pharaoh brings about the destruction of his own empire and the end of his royal line. Like Lori and James, he creates the very outcome he feared.

Because the ego-mind is cut off from Spirit, its actions are necessarily shortsighted. It tries to peer into the murky future, desperately seeking to know what lies ahead, because to the ego, the future is a very scary place. Death lurks out there somewhere, waiting to pounce. Therefore, the ego expends tremendous energy trying to manage the future. It's constantly planning for worst-case scenarios, often without regard for actual circumstances. With eyes so fixed on the future, the ego overlooks the present—what's happening *now*—and its actions are doomed to fail.

The Anatomy of the Ego

Like the Hebrews, we too begin life in freedom. Our minds are open and receptive—unencumbered by fear. By the time we reach school age, however, we're already in bondage. We're enslaved by a host of restrictive beliefs and roles that govern every aspect of our lives. They come to us from parents, friends, teachers, and the media. They determine how we look and dress, the way we speak, whom we look up to, whom we disdain, what we hope for, and what we dread. Somehow, without our permission or even our awareness, we've become slaves.

The parable of Exodus tells us that this force enslaving us—this new Pharaoh—is the ego. When we're cut off from higher guidance, when we forget our true nature, we grow fearful. Enter the ego to rescue us from our fear. The ego promises security. Stability. Control. Ego then is, first and foremost, a response to fear: the fear that comes from being cut off from Spirit. It is a mechanism to ensure survival in a world perceived as dangerous.

𖣔

The ego-mind develops early on in life. Initially, it is a tool for organizing perception. In order to survive, we must learn to integrate the raw data that our five senses bring to us—shapes, colors, sounds, sensations, odors, and tastes. We need to understand what they mean, and we accomplish this by forming associations. Rumbling in the stomach means hunger, and it goes away soon after we feel the touch of the person who nurses us. Lying in a wet diaper is irritating, and although we don't understand the source, we do know that we feel pain, which in turn makes us cry. If someone changes the diaper, we feel relief. If they do so regularly and predictably, we learn that our cries of distress elicit a positive response, and we feel cared for. If no one hears us or wants to be bothered, we learn that discomfort is out of our control. We suffer, and can do nothing about it.

As we grow older, these associations become more complex. We categorize people by how they've treated us and places by what we've experienced there (for example, the antiseptic smell of the doctor's office means humiliating examinations and painful vaccinations). This amalgam of experience and its associated emotions becomes the basis of a concept of self: the fledgling ego-mind.

The ego's beginnings, then, are to be found in the body and its perceptions. Ego is the software—the operating system—for organizing perception and pairing it with emotion to enhance survival. It helps us develop a schema of our physical body and its place in the world. And if that were the extent of it, there would be no problem.

But the ego doesn't stop there. It identifies with the body. The body now becomes *my* body, unique to me and distinct from all other bodies. Only *I* can feel what it feels. Its pleasure and pain are *my* pleasure and pain, and I crave the former but shun the latter. Through such a process, the physical body becomes the foundation for the developing sense of self.

When we learn to speak, the ego grows even stronger. Language assigns names to the things in our world. It helps us navigate safely through life. For example, snakes are dangerous, skunks smelly; Grandma is nice and gives me candy; the kids on the school bus are mean, especially the one named Billy. With language, our ability to organize and understand experience takes a giant leap forward. But our ability to grasp the interconnectedness of all things fades, the casualty of a world divided into separate entities each bearing its own name.

With language at its disposal, the ego actually begins to communicate with us. And once it starts talking, it never stops.

It provides a running commentary on our experiences, real and imagined. It cautions us, scolds us, praises us, and urges us toward one course of action over another. This ego voice, this inner monologue, stays with us practically to the point of death. It's very difficult to turn off—as anyone learning to meditate can tell you. Before long, we come to identify with this voice, as if it really were somehow us. After all, we're the only ones who can hear it in our heads. It seems to have strong opinions about what we do, and is present just about every waking moment. So who else could it be but "me"? Our self-concept expands now to consist of a body that interacts with the world under the direction of a voice that resides in our head—both of which seem to be uniquely us.

There's one final element in the formation of the ego, and it's perhaps the most difficult to comprehend. It is our sense of continuous memory. Psychology is very clear that memory is not a continuous stream, nor is it even factually accurate. Our brains are not video cameras recording each passing moment with perfect veracity. Memories are formed, and then reconstituted and modified each time we call them up.

Memory is malleable. It's easily shaped by suggestion and subsequent experience, including what we've read in books or seen on television or the Internet. In any family, it's not uncommon for a younger sibling to claim to remember an event that he or she has heard about repeatedly from an older brother or sister, but was in fact too young to actually recall.

Memory is also fallible. Studies of eyewitness testimony have made this abundantly clear. A well-meaning but overly zealous police officer can prod a witness into identifying a suspect from a mug shot with far more certainty than is truly justified. And once identified, the memory sticks, even when the witness is later confronted with facts disproving the allegations.

Nonetheless, we regard our memories as accurate and continuous, stretching back in a seamless line all the way to early childhood. Like our unique physical body or the voice in our heads, this long stream of memories becomes incorporated as part of the self-concept. For example, five years ago such and such an event happened to *me*. This is now part of *my* life. Through memory, the ego ties us to the past in ways that can be destructive and very difficult to reverse: "I can't help it. That's the way I've always been."

When we combine our seemingly continuous chain of memories with our inner voice and our physical body, the self-concept is complete. Ego is now fully formed. But no longer does it function as a simple interface for organizing perception and emotion. *It's taken on a life of its own.* It truly believes that it runs the show and does so all by itself. In this sense, the ego has become a god unto itself—a false god that's not only separate from Spirit, but threatened by and in competition with Spirit.

Imagine if your computer's software decided that it was its own living entity. You give it commands, typing furiously, but nothing happens. The machine has cut itself off from its source of direction: you. Now it cannot accomplish anything of real value. It requires a program to run, a task to complete, but that's no longer how it sees itself. Likewise, once the ego-mind is fully formed and views itself as a separate entity—once this new Pharaoh comes to power with no knowledge of Joseph—Spirit is banished from the mind. It's not us, not part of the self. Ego is our new ruler, and we have become slaves who serve its agenda.

Slavery Cannot Recognize Itself

If we're enslaved to the ego-mind as the Hebrews were to Pharaoh, then why isn't it more obvious? Why can't we see this slavery and fight to break free?

If you're born free and only later in life clapped into slavery, you'll no doubt recognize that your life has drastically changed for the worse. You'll remember your days of freedom and long for their return. You'll tell your children about what things were like before your enslavement. Perhaps you'll actively plot your escape. At the very least, you'll hold on to hope and keep a sharp eye out for opportunities to flee.

But what if you can't remember freedom? What if you were born a slave to parents who were slaves, just like their parents before them, going back generations? What if every person in your world has known nothing but slavery? In that case, imprisonment is a given. *There is nothing else.* As a result, the idea of escape won't occur to you. It won't even make sense. Escape from what? To what? Does a fish try to escape from its enslavement to water? Does an earthworm long for release from the soil's bondage? Does either one dream of flying or running free in the wind?

Therefore, when we read Exodus as a parable of the mind, we must start by asking what slavery means for us *today*. In what ways are *our* minds in bondage? For if we cannot recognize the chains around our own minds, we will have no hope of escaping. So let's take a look.

Chapter 2

THE MANY FORMS OF SLAVERY

The Roman philosopher Seneca wrote, "Show me a man who is not a slave; one is a slave to lust, another to greed, another to ambition; all are slaves to fear."[1] His words apply just as surely to our lives in the 21st century as they did to the ancient Romans, for slavery today comes in many different guises. Let's examine some of the most common, those which affect us all.

Bondage to Possessions

Karl is not my patient. His daughter, Liz, has sought my help because Karl has filled his house with stuff. Old newspapers and magazines are piled high in six-foot stacks, crammed into every room and spilling out into the hallways. The place is unlivable, but of more concern to Liz, it's a fire hazard. Yet her father refuses to throw anything away. Should she sneak in and toss a pile or two into the recycling bin, he finds the items, retrieves them, and then becomes furious with her. He's even shoved her to keep her away from his precious piles of stuff.

Karl isn't motivated by sentiment. He doesn't treasure the things he hoards. He's motivated by fear. He's afraid that, should he dispose of something, anything, he'll discover later on that he needed it. Hidden amongst the stacks of junk mail lies an unseen check. And that seven-year-old magazine he's saving will turn out to be exactly the one with the article that can save his life. Karl lies awake at night, tortured by the thought that something of value might have slipped by him and been lost.

Zoe, on the other hand, loves her possessions. She's a genuine connoisseur of beauty. Whether it's jewelry, designer clothing, ceramics, or fine art, her taste is impeccable. Should she spy something that speaks to her, she must have it, no matter the cost. In pursuit of her aesthetic high, Zoe has run up a debt of tens of thousands of dollars, which she's kept hidden from her husband. Yet she can justify each and every one of her purchases as a good buy, an item of real value that she simply couldn't pass up.

Both Karl and Zoe are slaves—slaves to objects, to possessions. Their examples may seem extreme, but we can all recognize in ourselves the impulses behind them. Fear of loss. Craving that special something that will make life worthwhile—whether it be a ring, a car, or a new song we've just heard and need to download right away.

Our world offers so much in the way of things to be purchased and owned that it makes our heads spin. With such variety to choose from, how could this be slavery? Isn't slavery the absence of choice?

But our possessions are indeed a form of bondage. We become enslaved, not just to the things themselves, but to the desire to acquire and the fear of losing them. We have a seemingly infinite choice of brands and styles, but we have *no* choice about our wanting. This thirst for acquisition can drive us like the most relentless of taskmasters. We end up with so many things that it often feels as if *they* own *us*, rather than the other way around. And they never do satisfy for very long. Sooner or later, our eye is drawn to something new and we want it. Surely, this is bondage.

And, of course, to acquire all the things we want, we need money.

Bondage to Money

Jerry despises his job. It's not just the commute in rush-hour traffic or the overtime without pay. It's the people he works for and with. He can't stand their patronizing attitude, their smug sense of superiority. Jerry is low on the corporate food chain. His work serves no useful purpose apart from the bottom line. He'd love to quit and do something meaningful, like coach high-school basketball, but he can't afford to. He simply has too many obligations and too much debt. Besides, the benefits are decent. So he keeps showing up every morning, even though it feels like crawling into a sewer.

Hank has all the money he'll ever need. A savvy businessman, he built the company he inherited from his father to a level of success that neither could have imagined. At 55, he sold it for a small fortune, retired, and took up golf full-time. Most of us would be envious of such a life. But Hank isn't happy. He has millions invested in the stock market, and he lives and dies by its every fluctuation. His BlackBerry is constantly at his side so he can check his market positions. Yet his attempts to stay on top of his fortune leave him feeling all the more out of control. Should an occasion arise that requires him to spend big money, like helping with his granddaughter's college tuition or taking the whole extended family on vacation to the Caribbean, he'll do it, but not cheerfully. He lives in fear that one day his funds will run out. There simply won't be enough, and he'll die poor.

Jerry and Hank are slaves to money. Jerry is tied to his job with no hope of escape. Hank is tied to his fortune and the gyrations of the financial markets. Their money fears weigh on them as heavily as shackles.

What is it about money that creates such bondage? Why are we so willing to sacrifice our time and energy in order to make money? We treat money as if it were survival itself. If we don't have money, we can't buy food, shelter, and all those possessions that make life worthwhile.

Money also supports our self-image. It buys the props that define who we are: the car we drive; the clothing, watches, and jewelry we wear; the brand of beer or whiskey we drink; the places we vacation. So we work hard to get money. We pile up debt to the point where we dread opening the credit-card bills. We stockpile our scarce dollars against the hard times that surely lie ahead when we're older and retired—always fretting, like Hank, that it won't be enough. Could this be anything but slavery?

Bondage to Time

Sally came to see me after the sudden and unexpected death of her mother. She'd become acutely aware of the passage of time—how each year seemed to speed by faster than the last. Sally tried to push such thoughts aside and treasure the good moments with her children and friends, but when her weekends came up short each Sunday night, she plunged back into moody introspection. How many good times remained before death reached out again and claimed another of her loved ones, as it had her mother?

If money is scarce, then time is scarcer still. There are no millionaires in the world of time. We cannot bank it, saving up the hours and days to be withdrawn later and used when and where we need them most. Nor do we know the length of our days. We could live on well into our 90s, or we could find ourselves stone-cold dead tomorrow. Therefore, when we think about time, it's almost always with an underlying sense of urgency and foreboding.

Unlike Sally, Miriam has not a moment to spare in her day for abstract thoughts about the passage of time. Getting her four kids dressed and off to school; managing the shopping, cleaning, phone calls, and errands; picking up her youngest from preschool at noon; driving the others to their after-school sports and music lessons; and then dinner, cleanup, homework . . . by the time she collapses into bed, her day feels more like a long and weary year. Miriam suffers from chronic insomnia—the most common complaint I hear in my office these days. She needs medication to fall asleep. Why? Because as she lies awake in bed, her mind is busy scouting out the next day. She works herself into a panic thinking that if she can't shut it down and get a decent night's sleep, there's no way she'll be able to function.

In our high-speed, 21st-century world we move so fast that we need pills to slow down and ease into sleep. God forbid we "waste" any time lying there awake, accomplishing nothing. When morning arrives with the blare of the alarm clock, we gulp coffee to accelerate from 0 to 60 as rapidly as possible. We gobble down fast food. We tune in to instant news and entertainment. We exchange text messages and check e-mails dozens of times a day. Without a doubt, we squeeze more out of one day than any generation in human history. Yet even with all our time-saving devices, a mere 24 hours feels insufficient.

Consequently, we run around frantically, trying to get it all done and wasting not a second. We hope that *maybe,* when every item on the to-do list is checked off, we might be able to relax and focus on something meaningful—or even have fun! Then we'll have the opportunity to do the things we enjoy, time that's liberated from this frantic bondage. "Free" time.

Except that the to-do list is never finished. Like the many-headed Hydra of Greek myth, each time we lop an item off the list, two more sprout up to replace it. The dream of free time recedes, a lovely mirage, while we struggle on to the next task, the next day, week, month, and year, enslaved as ever.

Bondage to the Body

Heinz is 60 years old, yet he jogs daily, rain or shine. And not just a measly mile, but six—even more if he has the time. Twice a year he ramps up and runs a half marathon. Heinz eats free-range chicken and fresh vegetables, takes dozens of herbal supplements, does yoga, and sees his doctor for regular checkups. He insists on monitoring his cholesterol closely, even though it's never been a problem. He is proud of how young he looks and prouder still that he can keep up with runners half his age.

Frances is a true socialite. She thrives in the rarified air of high society. She looks great for her 40-plus years, and works hard to keep it that way. She spends 90 minutes every morning with her personal trainer, an hour on makeup, and a half hour on her hair. Regular Botox injections are a must. So too is plastic surgery when those wrinkles appear to deepen or her skin begins to sag. She's had four or five procedures already, and will probably have four or five more before she surrenders her body to age and gravity.

What do Frances and Heinz have in common? Both are slaves to their physical bodies. Heinz lives a healthy lifestyle—and there's nothing wrong with that. But behind his fitness and his dietary regimen lies a profound fear of illness, infirmity, and death. He intends to keep this unholy trinity at bay for as long as he can. However, no matter how far or how fast he runs, he can feel them at his heels. One misstep, one lapse in his routine, and they'll be on him.

Frances's bondage is of a different sort. It's not illness or death she fears; it's aging. Since she was a girl, Frances has thrived on compliments on her appearance. At parties, the men flock to her still. How could she live without that kind of attention? Who would she be without her good looks?

What if Frances could be free of her fear of aging—just like that? No more Botox, no more lengthy sessions in front of the mirror. How might that feel? She shudders when I pose the question. The blank, frightened look in her eyes speaks volumes. She'll choose the slavery she knows over the risk of unknown freedom every time.

Bondage to Relationships

Jen is about to graduate from college. She and Randy have been involved since high school. They've had their ups and downs, but through it all both have clung to the relationship like a life raft in icy seas. When she has one of her not infrequent panic attacks, it's Randy she calls. Just the sound of his voice on the phone will calm her in minutes. Jen loves Randy, but she isn't sure she's *attracted* to him. When they have sex, it feels like she's paying him back for taking care of her. She thinks a lot about moving on, but fears that if she does, she'll never find anyone as devoted to her as he is. At the same time, she's terrified that Randy will find someone else, someone unburdened by panic attacks, and reject her first. And then what will she do?

Bonnie is a devoted daughter. Her 89-year-old father has heart and kidney problems, but proudly insists on living alone. Dad will call Bonnie day or night to report his latest twinge of pain, and she will drop everything and drive 45 minutes to make sure he's okay. He expects nothing less. He also expects Bonnie to accompany him to his doctors' appointments . . . and to visit every Saturday . . . and stay for at least three hours. If Bonnie lapses in any of these duties, her father plays the sullen victim and she feels crushing guilt. As a result, Bonnie has almost no life of her own. Should she dare to say no and attend to her own needs, she's sure she'll lose her dad's love, or worse still, he'll die—and it will be all her fault.

Relationships are of course among the best things in life. No man or woman is an island. But when we find ourselves in a relationship with someone who controls us, or who offers dependency instead of mutuality, then we are in bondage. Spouses, parents, children, significant others, schoolmates, colleagues, those we love, and those we idolize—all can be sources of joy, but also potential bondage. They can enslave us as surely as lack of money or poor health.

Bondage to Beliefs and Values

Jack's dad was an alcoholic. He'd stagger home from the bar at night stinking of beer and awaken the house with his wild accusations about his wife, which she bravely ignored. Unable to pick a fight with her, he'd lay into Jack, his only son, who wound up at the wrong end of the belt on far too many nights. When Jack got to high school, his goal was to get top grades so he could win a college scholarship and get far away from his father. At college, he eschewed frat-house parties. He never let a drop of alcohol pass his lips, lest he turn out like his dad. Alcohol was dangerous; it made people lose control and do stupid, mean, and embarrassing things. That was Jack's firm belief, rooted in hard experience, and no one was going to change his mind.

Jill's father worked long hours and often came home late. He'd settle in and drink a glass of wine or two with her mom. They'd relax on the couch, chat, and catch up on the day. In Jill's experience, alcohol was a necessity. It put people at ease and let them shake off the stress of the workday. Like her dad, Jill made sure to enjoy a glass of wine or two every night.

Which belief about alcohol is correct: Jack's or Jill's? Because their beliefs match their experience, *each is right within the context of who they are.* But what if Jack and Jill happen to fall in love and get married? Could he tolerate her drinking every night? Could she accept his rigid abstinence? Even if they managed to forge an uneasy compromise, what happens when their kids reach drinking age? Whose belief will prevail?

Both Jack and Jill feel justified in their positions on alcohol. Once established, beliefs such as these become very difficult to change. Their truth seems self-evident, and the believer may become shocked and angry when others turn out to see things differently.

To hold beliefs is unavoidable. But to make ours "right" and theirs "wrong"—to view ours as the sole, exclusive truth—becomes a form of slavery. Such tightly held convictions act like blinders. They selectively filter out what doesn't fit. They cannot help but lead to conflict. Perhaps more importantly, they lead to a disregard for Spirit. Why? Because we think we already know what's best. We don't need any help.

❦

Values become even more of a problem. Values are beliefs elevated to the level of morality. Especially in the arenas of politics and religion, our most strongly held beliefs become enthroned as values. We're more attached to values than beliefs, because they define who we are. They're the backbone of our self-concept.

Americans value independence and democracy. The Chinese value community and Confucian principles of order. One person values the ability to make snap judgments no matter who gets hurt; another the ability to empathize and give the benefit of the doubt. One U.S. President values a tough, aggressive posture, while the next prefers a thoughtful, consensus-building stance.

Values inevitably lead to judgments. Those who share my values are judged as good people; those who don't are evil or morally defective. They pose a threat and, in the extreme case, deserve punishment or outright elimination. We wear our values proudly and defend them righteously. Seldom do we recognize them as a particularly insidious and stubborn form of bondage.

Bondage to Roles

Phil is a police officer. He loves putting on the uniform. He cherishes the power of pulling over a speeder—and the privilege of flashing his shield and getting a pass when *he's* the one pulled over. He loves that he can make a difference in the world, and that he's on the scene for the most difficult moments in people's lives. Asked what it might be like to retire or change professions, Phil says, "No way." There is no space between his professional role and his self-concept. He's a cop, and he's willing to die if called upon in order to live up to the role.

Many professions demand that we play a role. Being a doctor requires clinical objectivity in the face of death. The role of prosecutor requires brashness and aggression to get a conviction. Politicians are always in role—while pretending to look and act completely genuine. Surgeons, therapists, teachers, actors—all are professions in which the role can grow so dominant that it eclipses the person behind it.

Each of us plays many different roles in the course of a lifetime, or in the course of any given day, for that matter. Some roles we slip in and out of as easily as we change clothes: the friendly neighbor, the prudent shopper, the helpful classmate. Others are fixed and unyielding. Like our values, they're fundamental to our self-concept: the hard worker, the good daughter, the devout churchgoer. We grow so attached to these roles that we forget who we are. They become grafted onto our identity, and anything that forces us to separate from them causes pain.

۞

Joe came to me with a very unusual problem. He was enslaved to a role that no longer fit him, and he suffered deeply as a result. For six months, Joe refused to tell me his real name. He drove three hours to my office to make sure he wouldn't be seen by anyone he knew. He paid in cash. All of this came quite naturally to him. You see, Joe was a career white-collar criminal: an embezzler.

From childhood, Joe's dad had trained him to steal. It was the family profession, and both father and son felt a rush of superiority and pride when they pulled one over on the stupid, unsuspecting corporation that employed them both. Joe's only problem was having to hide what he did from everyone he knew. For him, close relationships were out of the question.

But then Joe met a woman, someone special whom he hoped to marry. How could he reveal to her that he was a thief? On the other hand, how could he give up the only livelihood he'd ever known? He had no other way of making money. Joe wanted desperately to shed the role of thief, but couldn't, because he had nothing to replace it with. (We'll return to Joe's story in a later chapter.)

When we're forced to give up a role, we become painfully aware of the extent of our attachment to it. Getting fired from a job, going through a divorce, becoming sick or disabled—all jolt the foundations of our identity. Even the entirely natural role of parent can become problematic if, as children grow older and no longer need us the way they used to, we can't let them go. When your two-year-old hurts herself, you kiss the boo-boo and make it all better. Good luck trying this with your 20-year-old when she catches her boyfriend cheating!

In the course of aging, many of our most cherished roles are taken from us. Our bodies don't function the way they used to. They no longer look attractive. Hearing and vision fail. Memory falters. We can no longer perform at our jobs. We feel robbed of so many roles: breadwinner, parent, lover. All are stripped from us. No wonder growing old is so difficult. When the familiar roles we've relied upon fall away, what's left? Who are we then? On what do we base our self-concept?

The problem, of course, isn't with the roles themselves. It's impossible not to wear a plethora of different hats in life. The problem lies with our need to identify with them. We become the role: "the shark attorney," "the winning coach," "the savvy investor," "the irresistible hottie," "the good listener," "the underachiever," "the loser," and so on. And when we identify with a role, we disconnect from our most authentic self: our spiritual essence.

Let's be clear. It's not that these roles leave us no time to be ourselves. It's that, after we play out all our myriad roles, *there's no self left*. When we're so locked into them that we give up entirely on the prospect of inner peace—when we become "human doings" rather than "human beings"—we're slaves in the worst possible way. We've relinquished all possibility of choice, and along with it our freedom.

🐑

To conclude, we are enslaved, just like the Hebrews in Egypt. We live in bondage to our possessions, money, time, the physical body, the many beliefs and values we cherish, and the roles that seem so pivotal in preserving our sense of self. Taken together, these form a self-concept—the ego's vision of who we are—and we toil in support of it. We chase after its goals, with little in the way of lasting satisfaction. Inner peace or a sense of meaning—these are not the fruits of our bondage. These are not gifts the ego can give us.

Once we recognize the full extent of our bondage, what can we do about it? How do we free ourselves from the chains of attachment and suffering? We can't look to others to do it for us, because they're trapped in the same web of ego, playing out the same losing game. We must learn to free ourselves.

But how? Do we spurn all roles and values? Should we abandon them and run off to live on an island somewhere? Shall we give away our possessions and join a monastery or ashram? Remember, the ego is crafty. It will gladly embrace a new set of roles and beliefs, including those of "spiritual seeker," to convince us we've changed, when all we've really done is rearrange the pieces of our self-concept. The slave exchanges one set of dirty clothing for another—and remains a slave.

The truth is that we cannot use the ego-mind to free ourselves from ego. Ego will simply spin off a new self-concept, different and more compelling than the last, to keep us entranced. A slave cannot escape using the tools of slavery. To escape the bondage of ego, we need help. We need what Joseph had: an unshakeable connection to Spirit. In Exodus, this help arrives in the form of Moses.

❧ ❧

Chapter 3

THE BIRTH
OF MOSES AND
THE MOSES-MIND

In Chapter 1 of Exodus, a new Pharaoh came to power, one "who did not know Joseph," and he enslaved the Hebrews. But making the Hebrews slaves was not enough to quell his paranoia, and so he issues a further command. The Hebrew midwives must kill all male infants born to Hebrew mothers.

The midwives secretly refuse. They lie to Pharaoh, telling him that the Hebrew women give birth too quickly, before the midwives have a chance to get to the babies. However, this does not dissuade Pharaoh from his quest to destroy the Hebrew people. He next decrees that all male Hebrew infants are to be thrown into the Nile River. (He will graciously spare the girls.) Into this hostile environment is born the baby who will become Moses.

Moses's mother, fearing for her child's life, hides him for the first three months of his life.

But when she could hide him no longer, she got him a wicker basket and covered it over with tar and pitch. Then she put the child into it and set it among the reeds by the bank of the Nile. And his sister stood at a distance to find out what would happen to him (Exod. 2:3–4).

Soon enough, Pharaoh's daughter and her attendants come down to the river to bathe. They spy the basket with the baby, and Pharaoh's daughter proclaims that this must be one of the little Hebrew boys. But she does not obey her father and drown the infant. Instead, the baby's sister approaches her and offers to find a Hebrew nursemaid for the child. Whom else should she volunteer, of course, but the baby's own mother, also her mother.

One suspects that Pharaoh's daughter was not fooled by this ruse, but played along willingly. In fact, the entire scene unfolds as if all parties understood—with a wink and a nod—that this baby was not fated to die. Moses's mother no doubt knew the routine of Pharaoh's household and perhaps the disposition of Pharaoh's daughter as well. She placed her child in exactly the spot where he'd be found and offered protection by someone with the inclination and power to do so.

Then Pharaoh's daughter said to her, "Take this child away and nurse him for me and I will give you your wages." So the woman took the child and nursed him. And the child grew, and she brought him to Pharaoh's daughter, and he became her son. And she named him Moses, and said, "Because I drew him out of the water" (Exod. 2:9–10).

Moses is not unique in starting out life this way. The Hindu epic known as the Mahabharata describes how a king's daughter, Pritha, gives birth to a child fathered by the sun god. Fearing her parents' wrath, she places her baby in a waterproof wicker basket and sets it upon the river. The child floats ashore, is found, and adopted by a childless couple.[1]

A Babylonian text from around 2,300 B.C.E. (predating the events of Exodus by one thousand years) tells the story of Sargon of Agade, a mighty king.

[My mother] put me in a basket of rushes, with bitu-
men sealed me in. Then she cast me into the river, but the
river did not overwhelm me. The river bore me up, and
carried me to a drawer of water . . . [who] hauled me out.
He reared me as his own son.[2]

An Egyptian tale describes how the god Horus was threatened
as an infant by the god Seth and hidden away for his safety in a
thatch of papyrus near the mouth of the Nile.[3] There are many
other variations on this theme.

In the normal course of events, a mother should cuddle and
nurse her child, protecting him or her from danger. But in these
tales, the mother must let go of her baby, placing him in jeopardy
in order to save his life. The mothers of Moses and Sargon be-
queath their infants to the river—that is, to the forces of nature.
Figuratively, they release them into the hands of God.

The River as a Symbol

Picture a river. What is its defining characteristic? Why isn't
Moses set adrift on a lake or upon the mighty ocean itself?

Well, a river is a body of water that flows toward the sea. It
follows its own inexorable, mysterious course, day and night, un-
affected by the works of man. When we float on a river, we don't
stay in one place. We're carried along by the current and end up
somewhere different from where we started. The river, then, is an
apt symbol for life itself, for the spiritual journey, and for the notion of destiny. It flows toward some unknown objective, carrying
us along to wherever fate wills.

Therefore, when a mother gives her infant to the river, she's
entrusting the babe to the flowing forth of some grand design.
This child has a destiny, a direction to follow, someplace he's supposed to be; and in the fullness of time, he will reach it. No Pharaoh can alter that. You can't shift the river from its course.

When the hero is drawn from the waters of the river, it's a symbolic rebirth (akin to the ritual of baptism)—just as the midwife

delivered him from the amniotic waters of the womb in his first birth. This second birth underscores that from this point forward, the baby's protector and guide is not his mother but Spirit. Or, rather, that Spirit is his true mother. And it is Spirit that steers the child into the arms of safe, loving, surrogate parents who will raise him and keep him safe until he is of age and ready to take on his true calling.

Ego Cannot Kill Spirit

Exodus is not the story of just any great hero, however. It is a parable of the human mind and its relationship to Spirit, a template for the spiritual journey. We must not overlook the role played by Pharaoh, the ego, in this drama.

Pharaoh has issued not one but two decrees to murder all Hebrew male infants. He fears them. He fears what they'll do to him and his kingdom. (Note the parallel to the decree of King Herod in Matthew 2:16 to kill all males under the age of two in an attempt to murder the baby Jesus.) Yet despite Pharaoh's murderous intent, baby Moses survives, saved by the river, his mother and sister, and, most of all, Pharaoh's own daughter!

Right from the start, Exodus offers us a powerful contrast between the workings of ego and Spirit. The ego—Pharaoh— commands and bullies. It issues top-down decrees, preemptive strikes designed to eliminate its opponents. Spirit issues no such commands. It neither coerces nor kills. In fact, it does just the opposite. It preserves life. Spirit works by simply arranging events so that, like the river, they flow naturally toward the intended outcome—in this case, the safety of the child who will become Moses.

The story assures us that Pharaoh (the ego) cannot kill off Moses (our connection to Spirit) no matter how hard he tries. He can bellow and stamp his feet and issue all the orders and decrees he likes; they will all come to naught. Pharaoh-ego simply doesn't have the power to vanquish our link to the eternal. His frantic efforts must fail. The baby Moses will live.

Water and the Feminine

Water is a universally recognized symbol for life. Without water, crops die, plankton cannot thrive, and the food chain itself collapses, taking with it all life on Earth. Therefore, Pharaoh's decree to drown all male Hebrew infants in the Nile represents a reversal of the life-giving properties of water. He would use this primal symbol of life to bring about death. His decree is perverse, a travesty against nature.

Yet it's not the river that defeats Pharaoh's murderous intentions. It's the women of Exodus: the midwives who secretly defy him; Moses's mother and sister, who conspire together to undermine his decree; and Pharaoh's own daughter, who delivers the final blow by rescuing the baby and, even though she knows he's a Hebrew, adopting him as her own son.

Is this really such a surprise? It is women who bring life into the world, who grow new life within their wombs and are intimately connected with flow (the lunar cycle of the tides) through their menses.

Pharaoh cannot subvert the nature of water. He cannot transform the symbol of life into the agent of death. Spirit, working through the feminine principle of flow—through the women—will stop him. And so Pharaoh's grim plan is turned on its head. He cannot kill Moses. Neither the Nile nor the women of Exodus obey his decree. The waters ordained by him for death instead support life. Moses, our link to Spirit, survives and thrives.

A Baby Adrift

The story of Moses introduces some significant new wrinkles to the theme of the infant-hero bequeathed to the river to escape death. For unlike Sargon or the other heroes mentioned earlier in the chapter, Moses is never really in danger. His mother does not truly abandon him to the river. He floats among the reeds at the river's placid edge under his sister's watchful eye. Moses is given to the river symbolically, just like the other heroes of myth; but unlike them, he remains safe the entire time.

Of course, from baby Moses's point of view, things may not have looked so rosy. All alone in his little basket, he may easily have *believed* he'd been abandoned—which would explain why he's crying when Pharaoh's daughter finds him. He *feels* completely alone, adrift upon unknown waters. His limited perspective doesn't let him understand that he was never in danger.

How often in our own lives do we feel so alone and uncertain? *Am I in the right career? Should I get married? Do I make the big move? What's the best path to follow?* When we look back at such times with the perspective of the years, we see that, for the most part, things did turn out okay—even when in the short run they didn't. That first job or marriage may have been a disaster, but it paved the way for the next. It helped us learn what we wanted and what we didn't want from life.

Even when we find ourselves stuck in seemingly impossible situations with no obvious way out, Spirit is standing by our side. We remain under its watchful gaze. Like baby Moses, we're never left untended—even though it sometimes feels that way.

The Name *Moses*

The key to unlocking the true meaning of Moses and his birth lies in his name. In the Hebrew Bible, names often suggest an individual's meaning or purpose. For example, Joseph names his firstborn son Manasseh, which in Hebrew means "causing to forget," because "God has made me forget all my trouble and all my father's household" (Gen. 41:51). The name marks Joseph's transition from the son wronged by his family to a mature, successful father with a family of his own.

The naming of Moses is peculiar, however, for several reasons. Although baby Moses was returned to his mother for nursing, the Bible never tells us what name she herself gave the child. Instead, Moses receives his name from Pharaoh's daughter. "The child grew, and [his mother] brought him to Pharaoh's daughter and he became her son. And she named him Moses, and said, 'Because I drew him out of the water'" (Exod. 2:10).

In Hebrew, the name Moses (Moshe) is understood to mean "drawn from" or "drawn out of."[4] The name alludes to the fact that Moses is the child of the river, of the waters of flow and destiny and Spirit. His name reflects what I've called his "second birth."

But why would Pharaoh's daughter, an Egyptian, give this child a Hebrew name? Does the name Moses mean anything in the Egyptian tongue? Yes, it does. It means, "gave birth."[5]

Ironically, the name Moses was incorporated into the names of several famous Pharaohs. It was used as a suffix, added onto the name of a god, in order to show that the god *gave birth to* that particular Pharaoh. A looser translation might be "son of." So, for example, Tut-moses (Thutmose) and Ra-moses (Ramses) were sons of the gods Tut and Ra, respectively. Their names testify to their divine lineage, as these gods "gave birth" to them.[6]

Yet what a peculiar name for Pharaoh's daughter to have chosen for a Hebrew child—especially one she did not herself give birth to. Besides, the name Moses, standing on its own without the name of any god preceding it, seems to defy Egyptian convention. What might this mean?

It could simply be that Pharaoh's daughter didn't know the identity of the baby's father, so she left it blank. But conventional Egyptian usage suggests that Moses is part of some divine lineage, descended from some powerful god. Yet whichever god "gave birth" to him remains unnamed.

In the Hebrew language, the name of God is never pronounced. Other names and acronyms are substituted for It and spoken aloud in Its place, such as Elohim, Adonai, or even simply Ha-Shem (the name). So when Pharaoh's daughter names this baby Moses, with no "god" as a prefix, perhaps the story is trying

31

to tell us something—specifically, that Moses is the "son of" the unnamed and unnamable God of the Hebrews.

The Moses-Mind

If in the parable of Exodus Moses represents some aspect of the human mind, then we're being told right from the start that this part of the mind is descended from God Himself. God "gave birth" to it. This part of the mind has never forgotten its true nature. It has, and always will have, a direct connection to Spirit. I call it the Moses-mind.

What is this Moses-mind like? It's difficult to describe, much less recognize, because we identify so closely with ego. And Exodus is not always clear, because it's easy to confuse Moses the man with Moses the symbol. But we can start by describing what the Moses-mind is *not*. It is not limited by time or space, or by the physical body. It doesn't fear for its survival, and therefore has no need to plan. It doesn't compare its lot with others. Where the ego yammers at us constantly, the Moses-mind understands silence. It guides, but never compels. It knows no guilt because it is incapable of doing harm. It operates through miracles, not forced action, and so the law of cause and effect does not apply to it. And it can express itself in all people.

How can we reach the Moses-mind in ourselves? By being open to it and asking for its help: by recognizing when ego is trying to call the shots and deciding to try a different approach. When we silence the incessant chatter of ego, the Moses-mind naturally comes to the fore. It's been present all along, but like a nightingale's song, it cannot be heard beneath the raucous jack-hammering of the ego-mind.

How can we distinguish the voice of the Moses-mind from the ego's voice? This can be difficult, especially at the start of the journey. As we've seen, the ego is capable of taking on many guises, even that of spiritual seeker. But there are some useful tip-offs.

The guidance of the Moses-mind *feels* very different from our usual decision-making process. There's no sense of urgency to it. No drama. Its guidance comes with a sense of certainty from beyond the level of the personality—deeper by far than the knowledge accumulated through experience. Convention and logic have nothing to do with it. We simply *know* and understand that this knowing is not of us. Most of all, it brings with it a deep sense of peacefulness. The question or problem we struggled with isn't so much solved; it ceases to exist. Seen through the eyes of the Moses-mind, there is no more question, no more problem. We simply misunderstood. And now, seeing clearly, our minds are at peace again. We can get out of the way and allow the miracle to come forth.

In the first chapter of Exodus, the Hebrews are enslaved. In the very next chapter, Moses, who will lead them out of slavery, is born. This juxtaposition suggests that, the moment the mind is enslaved by ego, the agent of its deliverance appears. Because once enslaved, we cannot escape on our own. The ego has hijacked the mind and caused us to forget our true divine lineage. We mistakenly believe the ego to be *us*. A slave who doesn't know he's enslaved, a slave who's never known the meaning of freedom, will never seek to be free. The enslaved mind needs help.

Enter the Moses-mind. Drawn from the ever-flowing waters of Spirit; nurtured and protected by the Feminine Principle of flow; descended from the unnamed, unnamable God Who gave birth to it; its purpose and its destiny are to lead the mind out of bondage and into freedom.

Chapter 4

MURDERING THE EGYPTIAN: FIRST RESPONSE TO SLAVERY

After Moses receives his name from Pharaoh's daughter, the text of Exodus skips ahead many years to his first significant act as an adult.

> Now it came about in those days, when Moses had grown up, that he went out to his brethren and looked on their hard labors; and he saw an Egyptian beating a Hebrew, one of his brethren. So he looked this way and that, and when he saw there was no one around, he struck down the Egyptian and hid him in the sand (Exod. 2:11–12).

The young Moses clearly does not live among his people, the Hebrews, nor is he enslaved as they are. The implication is that he's lived in the palace as the adopted son of Pharaoh's daughter ever since his naming. Then one day he visits his people and sees one of them being beaten by an Egyptian. The incident affects him deeply. It's possible that this is the first time he's actually seen the brutality inflicted upon the Hebrews. Or perhaps he's finally old enough to appreciate their plight as slaves. Either way, he witnesses a wrong against one of his brethren and goes about setting it right.

Of course Moses understands that murder is a crime. Otherwise, why would he look around to make sure no one was watching? And why try to cover up the evidence by hiding the body in the sand? Yet strangely, the fact that he has taken a life doesn't seem to trouble him all that much. It's only when he learns that his unlawful act has been discovered that he panics. This is hardly the behavior we'd expect from a man designated by God to lead his people to freedom.

Nonetheless, for Moses, this is a moment of awakening. He has a destiny to fulfill (although he doesn't know it yet): to free his people. Therefore, when he sees one of them victimized, he's driven to take action by doing anything in his power to help, even commit murder.

But Moses acts rashly, perhaps in anger, and certainly with no regard for the consequences. And what exactly does he accomplish by his action? Does the murder of the Egyptian spark a slave rebellion among the Hebrews? Do they rally to overthrow the tyrant Pharaoh? In fact, just the opposite occurs.

In the next verse, two Hebrews are fighting and Moses steps in to mediate. But to his surprise, one of them turns and challenges him.

> "Who made you a prince or a judge over us? Are you intending to kill me, as you killed the Egyptian?" Then Moses was afraid, and said, "Surely the matter has become known."
>
> When Pharaoh heard of this matter, he tried to kill Moses. But Moses fled . . . and settled in the land of Midian . . . (Exod. 2:14–15).

Because of the murder, Moses has forfeited the respect of his people. They view him, not as a peacemaker, not as someone whose wise judgments can resolve their conflicts, but as a killer—a man who can hurt them. The murder has rendered him unfit to be their leader. Worse still, Moses must flee Egypt to escape Pharaoh's punishment. Once in exile, he can do nothing for his people. His misguided attempt to help them renders him useless.

Imprudent Action

Moses demonstrates the pitfalls of rash, premature action. He makes an ill-conceived attempt to enforce justice for his fellow Hebrews . . . and it backfires (in much the same way as Pharaoh's efforts to kill him). But this should come as no surprise. Moses is still young and immature. He's not ready to lead.

Just as fruit needs to ripen before it can be eaten and enjoyed, so too must our desires. Of course Moses wants to help his people. He sees a wrong and wants to set it right. But a new desire, however noble, however sharp and urgent, is often unripe. Like hard, green fruit, if we act on it—if we eat it—it proves bitter and indigestible. We must spit it out or suffer a bellyache. Either way, our hunger goes unsatisfied. We end up worse off for having taken that foolish bite. We must learn to let our desires ripen.

Greg, 14 years old, wants to be a rock star. He pesters his parents to buy him an expensive guitar. At Christmas, they give in to his wishes. He's overjoyed. At first he practices avidly, but he can't get the notes to sound like the bands on YouTube. He lacks finger strength and fumbles the tougher chords. After a few weeks, Greg's frustration trumps his commitment. He sticks the guitar in his closet and decides to become a filmmaker instead. For his birthday, he wants a high-definition video camera.

Greg's desire to be a rock star, initially so powerful, is unripe. He lacks the maturity to be patient, to practice scales over and over again in order to develop dexterity and finger strength. By pushing ahead with unrealistic expectations for instant success, he not only fails to fulfill his desire, but makes it unlikely that he'll ever pick up the guitar to give it another try.

Sadly, tales like Greg's are not confined to adolescence. All of us fall victim to impatience when what we think we want lies beyond reach. How many adults have tried meditation, for example, only to conclude after a few frustrating sittings that it's impossible. They can't silence their minds, so they give up. They approach meditation like a cookbook recipe. Follow the steps—sit quietly, close your eyes, chant a mantra—and voila, instant inner peace. Only the mind refuses to cooperate.

When we embark on a path of true transformation, we cannot rush things along. We can't make it happen all at once. As Moses learned the hard way, we must be patient. We must let our desires ripen.

Going It Alone

When Moses murders the Egyptian, he's acting on his own. He sees the Egyptian beating the Hebrew and decides he must do something about it. He appoints himself judge, jury, and executioner. Moses does not seek guidance. How could he? He doesn't yet know it exists, much less how or where to look for it. He was raised in the palace of the Pharaoh "who did not know Joseph." What could he have learned there of God and Spirit? Instead, he assumes that going it alone is the best course of action. Only after the fact does he discover how wrong he is—how imprudent his action was—and by then, it's too late.

By contrast, recall the chain of events that saved Moses from Pharaoh's deadly decree as a baby. With flawless choreography, his mother, his sister, and Pharaoh's daughter all show up at precisely the right moments to play their parts. None of them could have accomplished this on their own. Only by their joint effort, under the direction of Spirit, was his life saved.

The power of Spirit expressed through the principle of flow will always overcome forced, unilateral action. When we find ourselves fretting, like Pharaoh, about consequences that may never come to pass—when we feel the need to plan obsessively or when we're triggered into angry, impulsive action as the young Moses was—we can be sure we're on the wrong track. We're misguided, literally. We need to step back from the problem and ask for guidance, as the mature Moses learns later on. Any action we take on our own, however well-intentioned, is prone to backfire.

Survival, Violence, and the Spiritually Immature Mind

In murdering the Egyptian, Moses gives us a dramatic example of the workings of the spiritually immature mind. He acts on impulse, driven by raw emotion, with no understanding of the big picture. Moses is like the Hollywood action hero who shoots first without any thought for the consequences. This may work out well in the movies, but seldom in real life.

When we resort to violence, we've embraced action of the most extreme kind. We've essentially concluded that if we don't intervene urgently and decisively *right now,* we'll suffer harm . . . or worse, wind up dead. We must strike before we're stricken, attack before we're attacked, kill before we're killed. No other solution seems possible.

The only circumstances that could possibly justify such violence are threats to survival. When faced with a true survival threat, the brain must react quickly. It doesn't have time to evaluate the nature of the danger and calmly weigh all possible responses. In the short interval between peril and response, we must rapidly process the limited information available and come to a decision. A rival tribe has sprung an ambush. The wolf pack is circling. Survival is on the line. Do you stand your ground and fight or run away?

Survival threats mobilize the most primitive parts of the brain, in particular a small, almond-shaped structure in the midbrain called the amygdala. It's the amygdala's job to determine when life is at risk. But it can only process information in a rudimentary, black-and-white manner. It's incapable of making fine distinctions or appreciating nuance. Based on its crude read of the situation, if the amygdala senses a threat, it generates a massive fear-rage response that primes us for violence.

Evolutionarily, this makes sense. Those who respond quickly to danger, with overwhelming force, are more likely to stay alive. In our modern world, however, true threats to survival are rare. The driver cutting you off on the freeway, the plate slipping from your hand and shattering on the floor, your two-year-old stubbornly refusing to get in her car seat—these do not put your life at risk. You will live through them, guaranteed! But to the amygdala, they process no differently than a charging rhino. They trigger unjustified terror or rage. What was at one time an adaptive reflex now works against us—as Moses discovered.

We react to survival-level threats with a fight-or-flight response, and Moses's behavior demonstrates both of these. When the Egyptian strikes the Hebrew, he reacts with murderous violence and fights. Two verses later, when he learns his crime has been discovered and that Pharaoh seeks *his* death, he takes flight.

What Exodus seems to be telling us is that neither fight nor flight is an effective response to the ego's slavery. They represent opposite sides of the same emotional coin. If we fight, we inevitably wind up taking flight out of fear of retaliation. And if we flee, we only postpone the confrontation that we tried to avoid out of fear. The story of Moses and the Egyptian cautions us that anger and violence are by their very nature unripe. They do not serve us on the spiritual journey. They will not set us free.

When we apply this lesson to our own lives, it's important to remember how frequently we perceive danger where none in fact exists. As we've seen, the ego identifies with many different roles and beliefs, each of which it considers an essential aspect of the self. Threaten *any one of these,* and the ego will retaliate as if life itself were on the line. Politically motivated violence, workplace rampages by fired employees, murders committed by jealous spouses—all reflect the ego's inability to walk away from some treasured role or belief.

Sadly, our culture is stuck at the same level of spiritual development as the young Moses. We react to wrongdoing with a knee-jerk desire for vengeance. If we hear of a heinous crime, we call for the death penalty, just like Pharaoh. Violence is a staple of our entertainment in movies, on TV, and in the gaming world. It's become so commonplace that few of us give it a second thought. We're more offended by sexuality than bloodshed.

Politicians promise to "fight" for us. They declare war on diseases or social conditions that seem beyond our control: "the war on poverty," "the war on drugs," "the war on cancer," and even, ironically, "the war on terror." We assume that our desire to vanquish these ills will somehow bring us peace. Our logic is flawed. As with Moses and his people's slavery, going to war does not solve the problem; it makes it worse.

෯

Violence is always unripe—an overreaction to threat. But it is really just an extreme example of the ego's predilection for taking strong executive action. The ego believes that action is the only way to solve a problem. "Don't just stand there, *do* something!"

Pharaoh certainly operates out of this belief. He fears that the Hebrews have grown too numerous, so he takes decisive action and enslaves them. Moses behaves the same way when he kills the Egyptian. He sees a threat and leaps into action. He's grown up in Pharaoh's palace, after all, the symbolic home of the ego, so it should come as no surprise that he reacts to provocation as the ego does: with shortsighted, murderous action.

By contrast, Spirit knows the big picture. It knows all the variables and all possible outcomes. When we entrust our lives to Spirit, we do not feel compelled to immediately attack every problem with some type of action. We don't need to go it alone. We can wait and allow circumstances to ripen. And when we finally do act, we're guided by the hand of Spirit. How could such action not be effective?

"Murdering the Egyptian"

In the parable of Exodus, "murdering the Egyptian" becomes a metaphor for *any* action that's not guided by Spirit. Whenever anger incites us to violence, we've murdered the Egyptian. Whenever we force the situation in order to combat a sense of powerlessness, we've murdered the Egyptian. Whenever we swim against the current instead of flowing with it, we've murdered the Egyptian. Indeed, even the most well-intended actions can hide a murdered Egyptian.

※

A woman in psychotherapy with me wants to confront her alcoholic father about his violence toward her mother. She doesn't see that confronting him will only fuel the fire. He'll deny her allegations, scream that she's insane, and, at best, nothing will change. At worst, after she leaves he'll take it out on her mother. Only when this woman develops inner strength will she be ready to meet her father's rage and lies with the calm face of truth.

Another woman asks me to hypnotize her to force her to remember the painful details of her childhood sexual abuse. She doesn't see that her request itself is a replay of the abuse. She'll lie there frozen, eyes shut tight, while I inflict on her the memories her own mind deemed too painful to remember. She'd rather confront her past in one swift blow and have it over with than do the difficult inner work necessary to come to terms with her abuse and truly be free of it.

After the disappointing failure of a five-year relationship, a man decides to marry a woman he's met only recently. He's getting older and doesn't want to waste any more time. And although their sexual chemistry is only so-so, she seems like a nice enough person. So he proposes, insisting they set the wedding date as soon as possible.

A runner recovering from a knee injury overrides the advice of her doctors and sets herself a very ambitious training schedule in order to qualify for the upcoming marathon. A few miles into her routine, she feels a twinge of pain, but she pushes through it. Pain is a sign of weakness. No pain, no gain, right? She's going to run that marathon if it kills her.

A young candidate for the priesthood prepares to take vows of celibacy, knowing full well that he hasn't come to terms with his sexual urges. But he hopes that somehow, by taking this vow, they'll magically disappear. He's too afraid to face them and deal with them. It never occurs to him that, if he must struggle to stay celibate, then he's not ready to give up his sexual identity. Instead, he pushes ahead with the ordination. He will murder his sexuality into submission by assuming the role of priest.

Jenna is new to Buddhism. She's read about the possibility of enlightenment and been powerfully drawn to the idea. And she's learned that the greatest obstacle to achieving enlightenment is her ego. Through meditation, she's determined to eradicate every last vestige of ego. She'll throttle her thoughts down to silence, keeping her mind empty and her spine stiff and straight. She'll storm the gates of enlightenment and force her ego to surrender to her Buddha nature. Enlightenment will be hers.

Jenna's ego has pulled a clever bait and switch on her. It has cloaked itself in the garb of spirituality in order to divert her from the spiritual path, and in the process make itself stronger. For *only the ego believes that spiritual wisdom can be won by force.* Only the ego would attempt to murder the ego. Instead, Jenna must allow her practice to mature, until she's no longer grasping for *any* outcome, but simply being present in the moment. She must ripen to the discovery that the journey is not one of doing, but of undoing.

In each situation, we goad ourselves into premature or misguided action because of our need (the ego's need, really) to achieve some outcome that we've decided is too important, too vital to our sense of well-being, to have to wait for. The fear, anger, or shame of going without it drives us to impulsive, reckless action. And this action rips us from Spirit and its guidance. Like the immature Moses, we murder the Egyptian. And like Moses, we suffer the consequences.

Moses and Buddha: Two Approaches to Awakening

The life story of the Buddha offers some intriguing parallels to that of Moses. The Buddha, born Siddhartha Gautama, also grows up in a palace. His father, the king, tries to shelter him from the harsh realities of life, so he reaches adulthood with no knowledge of human suffering. He has never been enslaved by fear.

As a young adult, despite his father's attempts to shield him, Siddhartha leaves the safety of the palace walls to visit with his subjects. He spies an old man, then a sick man, and finally a corpse. Faced with the realities of aging, illness, and death, Siddhartha decides he must leave his royal life of privilege. He embarks upon a self-imposed exile, determined to find a way to escape these maladies and gain true spiritual freedom.

Both Siddhartha and Moses venture out of their protected environments to unexpectedly meet with oppression and death. The encounter drives each into exile: Siddhartha by choice, Moses to escape punishment. Siddhartha's insight leads him, not to fight or flight, but (after many years) to enlightenment under the Bodhi tree—an awakening that strips away all sense of personal identity, all vestiges of ego. The man Siddhartha is no more; he has transformed into the Buddha.

Moses's story is a better fit for the Western mind with its penchant for action. It suggests that we gain spiritual insight not only by contemplation, but through a process of trial and error—that is, through life itself. When we act imprudently, without ripeness, we learn by the consequences of our action (exile) that we have erred. We conclude that there must be a better way to achieve our goals, and we set out to find it. Our spiritual journey advances in fits and starts—three steps forward, two back—as we make mistakes and learn from them, groping our way forward toward ultimate truth.

The Preconditions for Ripeness

There's one final question we must ask before moving on with the story of Exodus. Why was Moses so unripe? Why did he murder the Egyptian instead of trying to truly help his people? Exodus gives us the answer immediately after Moses settles into his new life of exile in the land of Midian.

The reason Moses can't free his people at this point in the story is because his people aren't ready. How do we know this? *Because they haven't asked for it.* They haven't recognized their need for help, and so nothing Moses or anyone else can do will help them. Their desire for freedom is also unripe.

At the conclusion of Exodus, Chapter 2, the old Pharaoh dies, and a hugely important transition takes place: the Hebrews ask for help.

> And the sons of Israel sighed because of the bondage, and they cried out; and their cry for help because of their bondage rose up to God. So God heard their groaning; and God remembered His covenant with Abraham, Isaac, and Jacob. God saw the sons of Israel, and God took notice of them (Exod. 2:23–25).

The Hebrews cry out, and God hears their cry and takes notice of them. He remembers His covenant. In reality, He'd never truly forgotten it. But without their appeal, He cannot act. As we'll see later, God cannot force His will upon them. He needs an invitation of some kind, an opening.

Now the Hebrews cry out. They want freedom—release from bondage—and they want it more than anything. Now they're ready. Now they're ripe. Now God can intervene on their behalf.

The same process holds true for our minds. Until we get desperate, until our suffering under the ego becomes so unbearable that it forces us to cry out for help, the Moses-mind remains in exile, distant and unreachable. Only when we cry out do we invite Spirit into our lives.

⚶

Bill Thetford and Helen Schucman, psychologists in the highly demanding academic environment of Columbia University, reached a moment of crisis similar to that of the Hebrews. Bill one day got fed up with all the competition and backstabbing. He walked into Helen's office and said, "There must be another way. Our attitudes are so negative that we can't work anything out."[1] And he made a commitment to finding this new way. He would no longer be drawn into the poisonous atmosphere of anger and criticism so endemic to the department. Henceforth, he would seek cooperation, not conflict. He would look for the best in his colleagues, not the worst.

Helen instantly agreed to join him. In a matter of months, the channeling of *A Course in Miracles* began. Had Bill not cried out, had he not given voice to his suffering and committed to finding another way, there would perhaps be no *Course* today.

Until we know that we're suffering and reach out for help—because all of our own devices and plans have come to naught—we will remain enslaved. This crying out is really the first conscious act of the spiritual journey. We recognize our bondage and our suffering, and with no agenda of our own—no plan, wish, or outcome in mind other than release from suffering—we cry out for help. We don't care what form it takes, as long as it offers relief.

When we cry out, we make real our intention for change. We've opened our minds to Spirit, and Spirit comes, bearing miracles.

☙ ☙

Chapter 5

THE BURNING BUSH;
AWAKENING TO SPIRIT

The Hebrews cry out, and God hears their cry. Now at last the time is ripe for Moses to return to Egypt and lead them out of bondage. Moses, however, has been living in exile in Midian for many years. He's married and has at least one son. He spends his days tending his father-in-law's flocks. The drama of Egypt is long behind him.

Moses has matured—a good thing, no doubt—but he's no longer focused on the plight his people. The passion for justice and freedom that once drove him to commit murder has given way to a comfortable domestic routine. Moses needs help to remember his purpose. He needs a wake-up call. In the very next passage of Exodus, he gets it.

Moses is out pasturing the flocks and leads them to the western side of the wilderness, where he happens upon the Mountain of God. What Moses finds there is one of the best-known events in the Bible.

> The angel of the Lord appeared to him in a blazing
> fire from the midst of a bush; and he looked, and behold,

the bush was burning with fire, yet the bush was not consumed (Exod. 3:2).

What a remarkable image this is: a bush blazing with fire, but not consumed by it. It's an apt symbol for the reawakening of Moses's passion—his *burning* desire to free his people, which has lain dormant for so many years. The angel of the Lord appears in order to *light a fire under him,* to get him *all fired up* about resuming his mission. The burning bush is his wake-up call. In the parable of Exodus, it represents an inner reawakening to the presence of God, a new openness to receiving the wisdom of the Moses-mind.

Such a fire activates us in a manner very different from the fight-or-flight response of the amygdala. It's not fueled by blind rage, nor does it lead to unripe action. It's not about survival. It's the fire that reignites our spiritual journey when we've lapsed into the familiar and comfortable routines of day-to-day life. And like the bush itself, this fire will neither consume nor destroy us. It restores us to our true purpose: the pursuit of spiritual freedom.

Turning Aside

The burning bush is not merely an inspirational image. It's a powerful experience with a very practical purpose: the burning bush gets Moses to pay attention.

> So Moses said, "I must turn aside now, and see this marvelous sight, why the bush is not burned up." When the Lord saw that he turned aside to look, God called to him from the midst of the bush, and said, "Moses, Moses!" And he said, "Here I am" (Exod. 3:3–4).

Moses "turns aside" because of the burning bush. He's curious. He experiences wonder, perhaps even awe, at this incredible sight and deviates from his normal routine to investigate it. In doing so, he takes a step toward God, and God responds.

But God waits until He sees that Moses "turned aside to look." Only then does God summon him. God does not compel Moses to pay attention. He doesn't confront him with a spectacle so grand and impressive that it can't be ignored. Niagara Falls doesn't materialize in the midst of the desert. Trees don't start walking around and talking to him. Such sights would certainly have caused Moses to turn aside, but not of his own free will.

By the same token, Moses could have simply dismissed the sight of the burning bush as no big deal—a common brush fire—and gotten on with his shepherding. Or he could have fled from it in fear. Yet he does none of these things. He turns aside, and he approaches.

Before we can establish a living connection with God through our Moses-mind, we must *choose* to take off the blinders and turn aside, however briefly, from life as we know it. We must be willing to suspend the daily routine and respond to the wonders of the burning bushes that come our way. These are the moments when a window to Spirit opens and the fresh breeze of the miraculous blows through, catching our attention, calling us to our true purpose, and reminding us to awaken.

⚉

Daniel and I had worked together in therapy for many years. He'd accomplished a great deal, changing from an anxious, depressed man trapped in an unrewarding job to someone with many interests, eager to embrace life. As a result of his shift, Daniel began to question whether he could continue at his job while remaining true to himself. He worked for a large state university where the demands consistently outweighed the meager rewards. Each year he was asked to take on more projects, requiring ever longer hours, with no additional compensation or thanks. The stress was suffocating him. He began to feel a desperate sense of panic when he awoke in the morning just thinking about the day ahead. The final blow came when he spearheaded a consolidation of services that would save the university tens of millions of dollars and got zero recognition for it—not even a polite note of appreciation from the president or provost. Daniel was a slave.

Realizing this, he decided to take early retirement. But he didn't have the savings to stop working for good. Instead, Daniel planned to supplement his modest pension by doing freelance consulting to private schools and universities. A few months passed, however, and the clients weren't exactly pounding on his door. Meanwhile, the bills kept mounting. Every time he picked up the checkbook, that old, familiar sense of desperation would grab him by the throat, and he feared he was going under.

One fine day in autumn, Daniel was out raking leaves. He paused briefly to glance up at the sky. The late afternoon sun filtered down through the tree limbs, illuminating the reds, yellows, and oranges of the leaves from within, as if they were jewels afire. It was a breathtaking moment, and it filled him with awe. The very next instant, however, Daniel's inner Pharaoh was back, taking him to task. How could he stand there gawking at the leaves when he didn't even have a job? He should be doing something productive, something to make money, instead of staring up at the trees like an idiot.

Fortunately, Daniel recognized the familiar voice of oppression. It had served him poorly in the past, and he knew that if he listened to it now, he'd wind up consumed by anxiety. Instead, he chose to challenge the voice. Sure, he'd love to find work. But how could he *not* enjoy the sight of the leaves? Job or no job, money or no money, a moment like that was precious. And so, Daniel made a promise to himself: From that day forward, whenever he felt trapped by money fears, he wouldn't fret. Instead, he would remember the fiery translucence of the leaves and what was really important in life. Did this insight solve Daniel's money problems? Not in the way we might think. (We'll catch up to Daniel and his journey in a later chapter.)

How many of us have seen autumn leaves catch fire at sunset as Daniel did? Or clouds streaked with orange, pink, and red? Or the full moon rising above a placid lake? How many of us have beheld wondrous sights . . . and walked right by them? When we fail to turn aside, we've closed the door on Spirit. We've ignored the invitation of the burning bush and lost a chance to encounter God.

A Miracle That Calls Our Name

The burning bush represents the first miracle of the Exodus journey. Its purpose, as we've seen, is to get our attention and pry us loose from our everyday worries and routines—to rekindle our awareness of the Moses-mind, which has been lost in exile while we let ego run the show.

But the burning bush is more than a generic wake-up call. Once God sees that Moses has turned aside, He calls his name aloud, and Moses responds, "Here I am." Moses is present. He's not afraid like he was in Egypt after slaying the Egyptian. He doesn't run away. He stands and answers God. He's willing to be seen, to be accountable.

The first miracle of the spiritual journey, the first that we encounter as conscious seekers, not only causes us to turn aside, it speaks to us directly in a highly personal voice. It calls our name, so to speak. Spirit knows us better than we know ourselves. It knows the best way to get our attention, how to wake us up without scaring us. This is important, because fear would drive us right back into the arms of ego.

I vividly recall the first miracle of my own spiritual journey. I was a college student on winter break at a ski resort. I'd just started working with *A Course in Miracles* and was having a lot of difficulty with its language and philosophy. I sat in the lodge, poring over the *Course* while my friends were out on the slopes. A janitor sweeping up—a kid even younger than I was—approached me and asked what I was reading. I was too embarrassed to tell him the truth. I wasn't comfortable with all that God stuff, not back then. Instead, I said it was a book about the mind. This led us into a pleasant discussion, the details of which are long since lost to me. Finally, turning away to resume his work, he muttered almost to himself, "All I know is that all real pleasure comes from doing God's will."

I immediately branded the guy a religious fanatic and, with relief that our conversation was over, returned to where I'd left off in the *Course*. The very next line read: "All real pleasure comes from doing God's will." That got my attention. I didn't necessarily agree with the statement, not at the time, but the coincidence was beyond striking. There was no rational explanation for it. I was shocked, intrigued, and not the least bit frightened. The form the miracle took was perfect for me at the time. It was compelling enough to convince me to stick with the *Course* despite my difficulties, but not powerful enough to scare me.

That incident—that miracle—helped cement my commitment to my own spiritual journey. Whatever else I might choose to pursue, whatever goals I might set for myself, this had priority. It also showed me, through direct experience, that miracles were possible. They didn't need to be awesome or terrifying to make their point. And no matter how insignificant I might feel, I was worthy of them.

Removing Sandals

After Moses responds, "Here I am," God orders him to remove his sandals, because "the place on which you are standing is holy ground" (Exod. 3:5). Most readers assume that God doesn't want Moses to defile this holy ground with his dirty sandals, but there's another way to understand it.

What makes this ground holy isn't the dirt or the location. It's what is taking place there: Moses encountering God. What could be more holy than that? Moses has turned aside to let God enter his life. Why then must he remove his sandals?

Recall that the whole purpose of the burning bush is to reunite Moses with his mission—to reawaken him to God. By removing his sandals, Moses experiences direct contact with this holy ground through the soles of his feet. The sandals that protect his feet out in the world have no use here. They can only obstruct. So the act of removing sandals is symbolic. It signifies his willingness to remove all barriers that stand between him and God.

In this sense, wherever we happen to encounter the miracle of awakening (and indeed, all the miracles that follow)—wherever we turn aside to meet Spirit on its terms, not ours—that place becomes holy ground. It is holy because it's where we let God in for the first time. And we want nothing to distance us from this experience, which inaugurates our spiritual journey. Therefore, we remove our sandals, symbolically setting aside the trappings of the world, in order to experience God as fully and directly as possible.

"I Will Be With You"

God next tells Moses why He has summoned him. He has heard the cry of the Hebrews and intends to bring them out of Egypt "to a good and spacious land, to a land flowing with milk and honey" (Exod. 3:8), namely, the Promised Land.

"Therefore, come now, and I will send you to Pharaoh, so that you may bring My people, the sons of Israel, out of Egypt" (Exod. 3:10).

God has assigned Moses his task. *Now* the time is ripe for Moses to return to Egypt, confront the new Pharaoh, and free his people.

But Moses resists. He questions God: "Who am I, that I should go to Pharaoh, and that I should bring the sons of Israel out of Egypt?" (Exod. 3:11). Moses doubts his ability to carry out the mission, and who can blame him? The last time he tried to help his people in Egypt, he wound up fleeing for his life. Now God instructs him to return to the land of his birth, where he is wanted for murder, in order to challenge the most powerful ruler on earth.

God reassures Moses, "Certainly I will be with you" (Exod. 3:12). These words are, I believe, the most important words in all of Exodus, and perhaps the entire Bible. God is letting Moses know that now, when he undertakes this seemingly impossible task, things will be different. He won't be going it alone. God will be with him.

Once we turn aside and take notice of Spirit—in whatever way that occurs—once we start down the road to freedom and the Promised Land, we leave our old life behind. We can no longer pretend that the daily routine is all there is. We've been summoned by name to our true purpose: to free our minds from the ego's slavery. This is a daunting task. Indeed, left to our own devices, we would certainly fail. But God assures us that we will not be alone. He will be with us. He will support every step of our journey. How else could it be? This is, after all, the journey to reclaim our spiritual inheritance, our true identity in God. How could He, our constant companion, not accompany us?

Yet seldom are we aware of God's Presence. And, like Moses, even when we are aware, too often we feel uncertain. Considering the enormity of the task and the challenges it will require of us, the knowledge that "I will be with you" can feel like cold comfort. We want more than perfunctory reassurances. We want proof of God's support. We want to know that He'll really be by our side when the going gets rough.

Moses Objects

God's words—"I will be with you"—fail to console Moses. He has very specific fears that he needs addressed. He worries that the Hebrews won't believe him when he says that God sent him. He's concerned that they'll demand he tell them God's name. So God reveals His Name: "I AM WHO I AM. . . . Thus you shall say to the sons of Israel, 'I AM has sent me to you'" (Exod. 3:14).

But Moses isn't satisfied. "What if they will not believe me, or listen to what I say? For they may say, 'The Lord has not appeared to you'" (Exod. 4:1). So God offers Moses two miracles to perform by way of proof. His staff becomes a serpent, and his healthy arm turns white with leprosy. God even provides Moses with a third miracle as a backup—changing water into blood—in case the first two fail to impress the Hebrews. But none of these mollify his concerns.

And now, at last, Moses gets to his real objection, the one that's been troubling him all along: his shame about his speech difficulties. "Please, Lord, I have never been eloquent, neither recently nor in time past . . . for I am slow of speech and slow of tongue" (Exod. 4:10).

God reminds Moses that He will be with him, but Moses begs God to send someone else, *anyone* else. Now God grows angry. However, He obviously can hear how deeply ashamed Moses feels, because once again He offers a remedy. As if on cue, Moses's brother, Aaron, appears, ". . . coming out to meet you" (Exod. 4:14). Aaron is a gifted speaker, but he's no leader. The task of freeing the Hebrews still belongs to Moses. Therefore, God tells Moses to "speak to him and put the words in his mouth. . . . Moreover, he [Aaron] shall speak for you to the people; and he will be as a mouth for you, and you will be as God to him" (Exod. 4:15–16). And then, for the third time, God promises that when Moses confronts Pharaoh, He will be with him. Moses finally has what he needs. He can depart for Egypt.

⚭

What's the meaning of this back-and-forth between God and Moses, and how does it relate to the spiritual journey?

Moses shares his fears with God, and God offers him four remedies: the fact of His presence ("I will be with you"), His name ("I AM THAT I AM"), His miracles (the serpent, leprosy, and turning water into blood), and finally, the specific remedy needed for his own sense of inadequacy (Aaron to serve as his mouthpiece).

When we take our first steps on the spiritual journey, we're often fearful. We feel inadequate to the task. Like Moses, we ask, "Who, me?" and "Why me?" God responds, first by giving us knowledge of His constant Presence: "I will be with you." Wherever we may go, we will not be alone. Next, He offers His name. God is infinite. Words cannot express His being. Yet for Moses's benefit, that is, to meet our human needs, God will take on a name, which functions rather like a business card or Internet address. Knowing the name, we know how to reach its recipient. God calls out, "Moses, Moses," and Moses replies, "I am here." Now Moses can call upon God's name and trust that he will receive an answer. A reciprocal relationship has been established. God then gives Moses three miracles he can use to prove that he really does speak for God. The need for proof is important. Without it, how can we be certain that the journey is real—that we're not delusional? Miracles provide the proof we need. They reassure us. And they become the means by which Spirit leads us out of the ego's bondage.

⚜

A friend named Donna had recently started working with *A Course in Miracles*. One morning while driving to work she was mulling over some of its ideas with a fair degree of skepticism. As a test, she remarked aloud, "If this really is the truth, then I need proof—something that will stop me in my tracks." The very next moment her tire blew out. Indeed, this stopped Donna in her tracks. She wasn't injured, and other than the flat tire, her car wasn't damaged in the least. But she had her proof.

Helen Schucman, the psychologist who channeled *A Course in Miracles*, also needed proof. As a child, she visited the healing shrine of Lourdes in France with her parents. She was so inspired by the miraculous healings that had taken place there (testified to by the piles of discarded crutches) that she bought herself a Catholic rosary—despite the fact that she was Jewish. She describes her experience as follows.

> That night in my room I stayed up in the dark with my rosary in my hand . . . and I thought about God. . . . Suddenly I had an idea. This was a wonderful place, and perhaps if I asked for a miracle for myself I would get it. . . . "Please, God," I said aloud, "I'm not a Catholic, but if all this is true, would you send me a miracle so I can believe in you?" I had already decided what the miracle should be. I would close my eyes and say three

Hail Marys; if there was a meteor in the sky when I opened my eyes, that would be my miracle. I did not really expect to find the meteor, but I closed my eyes and said three Hail Marys anyway. When I opened my eyes again, the sky was full of shooting stars. I watched in stunned silence, and then whispered, "It's my miracle. God really did send it."[1]

Sadly, Helen later discounted her miracle. She recalled that her tour guide had mentioned the possibility of meteor showers at that time of year, and so she questioned whether what she'd seen was truly miraculous. But there's little doubt that both Helen and Donna received exactly the confirmation they requested.

The Miracle Moses Needs Most

The need for proof is not Moses's main concern, however. He's already turned aside at the sight of the burning bush. He has engaged with God and is willing to do the job; he's just feeling insecure. The most important miracle for him—and for us as well—is not the one that offers proof, but the one that removes the obstacles to going forward. In Moses's case, the obstacle is shame about his speech. Until God addresses this, all else that He has offered in the way of assurances and proofs means little. Moses will remain paralyzed by his self-consciousness. The miracle Moses needs most is Aaron. Once his brother appears, Moses's shame is relieved, and he can do what God asks.

It's surprising how often the miracle we need lies no farther away than our "brother." That is to say, it's right around the corner, waiting for us where we least expect it. The solution to our greatest impediment lies not in some distant corner of the earth. It's already in our vicinity, hidden in plain sight among the familiar. And *it's coming to find us*. We don't need to go out and search for it. We don't need an action plan. Indeed, if we try to seek out this miracle, it's certain that ego will climb aboard and find some way to hijack it. The moment we commit to the journey, the miracles we need will find us. And they'll frequently come through those we know: symbolically, our brothers and sisters.

My good friend Rachel felt guided to sell her house in New Jersey and move far away. She'd had a long and fruitful career as a therapist and now felt called to join a loose community of like-minded spiritual seekers living out on the West Coast. She fixed up the house, getting it ready to show, and dutifully listed it with a Realtor—who proceeded to tell her that it would take at least a year to sell, because the market was at an absolute standstill.

Intuitively, Rachel knew this couldn't be right. Her guidance was quite clear, and it simply didn't make sense that she'd have to mark time and put her journey on hold for an entire year. For some reason, she kept picturing her hairdresser living in the house. So, at her next hair appointment, she casually mentioned that her house was for sale.

As it turned out, her hairdresser was looking to buy her first house. She toured Rachel's place with her family, and they all fell in love with it. The very next day they agreed on a price, and Rachel was headed west. The help she needed was right there waiting, already in her life. Her connection to Spirit let her find it, trust it, and act on it.

Of course, in reality, we're all fellow travelers making the journey together. In this sense, *everyone* is our brother (or sister). Whoever shows up to answer the call, whomever Spirit appoints to help us with our problem, is revealed as a "brother." Joined together in this way through miracles, Spirit demonstrates that we are all brothers and sisters to each other.

You Get What You Need (for the Journey)

God answers each and every objection that Moses makes. God hears his fear and shame and addresses each in turn. Such is the case with our own spiritual journey as well. We may start out convinced of our inadequacy. Maybe we feel we're not strong enough or smart enough to overcome the many Pharaohs in our lives and our minds—that we don't have what it takes. We think we need a graduate degree, a small fortune, or an amazing spiritual mentor before we heed God's call to escape from bondage.

Exodus tells us that this is not so. It's just our shame putting up roadblocks, like Moses with his slow speech. We lack the perspective to evaluate our own strengths and talents, much less to understand how Spirit might put them to use. Spirit knows who we are and what we're capable of. As slaves, we do not and cannot know.

Therefore, if we truly lack something essential for the journey, Spirit will provide it. If God could send Aaron to Moses, Spirit will surely send our way the "brother" best suited to our circumstances. Whether we think we lack ideas, skills, or resources, if we trust God's promise of "I will be with you," then all things become possible. We get what we need.

Many years ago, my friend Patricia Hopkins was preparing to coauthor with Sherry Ruth Anderson the book *The Feminine Face of God*. Their plan was to travel the country interviewing women from diverse backgrounds about their spiritual journeys. There was only one hitch: they had no funds for such protracted travel, and without money, they simply could not proceed. But they remained committed to the project and kept working on it to the extent that they could.

Then one day a dainty little envelope lined with tulips arrived in the mail. Neither of them knew the woman who sent it, but she wrote that she'd heard about their project and wanted to do what she could to support it. She enclosed a check—in the amount of $20,000. Just like that, they had the funds. Without seeking it, a sister had come to them bringing exactly what was needed for their journey.

The Beginning and End Are One

The voice of the burning bush has one more command for Moses and one more lesson for us. The voice instructs Moses, ". . .

when you have brought the people out of Egypt, you shall worship God at this mountain" (Exod. 3:12). Before the Hebrews' journey has even begun, God makes clear that the goal is not just freedom from physical bondage, but the ability to join with Him and worship Him freely on holy ground, as Moses did, far from the site of their captivity.

True freedom means more than escaping bondage. It comes when our minds and hearts are also free to reestablish a connection with their Creator. This is the real goal of the exodus from Egypt. Leaving Egypt does not itself make us free. Freedom comes from leaving Egypt *and* worshipping God on His mountain. The first without the second means nothing.

❀

When God tells Moses that he will return with his people to this very mountain—the site of the burning bush—He employs a powerful technique commonly used in sports psychology, namely, to visualize and mentally experience the outcome one intends *as if it has already occurred.* The Olympic diver sees herself flex atop the board; feels the tension in her muscles as she springs into her dive; the exquisite balance of her body as she lifts, arcs, and plummets; the delight of knifing through the water's surface with barely a ripple . . . and the swell of applause as she steps out of the pool—all before she ever climbs the ladder for her gold-medal dive. God does not say to Moses, "If by some miracle you manage to pull this off, come by and worship me on Saturday." It's not a question of *if,* it's *when.* We begin the journey secure in the knowledge of its successful conclusion.

This technique links the future and the present in one continuous loop. We learn to see time as God sees it—a seamless, eternal whole, as opposed to the ego's string of days lined up back-to-back, with death waiting at the finish.

The ego must fear the future, because it cannot control what lies unseen along that procession of days. God, by contrast, is omniscient. His being encompasses every event that ever was or will be. From His perspective, the journey to freedom is not just foreordained; it has *already happened.* In God's eternal present, the journey is over the instant we take our first step. The moment the Hebrews cry out, the Promised Land is theirs. It's only a matter of time. And from the perspective of eternity, time is really no big deal. Moses may question his fitness to lead his people from bondage, but God has no doubts, because He already knows the outcome. His will has been done, is being done, and will be done through the man Moses and the Moses-mind.

※

In summary, when the Moses-mind reawakens in us at the burning bush, it is endowed with: a direct line to God through His Name; the knowledge that it cannot be split apart from God, that He accompanies it always ("I will be with you"); and the capacity to work miracles in His Name. Lastly, it is given a way (symbolized by Aaron) to fluently and eloquently address Pharaoh-ego in its own language, the familiar language of our inner dialogue—that is, the spoken word. With these attributes in hand, the Moses-mind has all it needs to reenter the ego's Egypt and lobby for our freedom.

※ ※

Chapter 6

CONFRONTING PHARAOH

Following the command of God at the burning bush, Moses returns to Egypt. With Aaron at his side, he confronts Pharaoh and demands the release of his people.

> . . . Moses and Aaron came and said to Pharaoh, "Thus says the Lord, the God of Israel, 'Let My people go that they may celebrate a feast to Me in the wilderness.'" But Pharaoh said, "Who is the Lord that I should obey His voice to let Israel go? I do not know the Lord, and besides, I will not let Israel go" (Exod. 5:1–2).

Pharaoh claims not to know this god of the Hebrews, therefore, why should he obey him? Pharaoh then issues orders that make the lot of the Hebrew slaves even worse. They will receive no more straw for their brick making. They must gather their own straw, however much time it takes, yet still produce the same number of bricks. And should they fail to meet their quota, they'll be beaten.

Pharaoh's response is typical of the ego-mind. First, he baldly states that he doesn't know God. He goes even further than his predecessor, the Pharaoh who did not know Joseph. The self-important ego does not recognize any authority outside itself. God's call for freedom is heard as a challenge—an affront to its self-proclaimed sovereignty.

Pharaoh then reasserts his kingly power by assigning the Hebrews an impossible task. He'll show them and their upstart deity who's in charge. When they complain about his new decree, he accuses them of laziness. The request to worship God with a feast in the wilderness, away from Egypt, is recast by Pharaoh as an excuse to get out of work. In the ego's view, this is all we're good for: to labor like slaves. Should we ever dare ask for freedom, our insolence will be punished.

Yet it is not Moses, but Pharaoh, who demonstrates true insolence. Moses is simply following the will of God. There's nothing insolent about that. Pharaoh, on the other hand, proclaims his ignorance of God and proudly defies His command. The ego-mind will not bend—not to Moses, not even to God. This is arrogance of the highest order.

The Hebrew Foremen

It's no surprise that Pharaoh reacts as he does. He's a king, descended from the gods of Egypt, and he bows to no one. More surprising is the reaction of the Hebrew foremen. Dismayed at having to gather their own straw, they rebuke Moses for this added hardship. "May the Lord look upon you and judge you, for you have made us odious in Pharaoh's sight and in the sight of his servants, to put a sword in their hand to kill us" (Exod. 5:21).

The Hebrew foremen do not recognize Moses as a liberator. His request for freedom leaves them frightened and angry—at him! He's a troublemaker, an outside agitator, someone who's damaged their reputation with Pharaoh and made their lives all the more miserable.

The foremen know only slavery. As slaves, their lives are painful but predictable. If they do as they're told, they'll get by. Enter

Moses. Because he's provoked Pharaoh, they fear that he's put their lives in jeopardy. (Figuratively, he's "put a sword in their hand.") They'd prefer that he just keep quiet and not stir the pot, since to a slave things can always get worse. Today it's no straw but just as many bricks; tomorrow it could be double the bricks!

The Hebrew slaves have no control over their destiny. They serve at the whim of their masters, the Egyptians. They depend on them for food and water—that is, for their survival. This dependency makes the foremen far more concerned with placating Pharaoh than winning freedom. They've identified with the Egyptians and placed their rulers' interests over their own. To survive, they must not upset their masters—which is exactly what Moses has done.

In psychology, this tendency to identify with one's oppressors is called "Stockholm syndrome." Hostages will seek to please their captors, who hold the power of life and death over them, even though this means working against their own best interests and diminishing their chances of escape.

The dependency fostered by slavery (or by being taken hostage) sets up a regressive relationship akin to childhood. A child's survival depends completely on his or her parents. As a result, children rarely judge their mom or dad to be neglectful, sadistic, or cruel, no matter how egregiously they've been abused. Their parents are too important to them. Instead, they'll blame themselves. If only they'd behaved better or gotten better grades; if she were prettier, or nicer; if he could have taken his beatings like a man without crying, then the parent would have been more kind. Then the children would have been loved and all would now be well. So in the future, they just need to try harder.

Like abused children or hostages with Stockholm syndrome, the Hebrew foremen side with their oppressor, Pharaoh, against Moses, the very person capable of setting them free. So long as this condition persists, freedom will obviously remain out of reach.

The First Impediment

The Hebrew foremen are threatened by Moses because he's turned the status quo upside down. He's asking Pharaoh to bow to the will of God and free his slaves. How brazen! And how dangerous. But are we so different from the foremen? When Spirit comes knocking on our door, asking to be let in, asking us to change, we become just as confused and upset.

Change is scary in any form. We don't trust it. Like the foremen, we assume that it will only make things worse, not better. And so we resist. We fight it.

Dr. Martin Luther King, Jr., was cautioned by many of his fellow pastors to cancel his civil rights marches for fear that they would only make the plight of blacks in the South worse. The New Deal was opposed by many as too audacious of a plan, one that would cripple the economy. The common wisdom is that it's always best to play it safe. Don't overreach. Better to live within the predictable confines of slavery, however painful, than to risk escaping into a new and unknown world, even if it just might offer something better.

In physics, this phenomenon is called inertia: the tendency of an object at rest to remain at rest and an object in motion to remain in motion. And it's the first impediment we meet when we set foot upon the spiritual journey. Why go to all the trouble of making a change when it's so much easier to just stay put? If you've tolerated your circumstances for this long, why change now? Leave well enough alone. If it ain't broke, don't fix it.

And yet, because we *are* slaves, we can't tell anymore whether or not our lives are broken. We've ceded our judgment to our master, the ego, and lost the capacity for discernment. And without discernment, we can't take stock of our lives and make a decision to move toward something better. We don't know what "better" means anymore. Instead, we throw up barriers to change.

The first stirring of freedom, then, is usually experienced as painful and unwelcome—a disruptive intrusion. For the first time, we experience conflict about the way we're living. Pharaoh-ego reacts by branding us lazy (or stupid, or a complainer, or a dream-er). It orders us to stick with the program, to keep our head down and get back to work. Who are we to think we deserve more?

Yet now there's a new voice in us—that of the Moses-mind—and it's telling us that indeed we do deserve more. We do have a choice. This voice has heard God's promise at the burning bush, and it's promising us that we're not doomed to slavery. There's a better way to live, and it will guide us there. Shouldn't we at least give it a chance?

I see this pattern frequently in abusive marriages. The wife comes to me hoping to improve the relationship, as if she's the problem, not her husband. Once she starts to realize that she doesn't have to put up with his anger, sarcasm, entitlement, and impossible-to-meet demands, she finds herself in a real bind. She can no longer accept the status quo of obedient silence and cow-ering self-blame. But if she protests and speaks aloud her discon-tent, if she brands her husband's behavior unacceptable, he shoves back—hard. He will not easily relinquish his dominance, nor will he set her free by granting her a divorce. Oppressors do not will-ingly release their slaves.

Instead, like Pharaoh, he'll up the ante. He'll restrict her from seeing her friends, or play the money card. He'll insist that they need to cut back on expenses and therefore can't afford her thera-py anymore (but his outings with the boys are off the table). If she initiates divorce, he'll go after full custody of the children, claim-ing she's unstable. He doesn't really want the kids; he just wants to hurt her. In the worst case, he'll threaten to kill her if she dares to leave him.

The first confrontation with the oppressor always seems to make things worse. In homeopathy (and Chinese medicine, too), when the underlying cause of a chronic condition is finally ad-dressed, the symptoms do not improve, not right away. Initially, they get worse. It's called a healing crisis. But this is not the time to give up. It's a sign to press on. Once we see that there's a real alternative to slavery, we must not turn back. The Moses-mind does not bow to the wishes of the Hebrew foremen, or to Pharaoh. It answers only to Spirit.

⊗

It's helpful to contrast Pharaoh's response to God with Moses's at the burning bush. When the Moses-mind gets its wake-up call, we turn aside and listen. We may balk, understandably. We may have doubts and questions. But God is patient, and He addresses each of our concerns in turn. By contrast, when the ego confronts God for the first time (through the medium of the Moses-mind), it tries to demean Him. *Who is this God? I don't know him. I'm not even sure He exists.* Then, like a stubborn toddler, it digs in and does exactly the opposite of what's been asked. It inflicts more suffering, more bondage.

God has nothing to prove. He's omnipotent and omniscient. He can address Moses's fears point by point, giving him exactly what he needs. Pharaoh, on the other hand, has a great deal to prove. He chooses to inflict more suffering to counteract his deep underlying insecurity (the same insecurity that we saw in his predecessor when he decided to enslave the Hebrews). Pharaoh knows he's not really a god. He knows he's not in control, and so he strives to prove that his control is absolute. He attempts to save face, even though this means challenging the will of God.

Hardening Pharaoh's Heart

Pharaoh's obstinacy persists throughout Exodus. In fact, were he more accommodating, there would be no need for ten different plagues. He would see his error with the very first plague, change his mind, and set the Hebrews free—end of story. But he cannot.

Why is Pharaoh so stubborn? What makes him that way? What does he get out of it? He may be insecure and trying to prove otherwise, but at a certain point, self-preservation should trump the need for a show of power.

God tells Moses no fewer than seven times[1] that He will "harden Pharaoh's heart" (Exod. 7:3) so that Pharaoh will continue to resist God. This will allow God to display His might and lead his people from Egypt.

> "But I will harden Pharaoh's heart that I may multiply My signs and My wonders in the land of Egypt. When Pharaoh does not listen to you, then I will lay My hand on Egypt . . . the Egyptians shall know that I am the Lord . . ." (Exod. 7:3–5).

> Then the Lord said to Moses, "Go to Pharaoh, for I have hardened his heart and the heart of his servants, that I may perform these signs of Mine among them, and that you may tell in the hearing of your son, and of your grandson, how I made a mockery of the Egyptians, and how I performed My signs among them, that you may know that I am the Lord" (Exod. 10:1–2).

Passages like these are among the most problematic in the entire Bible. Scholars have debated their meaning for centuries. Why would God harden Pharaoh's heart? Why would He force him to resist? It seems as if God is preempting Pharaoh and infringing upon his free will, just to show off how powerful He is. God comes off as arrogant, uncaring, and yes, egotistical.

"Hardening Pharaoh's heart" only makes sense if we read Exodus as a parable and recall that Pharaoh is not a human being, but a representation of the ego-mind. It's the ego's nature to be stubborn and inflexible, to be hard-hearted. Ego is a slave master. Without its slaves—us—it has no purpose. It will never set us free, because to do so would undermine its very identity. Therefore, when God says that He will harden Pharaoh's heart, it's best heard as a figure of speech. Pharaoh's heart—the essence of the ego—is *already* hard and unbending.

God makes Pharaoh as stubborn as possible in order to deliver an object lesson in the nature of ego. As slaves, we're fully identified with ego. We're all afflicted with Stockholm syndrome.

Therefore, we need to see in the most exaggerated manner possible the reckless destruction that results from trusting the ego to lead us. It will fail again and again, like Pharaoh, because that's its nature, while God by His nature must prevail. And so, as God says, "I may multiply My signs and My wonders," because that's what's needed to crack the ego's façade of power and fracture our identification with it. Will we allow the ego to continue to enslave us? Or will we see its weakness, its falsity, its arrogance, and choose freedom instead?

In this sense, the way we interpret "hardening Pharaoh's heart" becomes a litmus test of sorts, a window into our view of self. With whom do we identify, Pharaoh or Moses? Which part of our mind sees itself reflected in the story? Is Pharaoh a classic tragic hero battling against impossible odds, the victim of a bullying, tyrannical deity? Do we admire his intransigence, his refusal to bow before a superior force? It's an appealing image—to the ego. But if we view the story this way, through the eyes of ego, we're bound to suffer plagues that grow ever more devastating. Or do we identify with Moses instead, relentless in his quest for freedom, secure in his goal because he knows that God will be with him? Such is the choice Exodus presents us with.

Pharaoh, Ego, and Free Will

If Pharaoh and the ego are by nature hard-hearted and inflexible, then another, more fundamental question arises. Why must God bother to convince Pharaoh to release the Hebrews at all? If God is all-powerful, as He obviously must be, then why would He need to *persuade* anyone to let the Hebrews go? Why not simply reach out and free them Himself, with a flick of His mighty finger? After all, the plagues in and of themselves do not set the Hebrews free. They only push Pharaoh toward submission. So why must God convince Pharaoh at all?

We human beings are endowed with free will. God does not impose His will upon us. He doesn't force us to relinquish our identification with ego, for that would violate the very nature of His creation. It would become yet another form of bondage. God gave us free will; why would He now abrogate it?

We believe in the ego. We believe that it is us. If God forcibly intervened to overthrow it, then it would seem as if God were attacking *us*—not a good way to go about bringing us closer to Him.

God wants us to come to Him of our own accord. He wants us to see for ourselves that the ego is unworthy of our trust and affection—that its promises of security and happiness are empty—so that we'll *choose* to let it go by our own free will.

The Hebrews had to take that first step and cry out before God could help them. Moses at the burning bush had to turn aside of his own free will before God would speak to him. The same holds true for us. God cannot help us until we choose Him over our stubborn, callous egos.

◈

This leads to another, closely related question. Why does God need Moses, or any human being, to deliver His message to Pharaoh for Him? Why would the Almighty need to work through *any* intermediary? Why not descend on Pharaoh as a pillar of fire, or warn him through dreams, like the Pharaoh of Joseph's time?

God cannot reach Pharaoh directly because God and Pharaoh—Spirit and ego—inhabit different worlds. They speak different languages. But Moses and Pharaoh live in the same world and speak the same language; they were, after all, raised in the same household.

God and ego are mutually exclusive. As long as we're slaves to ego, God cannot reach us directly, at least not without violating free will. He knows only that our minds are cut off from Him, and His light cannot get through. "Light cannot enter darkness when a mind believes in darkness, and will not let it go."[2] God doesn't care about the ego's motives or its justifications for enslaving us and separating us from Him. All He wants is for us to be free of ego, as He created us.

But because we've blocked God from our minds, He can no longer reach us directly. He needs an intermediary to carry His message, someone or something with a foot in both the ego's world and His. Enter Moses and the Moses-mind. Moses is human, but God "gave birth" to him and claimed him as a baby on the river. Moses was raised in Pharaoh's palace, speaking Pharaoh's language, yet he's also able to speak directly with God. Moses (the Moses-mind) is the perfect intermediary to bring God's word to Pharaoh (the ego).

෯

Because of free will, God cannot intervene directly to liberate us from the ego's bondage. But the ego is likewise bound by the reality of Spirit. Once the Moses-mind awakens and calls out to us, the ego cannot shut it down. It can resist, it can bluster, it can distract, but it cannot silence or in any way banish the Moses-mind. In the parable of Exodus, this is reflected by what does *not* occur when Moses returns to Egypt to confront Pharaoh.

Moses and Aaron request an audience with Pharaoh. He agrees to meet them, not once, but many times. How can these two nobodies—an exile and a Hebrew slave—so easily approach the most powerful ruler on the planet? No doubt they're a nuisance to Pharaoh. Why then does he tolerate them? Why not have them arrested on the spot and tossed into prison? If you or I walked up to the President and insisted on a meeting, I suspect we'd be given a hard time!

But what if you once knew the President? What if you grew up on the same block or attended the same school? Then you might have a chance. And if the President's sister was your adopted mother, then you might have a very good chance indeed.

Pharaoh and Moses know each other well. In fact, this Pharaoh would have been almost like an uncle to Moses. So it's understandable that he would consent to a meeting. He'll at least hear Moses out, even if he doesn't agree with him.

In the parable of Exodus, the ego does not know God—but it *does* recognize the Moses-mind, which was present and active when we were very young, before the ego could fully develop and enslave the mind. Therefore, the ego knows that it lacks the power to suppress the Moses-mind, however much it might like to.

The Moses-mind stands in for Spirit, which is eternal and indestructible. Ego stands on its own, in opposition to Spirit. But the ego—however reluctantly—must allow the Moses-mind its say. And God, respecting the free will with which He created us, must work through the intermediary of the Moses-mind to convince Pharaoh-ego to release us, His people.

଒ ଒

Chapter 7

PHARAOH'S MAGICIANS: THE EGO'S SLEIGHT OF HAND

The first time Moses approaches Pharaoh, he makes a simple request for freedom which Pharaoh spurns. Instead, Pharaoh piles more hardship on the Hebrews, depriving them of straw for their brick making. A simple request from the Moses-mind carries no weight with the ego. A more forceful approach is necessary.

When Moses and Aaron next meet up with Pharaoh, their intention is to demonstrate the might of God. Aaron casts down his staff and it turns into a serpent.

> Then Pharaoh also called for the wise men and the sorcerers, and they also, the magicians of Egypt, did the same with their secret arts. For each one threw down his staff and they turned into serpents. But Aaron's staff swallowed up their staffs. Yet Pharaoh's heart was hardened, and he did not listen to them, as the Lord said (Exod. 7:11–13).

Aaron's serpent swallows up those of Pharaoh's magicians, proving its superiority, but Pharaoh is not impressed. He still will not free the Hebrews.

God instructs Moses and Aaron to up the ante. The following morning they are to intercept Pharaoh on his way to the Nile River and, if he still refuses to let the Hebrews go (and he will), God will inflict a more serious penance.

> Then the Lord said to Moses, "Say to Aaron, 'Take your staff and stretch out your hand over the waters of Egypt, over their rivers, over their streams, and over their pools, and over all their reservoirs of water, that they may become blood; and there will be blood throughout all the land of Egypt, both in vessels of wood and in vessels of stone'" (Exod. 7:19).

The next morning, Moses and Aaron carry out God's command. Before the eyes of Pharaoh and his officials, Aaron strikes the Nile River with his staff, and all the water in Egypt turns to blood. Fish die off; the waters become putrid and undrinkable. Not to be outdone, Pharaoh's magicians again duplicate Moses and Aaron's feat. They too can transform water into blood. As a result, Pharaoh turns his back on this powerful demonstration. His people now must dig holes in the ground to find untainted water, but he remains obdurate. He will not let the Hebrews go.

The Magicians' Tricks Exposed

Exodus tells us that Pharaoh's magicians are somehow capable of mimicking the miracles of God. This cheapens them in Pharaoh's eyes and undermines their power to change his mind. For if any decent court magician can turn water into blood, then what's the big deal? Why should he care?

The magicians work for Pharaoh. Their task is to affirm his absolute power as king—not only over his subjects and slaves, but over all of nature itself. Therefore, when Aaron and Moses perform miracles, Pharaoh's magicians must follow suit. They must prove that Pharaoh and the Egyptian gods are every bit the equal of this upstart Hebrew God.

We need to look more closely at the encounter with Pharaoh's magicians, however, because we're missing a key point. Exodus says that the magicians transformed water into blood. A careful reading, however, shows that this cannot be the case.

When Aaron strikes the Nile with the staff of Moses, *all* the water in Egypt becomes blood, from the streams and reservoirs down to the smallest vessels containing water, whether made of wood or stone. What, then, is left for the magicians to transform? Once Aaron raises his staff, there is no more clear, untainted water in all of Egypt. *It's all blood.*

The Bible doesn't address this paradox directly. Yet the inference seems clear. Pharaoh is deluded. His magicians traffic in illusions, not true miracles. And we readers, hearing the story with the ears of ego, are likewise fooled. We, too, believe the magicians' sleight of hand, that they have somehow performed a miracle on par with God's and transformed water into blood, even though this was not possible, because all the water had already been transformed by God.

The same pattern holds true for the second plague, the blight of frogs.

> So Aaron stretched out his hand over the waters of Egypt, and the frogs came up and covered the land of Egypt. And the magicians did the same with their secret arts, making frogs come up on the land of Egypt (Exod. 8:6–7).

Once again, however, if the land is *already* swarming with frogs, what more can Pharaoh's magicians accomplish? Picture this: the magicians wave their wands and cast their spells and, lo and behold, a fresh wave of frogs belches forth from the putrid waters of the Nile. But what distinguishes these particular frogs from all the others that came before them? Are they really the result of the magicians' powers? More likely, they're just the continuing manifestation of God's original miracle.

Pharaoh's magicians piggyback on God's miracles. They claim to produce frogs, but all they really do is take credit for a miracle already in progress. It would be as if an adult told a young child that he had magical powers and would soon blot out the sun and make the sky go dark, because he knew in advance that a total eclipse was about to occur. The child might well believe him and his awesome "magic," but this is no miracle.

Pharaoh's magicians are tricksters. They simply perform cheap illusions to reassure their ruler that he's still all-powerful—that the Hebrew God and his plagues are of no consequence and he has nothing to fear from them. No matter how convincing the illusions, however, they have no foundation in reality, and so they cannot compete with God's miracles. The two are not of the same order.

The Agents of Denial

What do Pharaoh's magicians symbolize for us? What can they tell us about our own minds? And how do they help keep us enslaved?

Well, if Pharaoh represents the ego, then his magicians must represent those aspects of the ego-mind that weave illusions of safety and power. They hope to convince us that ego does just as good of a job as Spirit in protecting us from danger. Because if the ego's magic is so powerful, then why would we ever need to turn to Spirit? We can manage fine on our own.

The magicians are the agents of denial.[1] They deny the reality of the plagues brought on by Pharaoh-ego's own stubbornness. They convince us that all is well, when it should be perfectly evident that things are anything but.

Denial is a brick-wall defense mechanism. We shut our eyes tightly to what we don't want to see and then proclaim it not there. We resort to denial when faced with the loss of someone or something so important to us that we just can't accept it. It's too painful.

When a loved one is diagnosed with a terminal illness, we refuse to believe it. *The doctors must have made a mistake. Our loved one will not succumb to this illness; she'll be the exception and beat the odds somehow, we're sure of it.* When we hear an ominous rattle in the car, but shrug it off as no big deal; when the smoker coughs up blood, but attributes it to allergies; when a hurricane threatens and we're warned to evacuate, but stay put because it can't possibly be that bad, we can be sure the magicians of denial are at work.

✲

Sandy had been sexually abused for years as a child by her stepfather. As a teen, she'd repeatedly run away from home to escape his nightly visits, until at last she was placed in foster care. When she tried to tell her mother about the abuse, she got smacked and was called a liar. Understandably, this left her with deep, abiding scars. Sandy had severed all ties to her parents long ago, but needed desperately to feel that she was still part of the family, and not a pariah. Consequently, she worked hard to maintain relations with her only uncle and his family.

Professionally, Sandy had embarked on a successful career with a well-known ad agency. She had several high-profile commercials to her credit, and was understandably proud of her achievements, especially given her turbulent past. At Thanksgiving or Christmas dinner, she would bring along a clip of her latest work to show her uncle and cousins, hoping for some scrap of positive recognition. The TV would play on in the background, but not one of them ever bothered to watch. They didn't even try to be polite about it. Yet every year she persisted, making excuses for them, hoping that maybe the next year would be different.

Sandy was in denial. Her uncle's family didn't care about her. They merely tolerated her presence. Not until her uncle, under the pretense of supporting her, tried one day to fondle her breasts did reality come crashing down. He was no different than her stepfather. Now, she really had no family to turn to, no place where she belonged, no place that was safe—but then, she never did.

In this instance, Sandy's successful career played the role of Pharaoh's magicians. It gave her a sense of accomplishment and hope. Here was a way she could finally prove her worth—that she was more than just a damaged sex toy—and get some healthy recognition from family members who cared about her. But it was false hope, and it blinded her from seeing their utter lack of caring and moving on. Worse still, it set her up for more betrayal. (We'll revisit Sandy and her journey later to see how she coped with this blow.)

※

My patient Rena was also in denial. Her husband, Sam (who refused to meet with me), berated her constantly. If she made him dinner, it was too little, too cold, or a lousy recipe. If she ordered out for pizza, he accused her of being selfish and spending his money with no regard for how hard he had to work.

When Rena tried to enforce limits with the children, like bedtimes or getting homework done, Sam undermined her. He'd let them stay up late and watch TV, so that he got to be the good guy. Then when the kids were exhausted the next morning and got in trouble at school for not completing their homework, he'd scold her, calling her a bad mother right in front of them. Sam traveled a lot on business and would always bring home lavish gifts for the children (demanding lavish praise in return), but never brought so much as a token for Rena. Worse still, she strongly suspected that he was having affairs on the road.

Most women in a situation like Rena's would confront their husbands. They might turn to family for support, or consult an attorney. They might even move out, taking the kids with them. But Rena refused to believe that Sam was a threat. She refused to admit that she'd made a bad choice in marrying him. He didn't mean to be so critical; he was just tired from working such long hours. And if he strayed into another woman's arms, it was probably her own fault for being so disinterested in sex. If only she tried harder, she was certain she could make the marriage work.

❦

Pharaoh's magicians will do anything to shield us from the truth, especially when it's painful or threatening to our sense of self. They'll try to convince us that we're better off ignoring the problem or that we can fix it if only we try harder. The magicians have a multitude of excuses for why things must be the way they are. They'll do anything at all to keep us from feeling the pain of our plagues, and thereby keep us from changing.

But imagine taking this approach with a fire in your home. You smell smoke, but shrug it off. *It's probably nothing—just the toaster or someone burning leaves outside.* You open a window and push the worry from your mind. You switch on the TV to distract yourself from the increasingly obvious smell. Eventually, the flames break through, and it's clear that there really is a fire. Your denial collapses in an instant. But by then it's too late; your home is gone.

Pharaoh-ego's magicians use this technique to blind us to our own best interests. Denial creates a false complacency. It may initially cushion the pain of an emotional blow, but in the long run it prevents us from dealing with it. When we deny plagues, they escalate like the fire.

Bananas and Other Magical Tricks

Pharaoh's magicians are indeed the agents of denial. But this is merely one of the many tricks they use to deceive us and keep us from the truth.

Over the years, I've worked with a fair number of patients who were terrified of flying. For them, walking down the Jetway to board a plane was like walking the plank. They tortured themselves with lurid visions of their flight crashing in flames. They imagined the horror on the faces of their spouse and children, the pandemonium in the cabin as the plane pitched into a nosedive, while they sat frozen, awaiting the cataclysm of certain, violent death.

These individuals go to extreme lengths to avoid air travel—driving long distances; shuffling schedules; making excuses to stay home; even putting up with arduous, overnight train or bus rides. When flying is unavoidable, they evolve complex strategies for managing their fear. One patient would track the progress of his flight on the Internet every day for a month prior to his scheduled departure. He hoped to reassure himself that, if the flight arrived safely for 30 consecutive days, then it would go well for him, too. Another would repeat the Lord's Prayer over and over in her head from takeoff to landing. She feared that, should she stop, the plane would plummet. They were each trying to assert control over an event that was out of their hands. This too is the work of Pharaoh's magicians.

Like all magic, such defense mechanisms ultimately prove ineffective. When the hour arrives to leave for the airport, or if the flight hits a nasty patch of turbulence, the floodwaters of terror overrun the levees of the magical defenses. The fearful must resort to more surefire remedies, such as tranquilizers or another round of Scotch. Yet with the next flight they're back to the same rituals. It's very hard for them to let go. Why? Because the plane didn't crash! They arrived safely and are still alive. That is to say, the magic worked.

Of course, my patients would have arrived safely without their rituals. They understand this intellectually, but they cling to their rituals when pressed. As with Pharaoh's magicians and the first two plagues, magic gets credit for something that would have occurred anyway.

⚕️

There's an old joke about a man standing on a street corner holding a banana firmly in one ear. His friend comes along and asks, "Joe, what are you doing with that banana in your ear?" Joe looks at him incredulously, as if the reason were perfectly obvious, and replies, "It keeps the tigers away." His friend laughs and says, "But Joe, there are no tigers here." Joe nods sagely. "See, it works!"

Psychological defenses are self-reinforcing. To the extent that the calamity we feared has *not* occurred, we assume that the magic worked. So we return to the same formula again and again whenever we feel threatened or out of control. Joe is never going to remove that banana from his ear. Why should he? Why take that risk?

Even the outer appearance of spirituality can mask the workings of the ego and its magical defenses. Repeating the Lord's Prayer or a mantra handed down by your guru's guru is not necessarily a spiritual act. Lighting candles in church or incense at the ashram, going on a pilgrimage or praying at the shrine of a saint—all can be nurturing for the soul, but can just as easily be the handiwork of Pharaoh's magicians: a sacred banana in the ear.

Magical rituals turn up in all kinds of situations. The tennis player who bounces the ball exactly four times before serving; the jogger who must do his miles, rain or shine, to prevent a heart attack; the job seeker who insists on wearing the same "lucky shirt" to each and every interview—all are hooked on magic.

The magicians' spells are seductive. They may strike us as harmless, but once embraced they can be tough to give up. Yet as long as the magicians remain in the picture, we will not see reality as it is or recognize the full extent of our bondage.

This is the double-edged sword shared by all defense mechanisms. They shield us from what frightens us, but in the process restrict our ability to judge whether or not the fear still makes sense. With that banana stuck in our ear, we can't hear very well. Our defenses block us from getting the information we need to realistically assess the situation. To do that, we must remove the banana. We must face our fear.

Removing the Banana

As a young child, I would lie in bed in the dark with my eyes shut tight, certain that burglars stood right by my bedside checking to make sure I was really asleep. If I dared to open my eyes, they'd know I was awake and murder me on the spot. I don't know how long I would lie there frozen like that, but it seemed like hours before I finally mustered the courage to take a peek and discover that the room was empty and I was safe.

How much suffering must we endure before we open our eyes to the tricks of the ego's magicians? And what happens when we finally see through their illusions and give up our defenses? What happens when we remove that banana from our ear?

Without magic, we'll experience the fear raw and unfiltered—which is not a pleasant thing. Yet if we can hang on, if we can lean into the fierce winds of our fear and keep our eyes wide open, something remarkable takes place.

☙

Tony was one of my fear-of-flying patients. His terror of being confined in a flimsy cabin, hurtling at 500 miles per hour 30,000 feet above the ground, was extreme. He used every trick he knew of to avoid stepping onto a plane. This interfered with his personal life, because he couldn't vacation any place he couldn't drive to. But it affected his work even more. His company had major clients in Rome, and it's not exactly an easy drive from the U.S. to Italy.

When Tony felt ready to confront his fear, he booked an early-morning flight to Providence, Rhode Island, and intentionally got a window seat. For the entire 30-minute flight, he peered down at the ground far below, more elated than afraid. Upon arriving in Providence, Tony deplaned, walked a few gates, and boarded his return flight. He again kept his eyes open, looking out the window the whole time. In the space of a few hours, he was back home. But the man who returned was not the same as the man who'd left early that morning.

Tony had rejected his magicians' tricks. He'd made himself vulnerable to his fear, and he'd survived. He'd taken the banana out of his ear and discovered that—lo and behold—there were no tigers after all. Was his fear of flying cured? Not entirely. It still remained a struggle. But he'd reversed the momentum. He never again avoided a flight: he flew to Rome regularly on business, and vacationed on Hawaii with his family. No longer was he a prisoner of his fear, no longer the dupe of Pharaoh-ego's magicians.

❧

Stripped of our magical defenses, we're free to discover the safety that was always present. The anticipated calamity does not occur: the plane arrives without incident; we pass the exam; we don't get laid off. We learn to trust that all is well, and all will be well.

When we free ourselves from Pharaoh's magicians, however, there is another possible outcome. We may get a clear, unbiased view of the plagues that really do beset us and learn that our fears were justified. *There is a fire raging; it's out of control, and if we don't act right now it will consume us. My spouse is unfaithful, the marriage long ago dead. My kid is hooked on drugs and so distant I can't even talk to her. The medication isn't working. The money's running out.* But whatever form the fire takes, it's guaranteed that if we don't see it for what it is, we'll do nothing to stop it.

If we drop our defenses and face our plagues, we can at least see what we're up against and set an intention to change. Intentions are powerful, as we'll learn in a later chapter. But best of all, when we penetrate the illusions of the ego's magicians, we may find the door to Spirit and miracles. It's been there all along waiting for us.

This is the lesson that escapes Pharaoh, despite ten horrible plagues. His heart is hardened. He's incapable of learning, incapable of change. It's his nature—the ego's nature. Fortunately, however, *we* are not Pharaoh. We are not our egos. We *can* change our minds. We can exchange ego for the Moses-mind, plagues for miracles.

The Magicians' Final Trick

The first two plagues—blood and frogs—represent the stage of the journey where most spiritual seekers get stuck. They've encountered their burning bush, heeded the call of their Moses-mind, and asked for freedom from Pharaoh-ego. And yet they continue to identify with ego. When afraid, they turn to it instead of Spirit and wind up under the spell of Pharaoh's magicians, oblivious to the plagues that push them toward change.

But the ego cannot free us. It opposes freedom. Its magicians deal in illusion and prevent us from seeing our enslaved state and the plagues that it brings. The result? More plagues and more suffering.

By the third plague (lice, mosquitoes, or gnats, depending on the translation), Pharaoh's magicians admit defeat. They tell Pharaoh, "'This is the finger of God.' But Pharaoh's heart was hardened, and he did not listen to them . . ." (Exod. 8:19). The magicians can no longer keep up the pretense that their illusions are any match for God, nor can they shield Pharaoh from the consequences of refusing this God he claims not to know. Pharaoh will find no further refuge in their tricks. True safety does not come from denial, magical rituals, or bananas. It comes from a living connection to Spirit.

Consider the first lines of the 23rd Psalm: "The Lord is my shepherd; I shall not want. He makes me lie down in green pastures; He leads me beside quiet waters." Think for a moment about the relationship between the shepherd and his sheep. The sheep need never fret about which hill offers the richest grass or where the coolest streams may be found. They don't lie awake at night, obsessing about wolves attacking. They don't indulge in magical rituals for protection, nor are they in denial. The shepherd truly does care for them. He will steer them in the right direction. His safekeeping and skill assure that the animals will not only survive, but thrive.

From the perspective of the sheep, everything they need simply appears, without struggle or planning. Should our own lives ever go so smoothly, we would consider it a miracle indeed! Yet to the sheep it's wholly right and natural. They don't fret that the shepherd will abandon them. If he raises his voice, it's not because they've sinned, but because they've strayed. They don't dream of greener pastures and cooler streams forever beyond reach just over the next hillside. And they never assume that they can manage better on their own, without their shepherd. They trust in his care, not their own devices. If they were aware of his many actions on their behalf, their sole response would be gratitude.

Our creature comforts today far exceed those of the sheep, and yet, by contrast, we rarely feel gratitude. We take for granted that we can travel thousands of miles in a single day; that with the turn of a handle we get hot running water, with the flick of a switch the room lights up. We don't see these things as the gifts of a bountiful shepherd, because they result from civilization and technology and have nothing to do with Spirit—or so we believe. We paid for them, after all. We earned that money. Therefore, we're entitled. No gratitude necessary.

In fact, the only time we *don't* take our bounty for granted is when things *stop* working: when the power goes out in a storm or when an earthquake or hurricane damages the water lines. Then we get scared. Or mad. *What's wrong with them, why can't they fix it? How come it's taking so long?* And then when the power finally returns, we don't cry out, "Thank God!" but rather, "About time!"

By taking our bounty for granted, we convince ourselves that we're in charge, that we're the ones who make it all happen. Our faith rests solidly in the ego and its magic. This blinds us to the presence of Spirit and shuts down the possibility of miracles.

This is the last, and perhaps the most subtle, trick of Pharaoh-ego and its magicians. They've fooled us into believing that through technology they can and will meet our every need. Never again need we fear plagues. Magic works. It will protect us and solve all our problems. Ego, our king, shepherd, and master will defend us against the world's ills. Forget Spirit. Worship at the altar of ego instead.

Such is our modern-day equivalent of slavery under the deception of Pharaoh-ego's magicians. Our lives are certainly more comfortable than the Hebrews'. Our prison cells are heated and air-conditioned. They come loaded with all the amenities. We need never fret over finding enough straw to make bricks. But we do fret about other things, like health and money. We fret all the time, and we no longer appreciate the hand of the shepherd that can steer us to greener pastures. Most of the time we don't even remember he's there.

When we're no longer enthralled by Pharaoh-ego's magic, we can begin to receive the miracles of the Moses-mind. These will satisfy us in ways we could never have imagined while imprisoned in the ego's Egypt. They will inspire genuine trust and take us all the way to the Promised Land.

Exodus tells us, however, that neither Pharaoh nor the ego gives up easily. Three plagues are hardly enough to overcome their ironfisted rule. They must be driven to their knees and their powerlessness exposed for all to see. That, unfortunately, will require more plagues.

⚇ ⚇

Chapter 8

THE PLAGUES: BREAKING FREE OF EGO

Pharaoh and the Egyptians suffer through ten plagues. We've already looked at the first two—water turned to blood and an infestation of frogs—and the role played by the magicians in deflecting their impact on Pharaoh. The remaining eight plagues are: lice (or mosquitoes or gnats), flies, cattle blight, boils, hail, locusts, three days of darkness, and the death of all Egyptian firstborns. These plagues result from Pharaoh repeatedly denying the Hebrews their freedom. Each time he refuses (or agrees, only to change his mind later), God tells Moses how to bring about the next plague. It's a duel between Pharaoh and Moses, a contest of wills, with Moses backed by God.

The battle between these two figures is central to the parable of Exodus. It demonstrates the process by which we break free from our bondage to the ego. The plagues are the spasms of suffering—the labor pains, if you will—that the ego will endure and try to overcome before it finally surrenders.

The Purpose of Plagues

Many people view the ten plagues of Exodus as punishment from God. Pharaoh behaved badly; therefore, like any willfully misbehaving child, he deserves to be punished, and God has that right. However, this is a limited understanding that makes sense only if Pharaoh is a real person (and God a strict parental figure). But Pharaoh represents the ego; how then can God punish a part of the mind—especially one that we believe to be our self?

It's more helpful to think of the plagues as feedback that results from our identification with the ego. When we operate by its rules, enslaved under its "guidance," we experience tribulations, that is, plagues. They don't happen all the time, but inevitably things go wrong. Our best-laid plans derail; our hopes run aground; and we suffer frustration, disappointment, and loss. Plagues are the natural consequence of serving out a life sentence in the prison house of Pharaoh-ego. Only unlike the blind suffering of slavery, plagues carry within them the seeds of change.

Jesus of Nazareth said, "You will know them by their fruits" (Matthew 7:16). The plagues are the fruits of ego and its worldview. If we deny their reality, as Pharaoh does, then more are sure to follow, bringing ever greater suffering and loss . . . until at last we pay attention. It's a simple feedback loop.

Therefore, as spiritual journeyers, when we encounter hardship in any form—illness, loss, financial setback—there's no need for guilt. God is not punishing us. We're receiving feedback: an indication that we forgot Spirit and let ourselves be guided instead by ego. When we realign with Spirit, the actual "plague" may or may not abate, but the suffering we experienced from it surely will. We will understand our situation differently, in a way that supports the journey. Plagues are the sharp-edged rocks that strike our feet when we stray from the path. They're a pointed reminder to get back on track and remember Spirit.

Pharaoh Responds to the Plagues

When Pharaoh's magicians fail—when they inform him during the third plague that they can no longer duplicate the miracles of God—how does he react? Does he back down immediately and submit to God's will? To surrender would be no shame. After all, his magicians have failed, and he can no longer maintain his denial about the plagues. Or does he remain stubborn and unyielding? The answer is: a bit of both. Pharaoh's response is complex, and it tells us a great deal about the inner workings of the ego.

As early as the second plague Pharaoh's resistance to God begins to waver. Even though his magicians appear to have duplicated the miraculous infestation of frogs, he nonetheless calls for Moses and Aaron and tells them that he will let the Hebrews go, if only God will remove the frogs. So Moses appeals to God, and the frogs die off. "But when Pharaoh saw that there was relief, he hardened his heart and did not listen to them . . ." (Exod. 8:15).

The third plague (lice, mosquitoes, or gnats) does not budge Pharaoh at all. He remains unyielding. But with the fourth plague, an infestation of flies, he again relents. Well, sort of. He tells Moses and Aaron that they may go and sacrifice to their God—but they must do so within the borders of Egypt. Moses protests. Pharaoh gives in a bit more. They can leave Egypt to sacrifice to their God, but they mustn't go far—not the three days' journey that Moses had originally requested.

Interestingly, Pharaoh also now asks Moses to, "Make supplication for me" (Exod. 8:28), that is, to pray for him. He sounds repentant, as if he's finally coming around. Yet the moment God clears the air of flies, Pharaoh's heart hardens once again, and he backtracks on his promise.

Pharaoh's heart remains hard through the fifth and sixth plagues: a cattle blight and boils on the skin. In the seventh plague, a lethal hailstorm hammers Egypt, but not Goshen where the Hebrews live. This gets Pharaoh's attention, and he goes so far as to admit he's wrong.

I stand guilty this time. The Lord is in the right, and I and my people are in the wrong. Plead with the Lord that there may be an end of God's thunder and of hail. I will let you go; you need stay no longer (Jewish Study Bible, Exod. 9:27–28).

As soon as the hail ceases, of course, Pharaoh changes his mind.

In the eighth plague, cowed by the threat of locusts, Pharaoh agrees to unconditionally release the Hebrew men, but not the women, children, or livestock. Moses says no. How could the Hebrew men leave behind their families? So locusts swarm across Egypt, devouring whatever crops the hailstorm left standing. Pharaoh again calls for Moses, admits his guilt, and begs Moses to pray for him. Yet when God drives the locusts into the Red Sea with a strong wind, Pharaoh once again refuses to let the Hebrews go.

During the ninth plague's three days of darkness, Pharaoh magnanimously consents to let *all* the Hebrew people go, even the children—but not their flocks and herds. What at first appears to be a meaningful compromise is really not worth very much. If the Hebrews leave behind their flocks and herds, how will they survive? How will they perform the ritual sacrifice God has asked of them in Exodus 10:25? Worse, they'll have capitulated to Pharaoh. His word will have triumphed over God's, making the Hebrews' freedom a sham. Pharaoh's offers of compromise are simply a more subtle form of resistance. He remains incapable of submitting to the will of God.

This back-and-forth reveals a very different aspect of Pharaoh. No more the arrogant ruler who disdainfully orders the Hebrews to gather their own straw, he now hedges his bets. He bargains. He begs for supplication. He makes promises. But his words lack substance, because the moment the plague is lifted and the danger gone, he reneges. He's back to his old self. He's learned nothing.

Plagues and Addiction

Where in our world do we find the sort of behavior demonstrated by Pharaoh? We need not look far. It's the fundamental pattern underlying addiction.

Addicts start out content and complacent. The drug (or other object of addiction, such as sex, food, money, or fame) seems to bring satisfaction. It soothes anxiety and balms misery. The addict's only real struggle is to find more of the drug—to guarantee a steady supply.

But this situation does not last. Soon enough, addicts find that they need ever larger doses to achieve the same high. Their craving increases, while the sense of relief grows ever more fleeting. Their addiction now creates more suffering than satisfaction.

By this time, however, they are enslaved. They make a stab at quitting, only to find, much to their surprise, that they can't, because the addiction won't let them go. More to the point, they're not 100 percent committed. Given the choice, they'd still prefer the drug—if it would only satisfy them the way it once did. They haven't suffered sufficiently to want freedom at any cost. This is where the plagues come in.

☙

Brenda is smart, slim, and attractive. She's married to a successful patent attorney and has a magnificent home with a great view of Alcatraz and the Golden Gate Bridge. Her kids attend private school. To an outsider, she has it made. There's just one problem: Brenda is an alcoholic.

She'll freely admit she has a drinking problem. She's made frequent promises to quit—to herself and to her husband—and twice she's managed to pull off a few months of sobriety. But invariably she starts up again. Brenda has eliminated the hard stuff, rationalizing that wine is good for her health, but refuses to go to Alcoholics Anonymous (AA), because she tried it once and "it just wasn't for" her. Besides, what if she ran into someone she knew?

Brenda has dabbled in all kinds of treatments—medications, herbal remedies, behavioral regimens—but she's never stuck with any of them for long. She's attended rehab at the local psych hospital, but refuses to commit to a serious, monthlong, in-patient program, since it would take her away from her kids.

Meanwhile, Brenda's life is crumbling around her. She's made a spectacle of herself at parties, flirting inappropriately with other women's husbands, and on one occasion creating a scene by passing out. As a result, she's lost most of her friends. Recently, her husband threatened to leave if she didn't stop drinking. He even consulted a divorce attorney, which infuriated her. But despite it all, she still maintains that she could stop on her own whenever she wanted to.

Like the Pharaoh of Exodus, Brenda is stubborn and impervious to reason. She refuses to admit she's lost control over her drinking. The addictive need for alcohol has taken full possession of her mind, shoving aside all other considerations.

How much damage will it take before Brenda finally owns up to her problem and commits to getting real help? How many more plagues must she suffer? She's already experienced the loss of friends and a threatened divorce. Does her husband actually need to walk out or take custody of her kids? Will she wind up killing someone in a drunken car accident—one of her own children, perhaps? What will it take before she "hits bottom," as AA puts it, and realizes that to go on living she must break free from her bondage to alcohol? What calamity will become her tenth plague?

Brenda's addiction could just as easily have been gambling, risky sex, binge eating, impulsive spending, or workaholism. But no matter the object of addiction, the struggle remains the same. Addicts will suffer plague upon plague until they hit bottom and finally commit to freeing themselves.

But the addict's struggle doesn't really apply to the rest of us, does it? We're not addicted, are we? As a matter of fact, we *are*, and this is exactly the difficulty we face. We're ego-addicts. We're completely dependent on the ego to keep us satisfied and content. We've let it become so much a part of us that we might as well have mainlined it straight into a vein. It's possessed us and repro-grammed our minds to pursue *its* dreams, *its* goals, and *its* agenda. And when we finally realize that we are its slaves, it won't release us—at least not without a fight.

In this sense, the plagues that come our way are akin to a rehab program. They force us to confront our addiction to ego. Each one exposes some area where we remain dependent on ego and reminds us by our suffering that the drug no longer works. We need to be free of it. Each plague becomes another opportunity to break the ego's hold over us—another appeal to come clean, into the arms of Spirit.

The Ego Cannot Change

When Pharaoh's magicians admit defeat and the ego's defens-es fail, when we endure hardships beyond our control and come face-to-face with loss and death, when plagues seem to stalk our every move, we're forced to confront the ego's ultimate powerless-ness. But it won't let go right away. The ego takes countermeasures. It fabricates excuses and promises to do better. Like a slick used-car salesman, with the ego there's always a catch, because the ego doesn't want real change. *It's terrified of it.*

As we saw with Brenda, the ego will downplay the seriousness of any plague. Like Pharaoh, it prefers to strike bargains and make compromises (AA calls these "half-measures"), rather than taking that first step of admitting its helplessness regarding life's plagues and turning them over to a Higher Power. The ego does not rec-ognize any power higher than itself. Were it to own up to its lack of control, it would willingly surrender to the obvious superiority of Spirit. But it can never do this, because to the ego, surrender means annihilation.

The duel between Moses and Pharaoh in Exodus is an object lesson in the ego's inability to change. Its purpose and its func-tion are to defy real change. Because if the ego must change, then it must have been wrong; and if that's the case, then clearly it doesn't know what it's doing. Its promises of protection and happiness are exposed as phony. The ego cannot tolerate being wrong. It would rather die, and take us along with it.

Moses Responds to Pharaoh

In Exodus 2, Moses's passion to free his people led him to commit murder: an immature act that drove him into exile. But Moses has now matured, and God Himself has sent him on this mission. How then does Moses respond to Pharaoh, and what can we learn from him?

Pharaoh repeatedly reneges on his promise to free the Hebrews. Does Moses explode with rage? Does he argue with Pharaoh or try to reason with him, bribe him, beg him, or threaten him? None of the above. Each time Pharaoh backtracks on his word, Moses turns to God and lets Him decide the next step.

This is a very important point. The immature Moses makes rash decisions. He reacts from fight-or-flight mode and takes matters into his own hands. The mature Moses, secure in God's promise of "I will be with you," behaves entirely differently. He makes no decisions on his own, because he knows that he doesn't have the answers. Instead, he brings every choice to God. He lets Him pick the plagues and tell him exactly what Aaron should say to Pharaoh. Moses never questions God's instructions. He has no personal stake in the outcome—no ego investment. He's content simply to carry out God's plan.

As a result, Moses has no worries. He doesn't second-guess God's choices when they appear not to work. He trusts that they were necessary and right, because they came from God. He doesn't fret about future outcomes by wondering *What if the next plague fails and Pharaoh reneges again? What will we do then?* Nor does he dream of future success—how great things will be in the Promised Land. He takes it one day at a time, one plague at a time. He trusts that God will tell him all he needs to know, at precisely the time he needs to know it.

In our own lives, the ego likes to play commander in chief. It wants to make the big decisions (okay, the little ones, too), and we've allowed it that privilege. It makes thousands of judgments every day based on nothing more than its own limited experience. Unlike Spirit, which is all knowing, the ego operates on scanty data, and so its decisions are bound to be faulty. *A Course in Miracles* describes the utter folly of relying on the judgments of ego:

> In order to judge anything rightly, one would have to be fully aware of an inconceivably wide range of things; past, present and to come. One would have to recognize in advance all the effects of his judgments on everyone and everything involved in them in any way. And one would have to be certain there is no distortion in his perception. . . . Who is in a position to do this? Who except in grandiose fantasies would claim this for himself?[1]

If we allow our ego-minds to judge, our decisions will at best lead us into exile from Spirit, like the immature Moses. At worst, they'll set us on a course toward death, like Pharaoh. Only when we know that we don't know—and cannot know—do we practice true wisdom. Then, like the mature Moses, we're able to push aside the faulty judgments of our ego-minds and take our problems straight to Spirit.

Plagues and the Spiritual Journey

It's not possible to live a life free of plagues. They offer us the chance to learn and grow. No, the ego can't change, but *we* can. Each time we encounter a plague, we have a choice. We can take Pharaoh-ego's advice . . . and suffer more. Or we can follow the guidance of the Moses-mind.

Beginning with the fourth plague, God makes a clear distinction between the Egyptians and the Hebrews. He will inflict plagues upon the Egyptians, but spare His people, the Hebrews.

> But on that day I will set apart the land of Goshen, where My people are living. . . . I will put a division between My people and your people . . . (Exod. 8:22–23).

Every plague suffered by the Egyptians is in fact a miracle for the Hebrews. Each one demonstrates to them the wonder and might of their God. Each brings them a step closer to release.

In the parable of Exodus, we are not Pharaoh-ego, nor have we yet become the Moses-mind. We are the Hebrews. God has made us a promise that He will lead us home to the Promised Land. If we experience adversity along the way, it's only because we still identify with ego. Plagues help break this identification. They weaken our attachment to ego and wean us from this addictive dependency. When we step back and view our plagues through the eyes of Spirit, each one holds a hidden blessing. Each becomes an invitation to a miracle.

Visionary poet William Blake succinctly captures this idea in his poem "Auguries of Innocence."

> *Joy and woe are woven fine,*
> *A clothing for the soul divine;*
> *Under every grief and pine*
> *Runs a joy with silken twine.*

When we shift our perception, we no longer see plagues. Our "grief and pine" give way to reveal the joy beneath. The flip side of every plague is a hidden miracle. To find it, there's only one thing we have to do: change our minds.

Eleanor's Story

Eleanor is a poet and actress. She's in her late 70s, but you wouldn't know it to look at her. She remains active in a dizzying variety of charity and community events, including a local theater company. Her life is jammed with people to call, places to go, and things to get done. Recently, Eleanor was working out to a dance video in her second-floor study. The doorbell rang. She was expecting a package, and so she hurried down the stairs, not really paying attention, when she lost her footing and took a serious tumble.

Fortunately, her partner heard her fall and dialed 911. Eleanor lay unconscious at the bottom of the staircase for almost ten minutes before the paramedics arrived. She was admitted to the critical-care unit at San Francisco General Hospital with multiple fractures and bleeding in her brain. As serious as the injuries were, they could have been a lot worse.

Medically, Eleanor did well. After only five days, she was transferred to a rehab hospital. She couldn't walk and her memory was impaired, but she made rapid progress on both fronts. However, she grew quite depressed. She couldn't believe that this calamity had happened to her. How could she return to acting if she couldn't remember her lines? How could she help organize events and contribute to all of those causes she found so meaningful when she was too exhausted to even leave the house? She feared that the life she'd known was over. And if that were so, then what did she have left? What was there to live for?

Eleanor could do nothing to hasten the pace of her healing. It would take as long as it took. She had no choice but to accept her new limits. Yet when she did finally acknowledge what had happened to her—with all the restrictions it imposed—she arrived at some valuable insights.

Sitting at home, unable even to get to the bathroom without assistance, she could no longer leap up to answer the phone, make the bed, or prepare a meal. She couldn't participate in any of her usual social events. She was forced to sit, to do nothing, just to *be*. As a result, she began to glimpse just how much her life had been ruled by a compulsive need to be involved and stay active—to be *doing* something, anything, all the time.

Eleanor had been addicted to keeping busy. She'd used her compulsive activity to hold at bay a fear of inadequacy that dated all the way back to childhood. By staying perpetually in motion, she could prove to herself that she was okay—except that she had to keep proving it, over and over, every day. She dared not stop to rest for fear that her old insecurity would catch up with her.

Eleanor's fall revealed the extent of her enslavement to this demanding, addictive routine. Her amazing productivity hadn't freed her from her fear of inadequacy. Just the opposite, it kept her stuck in it. Now she saw for the first time that she had a choice. She didn't have to fill each minute of the day in order to have a meaningful life. She could relax. She could take naps. She could say no. Leisure was not laziness, nor was it avoidance. Through her fall and the restrictions it imposed, Eleanor received a miracle. Her plague brought her to a freedom she never even knew she lacked.

In this sense, the suffering we experience from plagues is different from the suffering of slavery. Slaves know only slavery, without end. They have no choice about it, no way to escape. Until her fall, Eleanor was a slave. She had no idea she was so driven by activity.

Once Spirit comes knocking, however—once the Moses-mind makes its first request for freedom—we no longer have the excuse of ignorance. Now, if we suffer, we at least know the cause. Plagues become an opportunity, a nudge from Spirit to unwind another layer of ego from our minds, to shake free of another encrusted role or self-image. With slavery, we're stuck. With plagues, we have a choice.

Plagues need not be major, life-changing events like Eleanor's fall. They can afflict us at any moment of any day. In fact, I encounter plagues every morning on my drive to work: a slow car in front of me, an aggressive tailgater behind, unexpected traffic, school buses picking up dawdling kids, and so on. Seen through the eyes of ego, each is an obstacle that frustrates my desire to appear responsible by getting to work on time. Each is a plague infecting my peace of mind.

When I shift and look through the eyes of Spirit, how different it all appears! I'm amazed at the choreography of so many cars and people moving about all at once without collisions. I notice the sky and the wind in the trees. I offer blessings to other drivers on their journeys. Because of my changed perception, miracles arise spontaneously—and not because I'm seeking them. The slow driver turns as I pull near. Lights stay green while I whiz through intersections. And if I do happen to run late, I'll find a message from my patient that they're running later still.

Whether our plagues seem grand and devastating or petty and inconsequential, each offers the same opportunity to change our minds. In this sense, when it comes to plagues, there is no hierarchy of suffering. The ego may judge one as worse than another, but to Spirit they're all equivalent. Each offers us the chance to shift the way we see things and to find, instead of suffering, a miracle.

Doug's Story

Doug worked security in a large office building in the city. He took his job seriously and performed well, but still he hated work. His co-workers harassed him mercilessly. Why? Because he set high standards and lived up to them, raising the bar for everyone else—and as a result he got paid more, too. Doug frequently thought about changing jobs, but given his seniority he knew he could never match the salary and benefits. There was no way out. He was trapped in his job: a slave.

Doug grew increasingly depressed. He'd come home at night an emotional wreck and withdraw in front of the TV. His wife complained, understandably, and they came to me for help. Through psychotherapy, Doug learned that the best antidote for his work situation was to put it aside when he got home and find enjoyment with his wife. Instead of watching TV every weeknight and spending weekends dreading the approach of Monday, they began doing things together.

One weekend they went camping at a scenic state park a few hours away. They'd been looking forward to the trip for weeks. They'd reserved a campsite in front of a beautiful lake where they could kayak. They pulled in right at sunset. The view was spectacular. Doug breathed deeply and felt relief wash through his body.

This would be a worthwhile getaway, a great chance to reconnect. They began unpacking their gear . . . and that's when the music started. Loud, angry lyrics on top of a pounding bass, it blasted at them from the next campsite over. Doug's weekend escape had been stricken by a plague.

His first reaction was incredulity. *Was this really happening? Can't I ever catch a break? God must truly have it in for me.* Doug would either have to march over and force them to shut off the music, probably starting a brawl in the process, or just forget the whole weekend, pack up, and go home. He noticed his wife eyeing him warily, anticipating the explosion. And in that moment, he made his decision. Doug began to dance. He gyrated and swayed and stamped his feet to the blaring music as if he had not a care in the world. His wife burst into laughter, then rushed over to join him in the dance. Needless to say, their weekend turned out to be fantastic, better than either could have imagined. It set the stage for a transformation of their entire relationship.

When Doug described this moment to me in my office, I congratulated him on becoming an alchemist. He looked at me puzzled. "An alchemist?"

"Yes," I said, "an alchemist. When you started dancing, you learned how to change lead into gold."

Doug had taken his leaden feelings of rage, disappointment, and hopelessness and made a decision to transform them into golden exuberance. He'd taken a plague, turned it around, and discovered a miracle.

When you walk your spiritual path with awareness, then each seeming plague becomes your teacher. It's a marker, a signpost, pointing to some area of your life where you still cling to ego. For Eleanor, it was her addictive busyness. For Doug, it was his chronic anger and despair. If you can accept the plague, that it at least has something to teach you, then you'll find lurking behind it some form of ego attachment or aversion—another link in the chain of your bondage . . . and, ultimately, another opportunity to break free.

❀

Zen master Adyashanti describes this transformational process with unusual clarity in his book *Emptiness Dancing*. He tells how, at an advanced stage of the spiritual journey, a plague helped him shed the last vestiges of an old ego identity. His many years of meditation and his dedication to Zen had already led him to a profound awakening. But that was not enough.

> I was an athlete, and I had a lot of identity wrapped up in being an athlete. So even after that awakening . . . I was still riding and training as if I was a competitive bike racer. And I started to question, why am I doing this? . . . I started to see that it was about some remnant of a self-image. . . . Then when I was about twenty-six years old, I developed an illness nobody could diagnose. It put me in bed for about six months. . . . At the end of six months, of course, there's not much of the athlete left. . . . And I realized, this feels great. It felt so good to be rid of that persona. It felt very liberating.[2]

Adyashanti could easily have experienced this illness as a terrible misfortune—a plague, quite literally—that had robbed him of an important aspect of his identity. He could have fought it, or, like Eleanor, grown depressed. Instead, he accepted the learning it brought him, and with that acceptance came a wonderful sense of freedom.

Adyashanti goes on to describe how, about a year later, without consciously intending it, he began to train again. He quickly saw what he was doing, but couldn't stop himself. That old self-image was too tenacious, too powerfully addictive. Like movie zombies or an infestation of fleas, our old ego identifications will rise up to haunt us again and again until we release every last vestige of them. But this is nothing to be afraid of. Nor is it a shameful failure. It's another chance to clean house—to throw out the old clothes that no longer fit, to affirm who we are and who we're not anymore.

And so Adyashanti got another six-month illness, this one even more serious than the last. By the time he recovered, his athlete persona was gone for good.

> To me, that's a spiritual unfolding. It's not getting rid of your self-image through meditation . . . it's just the school of hard knocks. It's an intelligence that takes over and puts all of us through whatever we need to go through to get us to let go.[3]

Adyashanti makes the point that our most profound lessons come, not from conventional forms of spiritual practice, like meditation, but from life itself. The plagues we suffer are essential for transformation. They expose our ego addiction for what it is and give us the chance to break free of it—the chance to make a different choice. They shine the clear light of Spirit upon the dizzying kaleidoscope of self-images the ego spins off to keep us entranced and compliant. Plagues teach us that *no* self-image can satisfy us. On the spiritual journey, plagues pave the way for freedom.

The Persian mystic Rumi expresses this idea succinctly and eloquently in a short poem, in which he refers to the spiritual journey as "the way of love."

> *The way of love is not a subtle argument.*
> *The door there is devastation.*
> *Birds make great sky-circles of their freedom.*
> *How do they learn it?*
> *They fall, and falling, they're given wings.*[4]

The doorway to freedom and the Promised Land is nothing less than "devastation": plagues—ten of them, sometimes more. But it's not *our* devastation. It's the ego's. Only when ego is wrestled to the ground by plagues do we discover—miracle of miracles—that *we* can fly.

※ ※

Chapter 9

THE TENTH PLAGUE AND THE PASSOVER: DEATH AND A NEW BEGINNING

When the ninth plague's three days of darkness fail to change Pharaoh's mind, God and Moses play their trump card. They have one final plague to inflict on Pharaoh and the Egyptians.

> Now the Lord said to Moses, "One more plague I will bring on Pharaoh and on Egypt; after that he will let you go from here. When he lets you go, he will surely drive you out from here completely" (Exod. 11:1).

This plague will prove so devastating that when it strikes, Pharaoh's resistance will collapse utterly. He won't just *allow* the Hebrews to go free, he'll drive them out! The tenth plague is the game changer. When it strikes, Pharaoh will bend and break at last.

Hitting Bottom

The tenth plague pushes suffering to its maximum. There can be no further question of resistance. Our defenses are overwhelmed, and we surrender without struggle. The tenth plague is the Godfather's "offer that can't be refused." In the jargon of addiction recovery, it's called *hitting bottom*. We've tried to cling to the old ways that seemed to work for us before, but they sure don't work anymore. Nothing does; nothing can stop our suffering. We're forced to let go—to surrender, fully and unconditionally.

Hitting bottom isn't confined to the world of addiction. When Sandy's uncle tried to molest her, she hit bottom. Her hopes of salvaging some morsel of respect from her relatives fell dead on the spot. No longer could she continue to pretend they cared about her. She knew for a fact that she didn't belong and never would. She'd met her tenth plague.

Sandy's incident with her uncle took place right before the holiday season—and her birthday to boot. It left her to confront her greatest fear: making it through Thanksgiving, Christmas, her birthday, and New Year's all by herself. Everyone else had loving family members to celebrate with, but not Sandy. She was alone and had to face the fact that no one in her family loved her; no one cared.

Sandy had no choice in this. The tenth plague leaves us no choice. She stiffened her spine and turned to face the bitter winds of loneliness. She'd just have to tough it out somehow and get through on her own.

As Christmas approached, Sandy cried nonstop. She raged and threw pillows. She even felt suicidal—*Why not just end it? Who would care?* But she was determined to stay alive for herself. She was worthy of love and respect, even if her parents and uncle and the whole rest of the world couldn't see it.

New Year's Day came and went. Sandy survived. And in the aftermath, she experienced a strange, new sense of confidence, an inner resilience she'd never known before. She'd weathered this stretch of desperate loneliness. She'd been alone on Thanksgiving, alone on Christmas, alone on her birthday, and alone on New Year's Eve. In the past, this would have proven to her just how worthless she really was. But she'd made it through. She'd endured her own particular brand of withdrawal—not from a drug, but from a cherished fantasy of belonging, a hoped-for love that could never be. Sandy actually felt proud of herself . . . and, for the first time, an inkling of self-love. Only by going cold turkey on her dreams and letting herself hit bottom was she able to discover that it wasn't *their* love she needed. It was her own.

🕉

My friend Marie also learned what it feels like to hit bottom. She worked in a printer's shop, which exposed her to toxic chemicals—but worse still, to a toxic boss. He was a master at dispensing criticism thinly disguised as "I'm telling you this for your own good" style advice. And he delivered his words of wisdom with the haughty air of an enlightened, superior male. It didn't help that he was also sexually inappropriate. Nevertheless, Marie was stuck there. How else was she going to pay the rent? If a new job opportunity happened along, terrific, she'd grab it. But until such time, she had no choice. However, just showing up for work each day was starting to make her sick. Increasingly, she saw that her job was a plague.

One day Marie's boss crossed a line. He intruded into her personal life, and although she immediately warned him to back off, he refused. Like Pharaoh, his heart was hardened. Suddenly, Marie found herself screaming at him. That's when she realized she'd reached a tipping point. The pain of staying at the job now outweighed the fear of leaving. Marie had hit bottom. She quit her job on the spot and walked away.

Marie was understandably anxious. She had no back-up plan and no savings in the bank. She still had to pay for rent, food, and gas. Beneath her anxiety, however, she felt relief, not regret.

She called a friend to commiserate, then hung up the phone, pulled out the "Help Wanted" section, and began looking for another job . . . when the phone rang. It was a woman she knew casually who owned a small bookstore that specialized in 12-step and spiritual literature. She proceeded to ask Marie if she would like a job working in her store. And if so, could she start the next day?

Without Marie's asking, her friend had made one call on her behalf. As it happened, this position had just opened up—and Marie had herself a new job. Her new boss valued her as both an employee and a friend, customers appreciated her insights and recommendations, her salary was higher, and she even got a discount on books! Now Marie awoke each morning looking forward to going to work. The job was a miracle. But to get there, Marie first had to hit bottom and say no to her Pharaoh.

☙

The point at which we hit bottom is of course subjective. There's no way to measure or compare degrees of suffering. One person's tenth plague is another's first. By definition, the bottom is the point at which we finally recognize and accept our powerlessness. Some people reach this point relatively quickly; others never reach it at all. Some quit smoking at the first sign of a chest cold and never look back, while others take their cigarettes with them to the grave.

If we were fortunate enough to have had early life experiences in which change brought relief from suffering, or even outright happiness—whether from a good parent, caregiver, or coach—then we're more likely to take on challenges and expect a positive outcome. Most of us could survive a lonely holiday season with nothing worse than a touch of disappointment. Not Sandy. Because of her abusive childhood, the absence of family during the holidays validated her worst fear: that she was unlovable. She didn't know how to change that, and so she hit bottom.

But what is it about the tenth plague that makes it so transformative? Or rather, when we hit bottom, what exactly shifts in us? It's not merely a change in behavior. Brenda can throw away her bottles and be back to drinking the very same night. No, when the tenth plague strikes, a much more fundamental transformation takes place.

The tenth plague is an endpoint. It's a death: the death of the old self. However, until that old self dies, it's the only self we know, and it will fight to stay alive. Not until this part of us dies do we discover that it *wasn't* us after all. During that stretch from Thanksgiving to New Year's, Sandy died, all alone in her little apartment, just as she feared she would. What emerged after the holidays was a new Sandy, born from that desperate sense of unworthiness, but also freed from it forever after.

The tenth plague signals a deep and painful recognition that our old self—the ego-self, or some aspect of it—has outlived its usefulness. It cannot take us where we want to go. We must release it in order to move on. We must let it die.

Death and the Ego

In Exodus, the tenth and final plague that God inflicts on Pharaoh is death.

> Moses said, "Thus says the Lord, 'About midnight I am going out into the midst of Egypt, and all the firstborn in the land of Egypt shall die, from the firstborn of the Pharaoh who sits on his throne, even to the firstborn of the slave girl who is behind the millstones; all the firstborn of the cattle as well. Moreover, there shall be a great cry in all the land of Egypt, such as there has not been *before* and such as shall never be again (Exod. 11:4–6).

The tenth plague brings about the simultaneous deaths of all Egyptian firstborns, including Pharaoh's own son and heir. When Pharaoh hears the wail of his people[1] and finds his eldest son lying dead, he hits bottom. He immediately agrees to all that Moses has asked. The duel is over, and the Hebrews are free to leave Egypt.

We have no trouble understanding why this particular plague would cause Pharaoh to surrender. The loss of a child is devastating—perhaps the worst thing that can happen to any human being. So of course Pharaoh gives in. But wouldn't it have been more just for God to simply strike Pharaoh dead? After all, it was he who defied God and Moses, not his son, and certainly not the other Egyptian firstborns who are all innocent. So why should they have to pay such an ultimate price?

Glimpsed through the eyes of ego, the tenth plague appears to be yet another example of God's callous cruelty, another good reason to fear Him. If we don't do as He asks, then, like a vengeful, angry father, He'll punish us by killing what we love most. He'll strike at the very heart of our vulnerability, taking the lives of our children while they sleep peacefully.

There's another way to understand the tenth plague, however, in keeping with the parable of Exodus. If Pharaoh represents the ego, and Egypt the kingdom ruled by ego[2], then the firstborns of Egypt (including the cattle) represent the offspring of ego: its creations, its works and deeds, everything it holds dear. And these all come to death.

🕉

As humans who are identified with ego, we try to cheat death and outlive the years allotted to us in many different ways. We pass along to our children our genetics, our last names, our cherished possessions, our personal values, and, of course, our memories. We hope that they in turn will pass them along to their children, and their children's children. This reassures us. It confers a limited sense of immortality.

We wish, too, that our accomplishments will live on long after we're gone—whether a work of art, a fabulous recipe, a home we built, a business we established, or an empire. One hopes his high school basketball record will stand the test of time, another that a street will someday be named in her honor. If our words and deeds can outlast our own brief life spans, then we will have achieved a certain kind of immortality as well.

Yet none of these bids for immortality is certain. The entire human race could perish in a heartbeat—from nuclear war, environmental collapse, or a random meteor strike like the one that ended the reign of the dinosaurs. No wonder the ego is insecure. Death stalks its every move.

Nineteenth-century Romantic poet Percy Bysshe Shelley portrays the fate of all ego-based attempts to win immortality in his famous sonnet "Ozymandias."

> *I met a traveller from an antique land*
> *Who said: Two vast and trunkless legs of stone*
> *Stand in the desert. Near them, on the sand,*
> *Half sunk, a shatter'd visage lies, whose frown,*
> *And wrinkled lip, and sneer of cold command,*
> *Tell that its sculptor well those passions read*
> *Which yet survive, stamp'd on these lifeless things,*
> *The hand that mock'd them and the heart that fed:*
> *And on the pedestal these words appear:*
> *"My name is Ozymandias, king of kings:*
> *Look on my works, ye Mighty, and despair!"*
> *Nothing beside remains. Round the decay*
> *Of that colossal wreck, boundless and bare*
> *The lone and level sands stretch far away.*

This great ruler Ozymandias, this king among kings, hoped to trumpet his fame to the ends of the earth. Surely his name would live forever—and he built an imposing stone monument to himself to guarantee it. The monument is now gone, toppled by time, awash in the desert sands: a symbol of the emptiness that undermines all the works of ego. "All is vanity," Ecclesiastes proclaims.[3] The ego's offspring, its firstborns, are as good as dead. The tenth plague will devour them all.

Like Ozymandias, the ego hopes to extend its reach as far into the future as possible. It seeks to defy death and live forever—in other words, to become like God. The tenth plague cuts it short. It's the one event that all of the ego's seeming might and power, all of its cunning and magic tricks, are powerless to defeat. The cold fact of death undercuts its goals and exposes them for what they are: Lies. Worthless fool's gold.

For ego-addicts like us, this is a hard bottom to hit. It forces us to go cold turkey. For if we continue to invest in the ego, loss and death are inevitable. The Buddha spoke of impermanence. Well, here it is. We will die. Our children will die, and their children, and their grandchildren. All our works will perish. In the ego's uncertain world, the only absolute is death.

And yet, according to Exodus, the tenth plague—death—is what makes possible our escape from Pharaoh-ego's bondage. How can this be? How can death lead to freedom? The answer lies in the festival of Passover.

The Choice to Follow God

In the last chapter, we saw how the plagues functioned as a means to leverage Pharaoh into setting the Hebrews free. They are a learning device designed to pry loose our identification with ego. In this sense, plagues strike the ego, but not our true self. They will afflict us only to the extent that we remain identified with ego.

Exodus makes this distinction using a geographic metaphor. Plagues four through ten strike only the Egyptians. The Hebrews, living apart in Goshen, are spared. They suffer no mosquitoes, no livestock losses, no hail, no three days of darkness. And they are spared the ravages of the tenth plague as well.

> "Moreover, there shall be a great cry in all the land of Egypt, such as there has not been *before* and such as shall never be again. But against any of the sons of Israel a dog shall not *even* bark, whether against man or beast, that you may understand how the Lord makes a distinction between Egypt and Israel" (Exod. 11:6–7).

The Egyptians will cry out, wailing in sorrow, while the Hebrews remain calm and undisturbed. God makes the distinction between Egypt and Israel—that is, between the ego and the true self—powerfully clear. Slavery obscures, but cannot tarnish, our true identity in Spirit. Like the Hebrews, we are God's chosen ones—all of us—and He will set us free.

Yet even for the Hebrews, the tenth plague is different. For plagues one through nine, the Hebrews could remain passive, doing nothing, hunkered down safely in Goshen while God lashed out at the rest of Egypt. Because their mind-set was still that of a slave, they lacked the ability to take action for themselves. So God and Moses had to do it for them.

With the tenth plague, however, passivity is no longer an option. Soon the Hebrews will be free, and they need to start behaving like a free people. Therefore, God tells them that not only can they take action, they *must*. This marks a significant change in status. For the first time they become active participants in His plan.

God prescribes a series of rituals to be performed if they're to escape the fate of the Egyptians—rituals commemorated in the Jewish festival of Passover. These mark the first steps in learning that their safety lies not with Pharaoh, but with God. And when the Hebrews perform these rituals, they will receive their first real taste of freedom.

The Passover Rituals

To survive the tenth plague, God tells Moses that each household must choose one perfect, unblemished male lamb (or ram), a yearling, and slaughter it. They must dab its blood onto the doorposts and lintels of their homes and then roast the entire animal over the fire—head, entrails, and all—and eat the whole thing before morning. If any is leftover, they must burn it (Exod. 12:3–10).

Why does God insist on this particular ritual? What is its meaning? Let's start with the blood on the doorposts and lintels. God tells Moses, "And the blood shall be a sign for you on the houses where you live; and when I see the blood I will pass over you, and no plague will befall you to destroy *you* when I strike the land of Egypt" (Exod. 12:13). The blood will distinguish the Hebrew households from those of the Egyptians.

But we already know that the Hebrews live apart in Goshen, a good distance from the Egyptians. God had no trouble telling them apart in plagues four through nine. Why now does He need them specifically singled out?

God says that "the blood shall be a sign *for you*" (my italics). It isn't there for Him; He doesn't need it. The blood is for the Hebrews, because they're the ones who need to remember who they are. They need to actively distinguish themselves from the Egyptians. With this ritual, they accomplish just that.

Unlike the previous plagues, God will no longer do all the work while they remain passive. By killing the lamb and dabbing its blood on their doorposts and lintels, they affirm their identity as God's people. They make a conscious choice to follow Him, as only a free people can do. They are *not* the Egyptians. God is their ruler, not Pharaoh, and they will obey Him and His commands.

A Taste of Immortality

In the second part of the ritual, God tells the Hebrews to roast the entire animal and consume it completely before morning. Why? What might this mean?

The animal sacrifice reprises a theme from Genesis 22, when Abraham, the progenitor of the Hebrew people, was ordered by God to prove his faith by sacrificing his firstborn son, Isaac. Both father and son received a reprieve at the last minute when a ram appeared to substitute for the child. In Exodus, the firstborns of Egypt will *not* be spared. They are the price to be paid for Pharaoh's intransigence.[4] The Hebrews, however, like their forefather Abraham, are once again offered a way out via the substitute sacrifice of the lamb.

To escape the mass death God will inflict on Egypt, the Hebrews must do more than just slay the sacrificial animal. They must roast it and consume it in its entirety, or burn whatever is left over. This seems like a peculiar command. Why would it be necessary?

The proper recipient of a sacrifice such as this is God. Yet here the Hebrews, mere mortals, not only offer the sacrifice, but then consume it as well. Thus, they take on the role reserved for the deity. By doing so, they become for this one night like God: impervious to death. Death will not touch them. It will "pass over" them. They're being given a taste of immortality.

By slaughtering and eating the lamb, the Hebrews affirm their commitment to God, and He in turn will protect them from death. This brief taste of eternal life is a fitting way to launch their journey out of Egypt to the Promised Land.

How does the Hebrews' sacrifice apply to our own journey? Well, when death—the tenth plague—splits us from the ego, we discover that *we*, in fact, do not die. God asks no mortal sacrifice of us. Just the opposite—he spares and protects us. Death, destroyer of all things of the ego, passes over us, and we take our first breath of spiritual freedom. Death is of the ego, not God. The Moses-mind, born of Spirit, is our true self. When we reconnect with it, we do not suffer the grim fate of the ego and the body.

❦

Many veterans of AA and other 12-step recovery programs can testify to the profound sense of freedom that comes after they hit bottom, face death, and decide to turn their addictions and their lives over to a Higher Power. In coming to this realization, however, many initially feel like they're making a tremendous sacrifice. The addiction has defined who they are. It's been the foundation of their self-concept, lending purpose, direction, and a reliable sense of comfort (however twisted) to their lives. How can they just let it go? Only with time and continuing abstinence do they learn that all they really gave up was their suffering.

To willingly part with an identity in which we've invested so much for so long feels like the ultimate sacrifice. Yet that's what Spirit asks of us. We are ego-addicts. As such, we must renounce and relinquish our lifelong dependency on the ego. But when we do, we'll find that we experience a sense of release and freedom unlike anything we've known—not loss, not sacrifice, and certainly not death. This is the essence of Passover.

Few have experienced such total release from ego. We can, however, get an inkling of what it might be like by looking at those times when we finally free ourselves from some more limited form of ego attachment.

۞

As a young man, I was afflicted by an intense, hopelessly unrequited crush on my best friend's sister. Looking back, I have no hesitation in labeling it addictive. After several years of painful disappointment, I forced myself to accept that nothing would come of it, and I tried to let go of my feelings and move on. But each time I found myself near her, the old longing would rise up to seize my heart once again.

As fate would have it, I wound up driving from California to the East Coast crammed into a VW Rabbit with my buddy, his sister, and her best friend. Some tiny part of me still hoped that she'd come around and return my love—that this trip could turn out to be my chance to win her over. A much larger and wiser part of me, though, knew that, in fact, it was my chance to break free of her.

We made a stopover at Bryce Canyon National Park in Utah, one of the most beautiful and unearthly spots on the planet. My three travel companions strolled off together, chatting happily, leaving me to experience Bryce on my own. Feeling very much alone and rejected, I wandered the majestic, red rock canyons, flanked to either side by tall, drip-castle spires. I took in the beauty of the place, and slowly my mood began to shift.

I realized that I was okay on my own without a girlfriend. In fact, I felt pretty good about my journey. I could appreciate myself, even if *she* could not. I didn't need her love to be happy. I really didn't. I was fine on my own. That was the lesson I needed to extract from my suffering. And so, in that moment, I chose to release her—fully and completely. The futile hopes and dreams, the drama and the longing, all of it had to go. I had to leave it behind, right there in Bryce Canyon.

I returned to the car feeling buoyant and eager to be on my way. But my friends were nowhere in sight, so I decided to meditate while waiting for them. I sat at the edge of a high ridge overlooking the canyon and basked in my newfound sense of freedom, oblivious to the darkening clouds, the cool gusts of wind, and the distant rumblings of thunder that grew ever louder.

All at once, the sky opened and it began to pour—not rain, but hailstones the size of marbles. They pelted down on me as I ran to the car and grabbed an umbrella. I stood in the midst of the storm—hail bouncing crazily all around, thumping madly off my umbrella—and belly laughed so hard my sides hurt and my eyes filled with tears. The weather perfectly matched my mental state. It was one giant catharsis—the sky releasing its pent-up energy, as if purging itself of all the hurt and pain I'd held inside for so long. I felt cleansed. Reborn. My relief knew no bounds.

My companions returned to find me standing out there under my umbrella, staring up into the hail, a wide, peaceful grin on my face. We piled back into the car and drove away from the park. The hail soon stopped, but off in the distance I spied a rainbow: symbol of God's forgiveness. Yes, I could forgive myself for my unhealthy attachment and the suffering it caused me. I already had.

The rainbow faded. I sat back contented . . . when I spied a second rainbow at another location on the broad horizon. It lasted perhaps ten minutes and, as it faded away, yet another appeared in a different spot. And then another!

Five rainbows in all escorted my departure from Bryce Canyon that day, each appearing just as its predecessor faded out. I'd come through the storm and finally let go of my attachment to my friend's sister. And my freedom was confirmed by the miracle of rainbows.

New Year, New Life

Chapter 12 of Exodus begins with God telling Moses, "This month shall be the beginning of months for you; it is to be the first month of the year to you" (Exod. 12:2). In other words, for the Hebrew people, time begins here and now with their release from Pharaoh's bondage. All that came before meant nothing. It's no longer relevant. This is the start of a new year; that is, a new era as a free people with a new identity and purpose.

We celebrate New Year's as a time of renewal, for clearing out the old and welcoming in the new. We make resolutions to change bad habits, turn over a new leaf, and reinvent ourselves. From the death of the old emerges the birth of the new.

But for the Hebrews, this is not just one among a cycle of years. This Passover night marks the start of their *very first year* as a free people. It's the beginning of a new calendar of days. Prior to this night, time was static, incapable of moving forward, because to a slave every day is the same. No real difference is possible, because the only thing that can truly change in the life of a slave is winning freedom. But from this night forward, the Hebrews *are* free. And so time itself has been liberated from bondage.

Recognizing this, God commands the Hebrews to celebrate this night down through the ages as the festival of Passover. The Passover prayer book (called the Haggadah) asks, "Why is this night different from all other nights?" It goes on to enumerate the various rituals to be performed and their meanings. But in fact, the night of Passover is different because each year it gives us another chance to reclaim our freedom and remember how we came by it. And where we are not yet free, it prompts us to break our bonds and seek freedom. Whenever we do this, we get a taste, within the framework of time, of our true, immortal nature as Spirit.

God also commands that from this night forward, all Hebrew firstborns are to be consecrated to Him. Here is the antidote to the tenth plague. The Egyptian firstborns die; the work of ego comes to naught. But our genuine firstborns, those tasks and relationships consecrated to God as part of our spiritual journey, these do not die; they live on forever. They are our only reality in God's eyes.

The yearly celebration of Passover, with its consecration of firstborns, confers an immortality entirely different from the ego's vain attempts. The freedom won on this night of the tenth plague extends in an eternal moment that comes around again every year, and that simultaneously passes on down through successive generations unto eternity.

Facing Death, Effacing Ego

Without the tenth plague, there can be no Passover and no freedom. The one makes possible the other. To be free of ego, we must confront and ultimately embrace the inevitability of death. Faced with its mortality, the ego cannot sustain its charade of self-importance. Death, then, holds the potential to awaken us to our true identity in Spirit.

Of course, for most of us the thought of death is terrifying. We try hard *not* to think about it. We push it from our minds and go about our lives as if it didn't exist. We prefer that people die in hospitals, where we don't have to see them. We pay funeral homes to insulate us from the reality of a cold, putrefying corpse by dressing and grooming it as if it were merely asleep. Glimpsed through the eyes of ego, death is indeed terrifying. And if we were nothing more than an ego confined within a body of flesh doomed to die, then denial might be a fitting response. How else could we cope?

The ego's fear of death is its deepest, most shameful secret. Behind all its bluster and bravado—its pose of always being right, always being in control, its grandiose schemes, its countless hidden anxieties, and its ultimate depression—lies the fear of death. It is absolutely powerless to stop this from coming, and it knows this. And so it tries to convince us that *its* end is ours as well. And yet, for those who've actually come face to face with death, a very different understanding emerges. Remarkably, they find that they're no longer afraid of it.

Much has been written about near-death experiences (or NDEs) by authors such as Raymond Moody and Kenneth Ring.

NDEs take place right at the brink of clinical death, most often resulting from an accident, near drowning, or heart attack. Those who experience NDEs feel separated from their bodies. They float above their lifeless forms, peering down in curiosity while medical personnel rush about frantically trying to resuscitate them. They then find themselves pulled through a tunnel, approaching a powerful light source that radiates pure, unconditional love. This light fills them with peace. They're usually greeted by a being—commonly identified as an angel or a religious figure like Jesus—or sometimes just by the light itself. This being offers them a panoramic overview of the lifetime they've just completed, its highs and lows, the lessons learned and unlearned—all viewed from the perspective of perfect love and acceptance. It then explains that they have a choice. They can cross over and die, or they can return, usually to complete some unfinished task. They choose to return (obviously), but do so with great reluctance and regret at having to part from this light. Once back in their bodies, they no longer fear death. They've had their own brief taste of immortality, and it frees them to experience each new day as a sacred gift. They have no need to exert control over an uncertain future. By facing death, they overcome it.

We don't have to undergo a near-death experience to find this sense of peace. We simply have to square off against the unavoidable reality of death, look it in the eye, and embrace it—for it will come. The body will die. The ego will die with it. We must keep our own death in mind as we go about our days and weeks—not as a fearful preoccupation, but as a reminder of the ego's frailty and our own eternal nature. Why invest in something that's doomed to die when you have a choice?

Death is the great prioritizer. It sorts the valuable from the valueless. Given its inevitability, we can appreciate the present moment as the only time there is—the only time that truly does belong to us. The past is over, the future yet to be. This moment—this *now*—is all that exists. Ever.

Therefore, we must ask ourselves this question: is what we're doing *right now*, thinking *right now*, feeling *right now, at this very moment,* of value? Does it serve our spiritual journey? Or does it serve the bondage of Pharaoh-ego?

Ego dies. Spirit does not. With which do you identify? Which are you? This is the paramount question you must ask yourself— the choice that death presents us with in every waking moment. Are you a body ruled by an ego that rushes about trying to pile up assets and accolades as an illusory bulwark against death? Or are you Spirit, the Moses-mind, eternal son of the Unnamed God?

Esoteric spiritual traditions have always placed great emphasis on embracing death. In indigenous cultures, to become a shaman the uninitiated must undergo a symbolic death. They die to their old identity and journey through the spirit worlds (in a process akin to the near-death experience) to reemerge as shaman, a healer with a new identity, born from and forever linked to the immortal realms of Spirit.

Hindu and Buddhist practitioners also understand what it means to embrace death. They seek out graveyards and spend entire nights meditating amongst the corpses to keep the thought of death near and remember the fate of the body.

I should withdraw to a burial ground
And meditate on the impermanence of my body
By thinking that it is really no different from a dead body,
For both are decaying moment by moment.[5]

The French philosopher Michel de Montaigne also saw value in keeping death close at hand.

And to begin to deprive [death] of the greatest advantage he has over us, let us take a way quite contrary to the common course. Let us disarm him of his novelty and strangeness, let us converse and be familiar with him, and have nothing so frequent in our thoughts as death. . . .

Where death waits for us is uncertain; let us look for him everywhere. The premeditation of death is the premeditation of liberty; he who has learned to die, has unlearned to serve.[6]

The Roman stoic philosopher Seneca (citing Epicurus) thought along similar lines.

"Think on death." In saying this, [Epicurus] bids us think on freedom. He who has learned to die has unlearned slavery . . .[7]

Only when released from the fear of death are we truly free. We can no longer be threatened, controlled, or manipulated. No tyrant can enslave us—especially not the ego.

Clearly, the passage to freedom and the Promised Land must run through the valley of death. We must traverse it with open eyes, as the Hebrews did on that first night of Passover. By embracing death, paradoxically, we escape its pull. We emerge with a new sense of who we are, as our true identity steps forward to reveal itself as Spirit: the Moses-mind.

༄

Several years ago I was deeply involved in the contemplation of death: how any individual moment could prove to be my last and, given this, what did I want from it? What did the moment have to teach me? What was truly meaningful?

At the end of a long and fairly typical day at the office, I climbed into my car for the short drive home. It was a cold evening in January. Darkness was already falling. As I turned out of the parking lot, I thought to myself, *In ten minutes, I should be home.* Then, for no apparent reason, came the afterthought: *Or, in ten minutes I could be dead.* And off I went, instantly forgetting this brief contemplation of my mortality.

Less than ten minutes later, I came to a tricky intersection, but one I navigate every day. The traffic was heavy, and I waited at the stop sign, my head turning back and forth searching for a break in the long line of cars so I could make my left turn. I saw my opportunity and pulled out fast. Suddenly, to my left, a car was bearing down right on top of me—there was no way to avoid it. The vehicle slammed into mine just in front of the driver's door and spun me around into the busy intersection. Somehow, I managed to coax my damaged car over to the side of the road. The woman who hit me sat unmoving, her car stranded in the middle of the road.

I knew immediately what had happened. I'd created an intentional brush with death. It was a demonstration of exactly what I'd been working on in my meditations. Just like that, with no forewarning, I could have been gone. Dead. The lesson was clear. That night I had faced my death, a bit rattled, but without fear.

As I sat shivering in the cold at the side of the road, I felt deeply certain that, despite the damage and the summons I'd received from the police, this accident would have no serious consequences for my life. After all, its purpose had been to face death, and I'd done just that. As it turned out, I was correct.

I tried to call my wife to let her know about the accident, and more important, to get a ride home, but couldn't reach her. A few minutes later, one of my patients happened to drive by. She saw me sitting there by the road and pulled over to give me a lift. I learned that the other driver had sustained only minor injuries (thank God), which my insurance company proceeded to handle without a hitch. My 11-year-old Toyota was totaled—hardly a surprise. But the substantial insurance check I received was indeed a most welcome surprise. It allowed me to lease a brand-new car, symbolic perhaps of a new beginning, and the fruit of this night on which death "passed over" me.

In March, I had to go to court. The prosecutor, judge, and woman who struck my car were all extremely understanding and helpful. I escaped with a minor traffic violation, a fine of under a hundred dollars, and no points against me on my driving record. My intuition had been accurate; I was free and clear of the accident. About a month after the trial, I celebrated Passover with friends and began work on this book.

Four years later, the only lasting scar I carry from this incident is an occasionally painful propensity to awaken with a stiff neck. At such times, I don't complain or bemoan my fate. I accept the tensed muscles as a remembrance of that night and a mark of my mortality: the promise of my physical body's eventual demise.

Exodus tells us that to escape the ego's bondage, we must confront death. We must release our attachment to the body and the things of this world: the firstborns of Pharaoh-ego. When we do this, we find that there was, quite literally, nothing to lose—nothing, that is, but our fear. Armed with this understanding, and with the experience of Passover, we're ready to make the transition to a new sense of self and a new way of being. We're ready to cross the Red Sea.

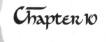
CROSSING THE RED SEA: BIRTH INTO FREEDOM

In the deadly aftermath of the tenth plague, Pharaoh orders the Hebrews to leave Egypt. "[G]et out from among my people . . . and go" (Exod. 12:31). From this point forward, they are slaves no longer. At last, they are free.

God guides them out of Egypt by a roundabout route in order to avoid doing battle with the Philistines. He doesn't want to frighten them at this early stage of their journey and give them an excuse to turn back to Egypt. He leads them, taking the form of "a pillar of cloud by day" and "a pillar of fire by night" (Exod. 13:21), until they come up against the banks of the Red Sea (literally translated as "the Sea of Reeds"). Here they make camp.

Pharaoh gets word of their meandering route and assumes they're lost. He's seized with a fit of anger. One last time, he changes his mind. He gathers his soldiers and charioteers, pursues the Hebrews, and catches up to them. But God keeps the Hebrew and

Egyptian camps separated through the night. What next takes place is perhaps the most famous miracle of the entire Bible.

> Then Moses stretched out his hand over the sea; and the Lord swept the sea *back* by a strong east wind all night, and turned the sea into dry land, so the waters were divided. The sons of Israel went through the midst of the sea on the dry land, and the waters *were like* a wall to them on their right hand and on their left. Then the Egyptians took up the pursuit, and all Pharaoh's horses, his chariots and his horsemen went in after them into the midst of the sea (Exod. 14:21–23).

Working through Moses, God divides the waters of the Red Sea to let the Hebrews pass. The Egyptian armies recklessly give chase, but God sows confusion among their ranks to slow them down. When all the Hebrews have made it across, He instructs Moses to again stretch his hand out over the sea "so that the waters may come back over the Egyptians" (Exod. 14:26).

> So Moses stretched out his hand over the sea, and the sea returned to its normal state at daybreak, while the Egyptians were fleeing right into it; then the Lord overthrew the Egyptians in the midst of the sea. The waters returned and covered the chariots and the horsemen, even Pharaoh's entire army that had gone into the sea after them; not even one of them remained (Exod. 14:27–28).

Thus ends the reign of Pharaoh and the oppression of the Hebrew people by the Egyptians.

What's the meaning of this miracle for the spiritual journey? Why do the Hebrews cross safely, but not the Egyptians? And why does Pharaoh die here and not earlier, for instance, during the tenth plague?

The Test of Water

At the start of Exodus, water played a major role in helping to preserve the life of baby Moses, saving him from Pharaoh's command to drown all newborn Hebrew boys in the Nile. With the parting of the Red Sea, water again enters the story. In a neat bookend, the current Pharaoh—presumably the son of the first Pharaoh—is drowned. The fate the father had decreed for the sons of the Hebrews is reversed and enacted upon his own son. The punishment fits the crime. The sin of the father has been visited upon the son. Justice is served.

There's a historical ritual alluded to here as well. In ancient times, whenever babies were accused of being illegitimate, a crude test was performed. They were thrown into water. If they floated and survived, they were considered legitimate; if they sank and drowned, they were not.[1] Baby Moses floats on the water. This "proves" him legitimate: the true offspring of the God Whose Name may not be spoken. Likewise, at the Red Sea, the Hebrews traverse the waters unharmed. They too prove legitimate. They are God's people. Pharaoh and the Egyptians drown. They are illegitimate, descendants of the false gods of Egypt.

This same theme shows up in the New Testament when Jesus walks across the waters of the Sea of Galilee. He doesn't sink or drown. He is the legitimate Son of the one true God. He doesn't merely float on the waters; he *walks* upon them. Who can doubt his divine lineage?

At the conclusion of the classic novel *Moby Dick,* the Pharaoh-like Captain Ahab (a portrait of the ego if there ever was one) is ensnared by the line from his own harpoon and pulled under the waves. He drowns when he tries to conquer what cannot be conquered: the great white whale. Yet the narrator, Ishmael, survives. Like Moses, he floats, buoyed by the coffin of his heathen friend, Queequeg, upon which is inscribed "a mystical treatise on the art of obtaining truth."[2] The truth that eludes Ahab supports Ishmael and saves his life.

In *Moby Dick,* as in Exodus, the ego goes under—a victim of its own mad, arrogant obsession. It has no relationship to God, and it can make no legitimate claim on Spirit. The ego is a poser, a false ruler, and when put to the test, it must fail.

The Power of Crossing Over

To cross a body of water is a powerful, symbolic act. In Greek mythology, those who have recently died must ferry across the waters of the river Styx to enter the underworld. The crossing confirms that they are indeed dead and may never return to mingle again with the living. The transformation brought about by death is permanent and irreversible. By crossing over, they've transitioned to a fundamentally different state of being.

Birth brings about an equally fundamental transformation. The baby leaves the safe confines of its watery environment and passes through the narrow birth canal to begin a new life. Indeed, the imagery of Exodus hints strongly at the birth process. When the waters pull back, they form two walls. "[T]he waters were like a wall to them on their right hand and on their left" (Exod. 14:22). The Hebrews pass through this narrow channel between these walls of water, to be born (or reborn) into a new identity that's different and distinct from their old identity as slaves.

When the waters return to engulf Pharaoh, we're also reminded of Noah's flood in Genesis, which wiped out the evil world. The flood was a death, a cleansing, and a rebirth into a new world all in one. Likewise, the Red Sea crossing is both a death and a birth: the death of Pharaoh and an end to slavery, and the beginning of a new life of freedom.

※

Julius Caesar crossed the Rubicon to invade Gaul (France). The expression "crossing the Rubicon" has since come to mean the making of an irrevocable decision. When Caesar crossed that river, he passed a point of no return. His decision was final, and there was no taking it back. He crossed the Rubicon . . . and changed the shape of the world.

When the Red Sea parts for the Hebrews and they march across, their fate is likewise determined. Once the waters rush back to drown their Egyptian oppressors, they can never return to Egypt, and they will never again be slaves. If the tenth plague opened the door to freedom, then crossing the Red Sea closes and locks that door firmly behind them forever. Pharaoh is dead, the way back to Egypt sealed off. The Hebrews stand on the opposite bank, a free people with no king or ruler but God.

If Pharaoh represents the ego-mind, then crossing the Red Sea marks the point on the spiritual journey where we're set free from the ego's dominion. Never again will it be capable of enslaving our minds without our awareness. Our eyes have been opened; we see too much. The ego may continue to grab at us, but its grip will not hold. No longer are we its prisoners.

In truth, crossing the Red Sea does not grant us freedom. That we already have; it's our birthright from God. What it does do is initiate a new phase of the journey in which we finally *claim* the freedom that we should have had all along. We transition to a fundamentally new and different sense of self. This is not just an outward change from slave to free person. It's a true transformation—a core shift in how we see ourselves and our place in the world.

What does this Red Sea crossing look like in our lives? What does it feel like to be born into a new sense of self? As you can imagine, such a transformation is not an everyday occurrence. It seldom takes place overnight, as it did for the Hebrews. It usually requires a long—sometimes lifelong—struggle with old self-concepts that fit us less and less well the farther we travel on our spiritual journey. It requires a growing awareness of just how constricting our old identity has become and how it brings us nothing but plagues and suffering. It often requires a tenth plague—hitting bottom. But above all else, it requires an unbending commitment to change: an intention to move forward into freedom, no matter the cost.

Recall my patient Daniel from the burning-bush chapter—the man who turned aside to marvel at the sight of autumn leaves catching the light of the setting sun, only to have his Inner Pharaoh lambast him because he had no job. Despite his psychological growth, Daniel's financial situation continued to deteriorate. His private consulting wasn't working out. Things got so tight that to save money he kept the heat in his house turned down to 50 degrees all through the winter.

Daniel grudgingly came to the conclusion that, if he and his wife were to survive, he had to find work. But the thought of going back to his old university job or anything remotely similar made him ill. I pointed out that his feelings were so negative, returning simply wasn't an option. It would be a betrayal of all his hard-won growth. With tearful relief, he nodded his agreement. Instead, Daniel sought and quickly found a new job, clerical in nature, wholly unlike his previous one. And although it didn't begin to make use of his considerable skills and experience, neither did it overwhelm him with desperation. In his own words, here's what his transition felt like.

> In recent weeks, I've felt much of the old care and worry melt away. For a greater and greater portion of each day, I can just enjoy the simple pleasure of being alive in this time and place. When the [money] worries come again, like clouds on a sunny day, they soon pass away. Most of the time, my cares just don't have the weight they used to have. The new job has been refreshing. I don't know if it will work out, but I'm optimistic. It's helped me wriggle out of my old administrator skin. Here's a funny thing: when I started the job, knowing I was going to meet new people, I thought about all the old stories that had been part of my self-presentation—and they just fell away. I had no interest in them anymore. I didn't reject them or feel ashamed of them—they just didn't seem relevant anymore. It was a good feeling.

Daniel had crossed over into a new sense of self. In doing so, the "old stories" that helped prop up his former self-concept "just fell away," like a snake shedding its skin or cleaning house and finally tossing out that favorite outfit you'd hung onto from so many years ago.

When we cross into freedom, we don't add to our self-concept. We simplify. We streamline. We offload old stories, beliefs, and roles, because they no longer fit. We don't need them any longer. We're comfortable with just being, without the ego trappings. Daniel helps us understand what freedom feels like from the opposite bank of the Red Sea. A good feeling indeed!

Let's turn to another journeyer and follow his transition out of slavery to freedom.

Barry's Story

Barry is a real-estate developer. He's not a big player. He buys run-down properties, fixes them up with an eye for design, and sells them for a profit. He's good at his work and has done well for himself.

Barry was raised by immigrant parents for whom money was the sole measure of success. When he left home and got his first job, they informed him, with straight faces, that they expected him to pay back every penny they'd spent on him growing up. His dad actually presented him with an itemized account of their expenses!

Coming from such a background, Barry understandably felt a fierce pride in his professional achievements and the financial independence they gave him. Beneath each successful real-estate deal, however, there lurked a terrifying anticipation of failure—a core fear, barely conscious, that he would not have enough, that one day he would run out of money. Unconsciously, this drove Barry to buy more properties and stockpile ever more money. But no matter how much he earned, his savings could never outrun his fear.

As a result, Barry began dreaming about making the big score—the kind of sale that would set him up for life. How nice to have that kind of security, to never again have to fret about money. Of course, this was his ego's pipe dream. Nothing outside himself could free him from his fear. But Barry, like most of us, had to learn this the hard way.

He found a century-old mansion in a great location. Although the price was well in excess of a million dollars, he stretched and bought the place, figuring he could double or even triple his investment. He remodeled the kitchen, replaced the bath fixtures, patched the old plaster walls, and added his usual dash of charm. The plumbing and electrical wiring were out of date, but too costly to repair. He listed the house for just under three million, with full disclosure about the antiquated plumbing and wiring.

In the meantime, the real-estate market took a nosedive. Seemingly overnight, buyers disappeared and home values plummeted. Barry received just one lowball offer on the house, from a wealthy divorcée, the ex-wife of a Wall Street multimillionaire. She was a woman with a reputation for trouble, and Barry's agent warned him to refuse her offer. But there were no other takers, and he felt desperate to recoup his investment, so he accepted the offer. He asked his attorney to draw up the contract very carefully. The woman signed without asking for a single change, even waiving her right to an inspection; she agreed to buy the house "as is." Barry was jubilant. He'd made a slim profit, nowhere near the windfall he'd hoped for, but he was out—free and clear.

Not long after the closing, the buyer approached Barry directly. She informed him that there were serious structural flaws in the foundation that would require a huge sum to repair. She accused Barry of knowing about these and intentionally hiding them from her. She didn't want to discuss or debate the matter. She simply wanted a check for one hundred thousand dollars.

Barry assured her that he had no idea about the foundation issue. He reminded her that she'd signed a contract and refused to give her any compensation. Two weeks later, she served him with a lawsuit—for a million dollars. Barry didn't have that kind of money. To lose a million dollars would wipe him out and plunge him into impossible debt for the rest of his life.

He assumed he was protected by the contract. He consulted several attorneys, specialists in the field, and learned that the divorcée was essentially accusing him of fraud, which would invalidate any contract. The attorneys, assuming he was a well-off real-estate developer, dragged out the case and milked him for tens of thousands of dollars in legal fees.

Barry watched his money hemorrhage away, powerless to stop it. He went through his entire savings. His mood darkened, and he felt trapped. Each morning he awoke in a panic over the lawsuit. He carried it in his mind throughout the day (reinforced by e-mails from his attorneys), and he tossed and turned in bed at night, ruminating, unable to fall asleep. He began taking sedatives, but still awoke in a sweat at 2 A.M. No matter what course Barry took, he couldn't escape this woman. She was relentless, and she had the funds to prolong the case and harass him for years. He was running out of options . . . and hope.

One day Barry ran into an old pal from high school who'd become an attorney. From him, Barry learned that his best chance to get out from under the lawsuit and its soaring legal fees was to declare bankruptcy. No sane person would pursue this case in bankruptcy court; to do so would be very costly and almost guaranteed to fail. So reluctantly, Barry followed his old friend's advice.

Several weeks passed and he heard nothing from the divorcée. His mood began to brighten. He began to hope that the bankruptcy filing had done the trick and gotten her to back off. Perhaps his trials were finally over. But when the deadline for filing claims arrived . . . there she was, marching into the bankruptcy hearing, her attorney at her side. She would pursue Barry even into bankruptcy! He was dealing with a crazy person, no, with the devil herself! She'd hound him to the grave and beyond if she could.

Barry hit bottom, and hit it hard. He felt completely helpless, like a little child. Nothing could keep his terror at bay. He saw no way out. Barry had met his tenth plague and he knew it would kill him. As a result, he fell into a deep depression. That's when he sought my help.

We reviewed his childhood and his parents' influence. We looked at his addictive relationship to money—his attempts to use it (like so many of us) to insulate himself from his survival fears. He saw that his real battle was not with the divorcée and the lawsuit. She was just the outer manifestation of an inner Pharaoh. The real culprit, the true source of his fear, lay within: in his ego-mind.

Therefore, there was nothing more Barry could *do* regarding the lawsuit itself. Any action he might pursue would only divert him from the true source of conflict. He really had no other option than to turn the whole thing over to Spirit. He might well lose everything; he might be digging himself out of debt into his 80s. But none of that mattered. The important thing now—the only thing that counted—was coming to grips with his fear.

With this realization, Barry began his transition to a new sense of self. Immediately, he started sleeping better. He still awoke in fear several times a night, but he was no longer afraid of the fear. He knew where it came from, and so he could simply allow it to be present without adding to it.

His perception of the lawsuit also began to change. Devastating though it was, it remained a powerful teacher. It laid bare his core fears in a manner impossible for him to ignore. Because he couldn't change his outer circumstances, he had to change what was inside. And this he knew he couldn't do on his own. He needed help. The lawsuit forced him to let go . . . into the hands of a Higher Power.

Mere hours after coming to this realization, Barry got an unexpected phone call from an attorney he'd never met. The attorney worked for the insurance company that had covered the mansion during the brief time he'd owned it. Barry had put in a claim back when the lawsuit was first filed, but nothing had come of it. Now, all of a sudden, and for no reason Barry could fathom, they'd decided they were going to take his case after all. They would cover all costs of his legal defense. It was a miracle!

Barry told me he felt as if he were in one of those old Western films where all seems lost . . . and then the cavalry rides in with trumpets blowing. For Barry, the Red Sea had parted, offering him safe passage through what had been an impossible situation. From the depths of his despair—his tenth plague—he'd managed to change his mental approach to the lawsuit. The problem was not the evil, wealthy buyer. It was his own mind.

With this insight in hand, he made a commitment to do his inner work *regardless of the outcome of the lawsuit*. And that changed everything. The door to Spirit opened; the waters miraculously parted. Barry learned that he was never truly alone. He had help, and it came from places he never could have imagined.

But Barry's work was not yet finished. He still fell back into fear, not fully trusting his new attorney and the insurance company. Would they really stand by him, or sell him out at the first opportunity? But as the months rolled by, he fretted less and less. And when, in a brief e-mail, his attorney informed him that the case was over, settled by his insurer for a pittance, he felt neither surprised nor jubilant. He'd learned that with Spirit, anything is possible.

The Death of Pharaoh-Ego

By crossing the Red Sea, the Hebrews transition to a new identity. But for Pharaoh, the Red Sea crossing has an entirely different outcome. Pharaoh first threatened and intimidated the Hebrews (no straw for bricks), then bargained and pleaded with Moses and God during the plagues, and finally surrendered and let his slaves go free. And yet, with his own firstborn lying dead and his people still in mourning, he decides to pursue the Hebrews once more and bring them back to Egypt.

It's one thing to continue to deny freedom to those already enslaved to you, it's quite another to try to impose slavery upon a free people—especially when you're the one who's just set them free! By changing his mind once again, Pharaoh proves that he's beyond hope of redemption. He cannot change.

Recall that God will not violate our free will. Because we accepted the ego into our minds and chose to identify with it, He will not challenge our choice. Instead, He works through the Moses-mind to show us that the ego is a false ruler who brings only suffering. Even during the tenth plague, He does not strike Pharaoh down. He refuses to attack and destroy the ego, because to do so would validate its reality and give it an importance it does not deserve. Nor will He pry us loose from our identification with ego by force. Force and attack are the ego's weapons. God doesn't need them. The ego is no threat to Him. He doesn't fear it the way it fears Him. He knows that it's literally nothing—a confusing, contradictory jumble of thoughts, behaviors, memory, and emotions . . . a software routine gone mad. He knows that without our belief in it, the ego has no reality, and therefore no real power either. And He knows that, once we awaken to this, we'll *choose* to relinquish it of our own free will.

Therefore, once the Hebrews are free, Pharaoh becomes irrelevant. God has no need to slay him. And yet, Pharaoh dies. He does so, however, *as a consequence of his own actions,* when he changes his mind one time too many and plunges into the Red Sea after the Hebrews. But he cannot help doing this. It's his nature, the nature of ego. His heart is hardened. In his arrogance, he tries to go where he cannot go and do what he cannot do.

Pharaoh is the agent of bondage. How can he follow the Hebrews and make the same transition they make to freedom? The ego cannot transform itself. A nothingness cannot somehow become something. Indeed, this is the essential lesson of the Red Sea: that we can, and must, undergo a transformation if we're to continue on the journey. The ego cannot. When we make the crossing, it must perish.

Joe's Story

The death of Pharaoh-ego represents the death of our slave identity. Therefore, if we persist in clinging to old ego roles at this stage of the journey—either because we're afraid to let them go or they're too important or entrenched—then we will not make it across. We will not transform, and must ultimately sink under their weight. If we remain stubborn and inflexible, or simply stuck, we'll never learn, never hit bottom. Like Pharaoh, we'll drown.

In the chapter on the many forms of slavery, I described my patient Joe as an extreme example of bondage to a role. Joe was a white-collar criminal: an embezzler trained from childhood by his father to steal from the corporation that employed them both. Being a thief was Joe's secret identity and, like an undercover agent, he wore it concealed beneath his outer appearance with pride. It let him feel brash and superior to all those "little people" who played by the rules and lacked either the gumption or the smarts to pull off what he routinely got away with.

But then Joe fell in love with Cheri, and his thief identity became a problem. This woman brought him more happiness than his grandest capers ever had. But how could he reveal to her his secret profession? How could he risk exposing this hidden identity? She'd reject him, he was certain of it. Yet if he did *not* share his whole being, how could he find the kind of closeness he so desperately sought? If Cheri loved him, but never really knew who he was, then how could her love be genuine? How could she truly love what she didn't know? And would her affection reach the deepest layers of his being and heal the loneliness there? He knew it would not. Joe could live a lie with everyone else, but not with her.

And so he made a decision. He would stop stealing. He rejected his father's legacy and committed himself to living off of only what he earned honestly. It was tough. Opportunities to steal came up frequently, but he had to look away. As a result, he was chronically short of cash. But that wasn't the hardest part. Learning to live without the thrill of pulling one over on the dumb company, to value closeness and warmth over cleverness and superiority, proved far more challenging. Joe quickly discovered that, without stealing, he didn't feel like himself. He didn't know who he was anymore, and felt worthless. His thief identity had so completely dominated every other aspect of his life that when he tried to get rid of it, he found there was nothing left.

Joe grew depressed. He felt unworthy of Cheri. To his credit, he never stole again, but he distanced himself from her, and they eventually broke up. Without Cheri, Joe was rudderless. He'd given up stealing for a life with her, and now what did he have to show for his efforts?

Joe's visits to me grew infrequent. I offered to lower my fee, but he admitted that he couldn't even afford the gas for the long drive to my office. The last time I saw him, he was trying to scrape up enough money to enroll in college and get a real degree (as opposed to the forgeries he'd relied upon in the past). Several months later, I learned that he was killed when his car went off the road for no apparent reason on a rainy night—a crash that may or may not have truly been an accident.

Joe could give up stealing, but he couldn't give up the ego-based identity of "thief." He'd relied on it so extensively and for so long that without it he was lost. He didn't really believe he could survive without stealing. His insecurity and self-doubt preempted the possibility of a miracle.

Joe hit his tenth plague. With Cheri, he briefly tasted freedom and made the decision to stop his dishonest lifestyle—to escape his Egypt. But he couldn't make it across the Red Sea. Unlike Daniel and Barry, he wasn't able to transform and embrace a new identity free of the oppressive past. Instead, like Pharaoh, he was pulled under.

A World Governed by Miracles

The miracle of the Red Sea crossing ushers in a new phase of the spiritual journey. Pharaoh-ego is gone. It rules us no more (although, as we shall see, its influence persists in other, equally pernicious ways). Now nothing stands between us and God.

Freed from the ego, the mind becomes open and receptive. We can experience a world governed not by logic, not by cause and effect, but by Spirit. On the opposite bank of the Red Sea, the journey proceeds according to the principle of flow, as we saw with baby Moses. Here miracles are natural. The act of making it across to the other side is our initiation into this new world.

In summary, by whatever path we arrive at the Red Sea crossing, from that point forward we're not the same. Our sense of self expands beyond the narrow confines of body and ego. Our goals shift. Things that once seemed of vital importance now fall by the wayside as trivial. The door to freedom is flung wide open for us. And although we may lapse into forgetfulness, we can never fully shut that door again, because our previous identity is dead. We've transitioned to a new one that's not limited in any way. We are God's chosen people, and He leads us forward with miracles.

ॐ ॐ

Chapter 11

MIRACLES

When we think about miracles, the parting of the Red Sea is the prototype. Unfortunately, it's so grand, so immense in scale, that the ego happily distorts its meaning. Instead of validating the possibility of miracles, it provokes skepticism and disbelief. How could the Red Sea have parted as the Bible describes? It defies scientific explanation; it defies common sense. Perhaps more to the point, it seems irrelevant. Who among us will ever have to transport six hundred thousand people across such a wide body of water?

Of course, as we saw in the last chapter, the true meaning of the waters parting is symbolic. It describes the entry into a new phase of the spiritual journey: a new state of being that's free from the ego's oppression and governed by miracles. If we are indeed entering such a phase, then the parting of the Red Sea has a lot to teach us about how miracles work.

Intention, Commitment, and Miracles

A good way to begin is by considering how we might accomplish the Red Sea crossing today. With all the technology and engineering skills of the 21st century at our disposal, how might we transport so many people and livestock across such a wide expanse of water?

We could build a bridge—an immense, remarkably sturdy bridge it would have to be. Or, alternatively, we could recruit a fleet of boats to ferry everyone across—another Dunkirk, perhaps, only on an even more massive scale. Either way, such projects would take years of planning. We'd need studies performed, blueprints drawn up, permits obtained. Funds would also have to be raised. The materials to construct the bridge or the boats would have to be purchased and somehow delivered to the site. The people themselves would need to be prepared and organized for a smooth departure. With luck, it could be done, but never in a single night.

Just thinking about the logistics involved is so daunting that it sucks the oxygen right out of us. Each step is contingent on the previous one. Should any of them fail or stall, the whole project grinds to a halt. With this level of uncertainty, our commitment to make the crossing falters and we begin to wonder: *Is it really worth the trouble?*

When we plan at the level of ego, we necessarily focus on all that can go wrong, and how to prevent it. What if costs go up? What if everyone panics? What if there's a storm or an earthquake? Every step of the journey is undermined by these fear-based, what-if scenarios. We become anxious and uncertain before we even get started.

Miracles, by contrast, arise from a mind-set of trust and commitment—a knowingness that with God by our side ("I will be with you"), all things become possible. Our goal is not just achievable, it's inevitable. The moment we commit, the ending is certain, even though we have no idea how we'll get to it or even what the actual outcome might look like. Our act of commitment allows us to cut through the ego's doubts and proceed with God as our guide, just as Moses did.

The mind-set of miracles, then, requires a profound intention for meaningful change on top of an equally profound conviction that such change is inevitable. From Spirit's perspective beyond time, our intention has already been fulfilled, the task already accomplished. (Recall God's use of the sports-psychology technique at the end of Chapter 5: The Burning Bush: Awakening to Spirit.)

Before their arrival at the Red Sea, the Hebrews had already pledged their commitment to God by following His instructions for the Passover. They've already taken this initial step toward freedom; God takes the next one. Had they not marked their houses with the blood of the lamb and consumed the sacrifice as God directed, they wouldn't now be standing on the banks of the sea with a strong intention to cross it. They would not be in position to receive this miracle. But they paved the way for it with their commitment.

Few among us can appreciate the power of focused intention that's uncontaminated by fear, doubt, greed, or need. A famous quote, widely attributed to the German poet Goethe, but in fact written by the Scottish mountaineer William Hutchinson Murray (in his book, *The Scottish Himalayan Expedition*) speaks to the power of commitment.

> Until one is committed, there is hesitancy, the chance to draw back, always ineffectiveness. Concerning all acts of initiative (and creation), there is one elementary truth the ignorance of which kills countless ideas and splendid plans: that the moment one definitely commits oneself, then Providence moves too. All sorts of things occur to help one that would never otherwise have occurred. A whole stream of events issues from the decision, raising in one's favor all manner of unforeseen incidents, meetings and material assistance, which no man could have dreamt would have come his way. I learned a deep respect for one of Goethe's couplets:

> *Whatever you can do or dream you can do, begin it.*
> *Boldness has genius, power, and magic in it.*[1]

Although Murray misquotes Goethe's couplet, he beautifully describes the process by which commitment gives birth to miracles. So in order to understand miracles, we must first understand intention and commitment.

An intention is not the same as a desire or need, both of which imply lack. (But with Spirit, what could ever be lacking?) An intention is a direction to travel in, not a wish we pray will come true. There is nothing desperate about an intention. It's not a lifeline. When Moses calls upon God with the intention of freeing his people, it's never out of desperation, but in calm certainty and trust. He remembers God's promise at the burning bush: "I will be with you." What more could he ask for?

Intentions precede miracles. They call them forth into our world. Without intention, nothing changes. The miracle is Spirit's response to intention—but not just any intention. The only one Spirit recognizes is the intention to be free, because all others simply reinforce the ego's slavery in a different form. When the Hebrews cry out at the end of Exodus 2, they express this intention in a powerful way, which is why God hears them and responds. All the miracles that follow spring from this one initial intent—to be free of suffering.

One of the more effective methods for focusing intention in order to escape bondage is the 12-step recovery program. First developed for AA, it has since been applied to a host of different addictions, including narcotics, gambling, sex, overeating, reckless spending, and others.

According to step three of this process, we "made a decision to turn our will and our lives over to the care of God as we understood God."[2] Such a decision represents a profound intention for change, one that the Hebrews would certainly identify with. In step six, we work toward readiness for God to remove our "defects of character." We must first be ready—that is, our intention must be pure and consistent—before we can actually go ahead and ask Him "to remove our shortcomings"[3] in step seven. Similarly, in step eight we must become *"willing* to make amends"[4] (my italics) to those we've harmed by our addiction before we go about actually *making* such amends. The commitment must take root in the mind first, as an intention, before it can move out into the world in the form of action. Intention is the prerequisite for change, for freedom, and for miracles.

Why Do You Want It?

We are blessed today with an abundance of self-help books that promise to bring us whatever our hearts desire—fame, fortune, endless vitality, and the perfect mate. Many of these offer specific techniques for honing intentions in order to make manifest our dreams. But let's be clear. Genuine intentions are never about the getting of things. That's the ego's game. An intention to win the lottery will leave you poorer by the cost of the ticket.

Genuine intentions are operating instructions for the deepest levels of self. I once set an intention for, and then manifested, a Caribbean vacation. Floating in 20 feet of clear, turquoise water, my mind as uncluttered as the cloudless dome of sky above, I realized that my true intention—my deepest level intention—was *not* to get away from it all, but to go about my day in peace. It was to be able to navigate the hectic pace of work and home with the same degree of inner calm that I experienced floating upon those waters. My true intention was not to run from stress, but to bring this peace of mind home with me, to carry it around inside and make it mine, a living part of me, no matter what brand of insanity happened to leap out and ambush me during the course of my day.

As my example demonstrates, seldom are we conscious of our true intentions. The ego and its magicians will try to hide them from us. They will distract us and keep us blind to our bondage. This creates a conflict between what we *think* we need—the thing that *we've* determined will solve our problem—and what we *really* need, which only comes from Spirit. How then do we distinguish the genuine intentions of our Moses-mind from those of the ego?

Here's a simple test. Whatever you think you need, whatever seems to capture your desire, ask yourself *why* you want it. What's it for? What will it do for you? Peel away the layers of the ego's misdirection and dig deep to the core of the desire. *Why do you want it?*

For instance, say you want a new car. Ask yourself, *Why do I want it?* Because your old car is breaking down and you're afraid it might quit on you altogether—no doubt in the pouring rain, late at night, and 20 miles from civilization in a mobile-phone dead zone. Your deeper desire, then, is relief from your anxiety about getting stuck. You want to be free of this fear and feel safe and secure. Now go deeper still: why do you want safety and security? Because they feel better than fear. They feel peaceful. Therefore, your most genuine desire is for peace of mind. That's the true intention behind wanting a new car.

But what if you want the new car to attract attention? You'd like people to stare as you drive by, to envy you, to admire you, to find you attractive and desirable. Again, ask yourself: *Why do I want that?* To be popular? Sexy? To impress the boss? These are not genuine intentions. They do not serve the journey. Dig deeper. *Why do you want* to be more popular, sexier, or to impress the boss? You clearly must not believe that you're capable of these things as you are now. You're trying to buff up your image, rather than facing and accepting your underlying insecurity. Your deeper-level intention is to feel better about yourself, to feel good in your own skin, to be at peace with who you are. This is a genuine desire, and it will give rise to an intention that could be answered in many different ways other than a new car.

In both instances, the intention to have a new car comes from a deeper intention for peace. *A Course in Miracles* states, "God's answer is [always] some form of peace."[5] Miracles bring our minds to a state of peacefulness. They resolve conflict, oftentimes conflict that we weren't even aware existed.

When we receive such miracles, we see firsthand that there's a power operating in our lives that understands us far better than we understand ourselves. It takes care of us in ways the ego-mind could never have imagined or planned. As a result, we feel deeply comforted.

Miracles—A Matter of Timing

By definition, a miracle is an event that doesn't conform to the common understanding of how the world works. It seems to defy rational explanation. And yet, many miracles are amenable to a scientific explanation, including the parting of the Red Sea.

Exodus states that, "the Lord swept the sea back by a strong east wind [blowing] all night, and turned the sea into dry land . . ." (Exod. 14:21). A path did not magically materialize for the Hebrews. The waters did not leap back of their own accord. They were *pushed back* by a powerful wind blowing hard all through the night.

In his book, *The Miracles of Exodus*, Cambridge University physicist Colin Humphreys makes an intriguing case for a phenomenon called wind setdown to explain the parting of the waters. A strong wind blowing continuously through the night could indeed have pushed the waters back sufficiently to expose a hidden underwater ridgeline, which then became a land bridge for the Hebrews to cross. (He even identifies a likely candidate for such a ridge, near Eilat at the northern end of the Gulf of Aqaba.)[6] As soon as the wind ceased, the waters would roll back very rapidly to engulf the Egyptians.

But doesn't an explanation like wind setdown undercut the miraculous nature of the Red Sea's parting? If it can be understood as a natural phenomenon, then how can it be a miracle? In fact, don't such scientific explanations invalidate the whole concept of miracles? Not at all. For the real miracle lies not in *how* these things occur, but in the why and the when. It's all a matter of intention—and timing.

❀

Theresa was a community organizer in a large West Coast city. She lived her life and pursued her work with saintlike devotion. Many years ago, when her organization had just gotten off the ground, a kind donor offered her a house to use as an office, which she gladly accepted. A dedicated office space would help

147

their mission immensely. There was a catch, however. In order to comply with city ordinances, she would have to remove a large tree from the property. If the tree was not gone by a certain date, she'd be forced to forfeit the house. Needless to say, her fledgling organization had zero money in the budget for tree removal!

The weeks passed with no solution in sight, and Theresa's co-workers grew increasingly anxious. They were going to lose the house, and with it this precious opportunity. But she had complete faith in God. She felt certain that, if they were meant to have the house, then somehow the issue with the tree would be taken care of.

The deadline approached, and still no one stepped forward with funds for tree removal. What were they to do? Theresa urged everyone to remain calm and trust in God. Mere days before the deadline, a thunderstorm struck, which is a rare enough event in that part of the U.S. Rarer still, this storm spun off a freak tornado. It touched down on the property, uprooted the tree in question, and then vanished back into the clouds—all without injuring a soul or damaging any other property in this heavily urban area. Just like that, Theresa's obstacle was gone, as surely and with as little effort as the waters of the Red Sea parting before Moses's outstretched hand.

Had a freak tornado spun down over Theresa's city and uprooted the very same tree a year earlier, no one would call it a miracle—an unusual event, yes, but not miraculous. Theresa's *intention* to keep the house for her mission, which in turn necessitated removing the tree by the deadline, made the tornado and its timing extraordinary. Likewise, the five rainbows I witnessed in Bryce Canyon would have been impressive to anyone on any day. But for me, they were a miracle, because they affirmed my intention to be free of my romantic longing. And a strong east wind may have blown all night across the Red Sea (or Gulf of Aqaba) many times before, exposing the very same land bridge used by the Hebrews, with no one present to notice or care. But when it blows with hundreds of thousands of people trapped against the banks, all holding a firm intention to cross over and escape the Egyptians, then it becomes a miracle indeed.

※

Miracles frequently show up in our lives as synchronistic events: helpful coincidences that are too unlikely to have occurred by mere chance and which seem to address our needs in a very personal way. We find ourselves in the right spot at precisely the right moment, without planning or effort. There are countless examples of such incidents.

Remember Marie, the woman who hit bottom taking abuse from her boss at the print shop and quit, only to land her ideal job at the bookstore? Had she quit a day earlier, the bookstore position would not yet have been available. Had she left a day later, someone else might have already taken it. The timing was perfect in a way that Marie herself could never have orchestrated. Let me offer two more examples.

I recently hosted a big birthday bash for my son. As it turned out, I bought several more gallons of water than necessary. I stashed the leftover bottles in the pantry, scolding myself for poor planning, figuring that we'd never get around to using them all. Four days later, we lost power in a storm. Without electricity, our well pump doesn't work, so we quickly ran out of tap water. But surprise! We had an abundant supply of drinking water in the pantry.

When I was a medical student, I planned to attend a Grateful Dead concert with a large group of friends. But on the night of the show, the friend who was holding the tickets was nowhere to be found. (This was before the days of mobile phones.) I had a car full of people, all pumped up to see the show, but no tickets. I had no idea what to do.

In helpless frustration, I pulled over to the side of the road and closed my eyes. I asked for help in the form of a miracle. Within moments, with my eyes still closed, I heard a tapping on my car window. I was startled and opened my eyes, expecting to see a cop . . . but it was my missing friend! He stood there grinning, waving the tickets in his hand. He just happened to be driving by, saw my car, and stopped—a simple matter of intention and timing, to be sure.

Obviously, these are not biblical-scale miracles. Life did not hang in the balance. However, if we refuse to recognize synchronicities such as these as miraculous and insist that only large-scale phenomena like those portrayed in the Bible are worthy of the name, then we'll overlook the many miracles that come our way in response to our intentions.

Judging Miracles

It's difficult to dispute the miraculous nature of Theresa's tornado or the Red Sea's parting. But what about my Bryce Canyon rainbows or Marie's bookstore job? It's easy to dismiss events like these as chance occurrences that we've invested with far more significance than is warranted. Yet for me, those rainbows were clearly a miracle. And Marie felt the same way about her job offer.

When someone claims to have experienced a miracle, it's natural to be skeptical. So how can we judge whether or not an unusual event constitutes a true miracle? The answer is simple. We can't. Not unless the miracle involves us. Otherwise, we cannot make that call.

The purpose of miracles is not to impress. They come to us in highly personal ways to support our own journeys, to clear the path ahead so that we can move forward, and to demonstrate God's "I will be with you" promise.

Therefore, they can be recognized only by those to whom they occur. Any attempt to evaluate them according to some objective standard is misguided. Nobody can stand outside our life and tell us that what we experienced wasn't a miracle. When it happens to *us*, we know it.

By extension, nobody can measure a miracle's degree of "miraculousness." We cannot rate them like Olympic judges on a scale of one to ten. We cannot say, "Her miracle was way better than his." As the *Course* so wisely puts it, "There is no order of difficulty in miracles. One is not 'harder' or 'bigger' than another. They are all the same. All expressions of love are maximal."[7] Miracles are expressions of God's love for us, which is by definition maximal. Love doesn't get any bigger than that! And from that love, Spirit will always find a way to meet our intention fully and perfectly, whatever that requires—whether it be rainbows, a new job, or the parting of the Red Sea.

We Cannot Choose the Form of the Miracle

The ego thinks it knows what's best in every situation. It will urge us toward all kinds of actions that offer the promise of security and happiness. And yet, when we achieve an ego-driven goal, when we run ego's race and cross its finish line, we find no prize awaiting us. Instead, we feel a gnawing sense of emptiness, an uneasy hunger for something more. Like a mirage of water in the desert, when we finally reach our destination, we find there's nothing there. Our striving did not slake our thirst.

If we think we know what we want, if we imagine that we know just the thing to make us happy, we're almost sure to be wrong. Our search for the perfect mate, the perfect job, the perfect vacation spot, the perfect outfit, the best doctor, the sharpest attorney, the ideal investment strategy, or even for that one perfect Faustian moment that makes it all worthwhile . . . these will never bring lasting contentment. Should we happen to achieve such goals, we're thrilled, of course. Fist pumps and high fives! But once the initial thrill passes (and it will), we're no longer satisfied. And if happiness does not last, if it evaporates to leave us chasing one goal after another, then it never truly was ours in the first place.

The ego-mind is incapable of abiding happiness. Spirit alone knows the path there, and it will gladly lead us forward—through miracles. But it cannot do so if we get in the way by demanding that its miracles conform to our own expectations of what we want. The moment we latch onto a particular picture of how things should be, we've blocked the miracle. Or more likely, it comes and we miss it, because we were so focused on our preconceived notion of what we wanted.

There's a joke that gives a wonderful illustration of this problem. It's about a minister, a good man who loudly and frequently proclaims his faith in God and miracles. One day, a severe storm hits his town, and in a matter of hours several inches of rain have fallen, swelling the river near his church until its banks overflow. Several of his parishioners come by to alert the minister to the danger. They knock loudly on the big door, and when he opens it, they warn him that the river is flooding. "Pastor, you need to evacuate. We've got room in our car. Come with us."

"No, no," the minister replies with a knowing smile. "I have faith in God. He will take care of me." And with a puzzled shrug, his parishioners drive off.

The flood waters continue to rise, all the way up to the church's second story. The minister peers out a high window, awaiting a sign from the Almighty, when a rowboat paddles over. The rescuers call out, "Get in, Pastor, we'll take you to higher ground."

Again the minister refuses. "No, my sons, I have faith in God. He and He alone will rescue me. He will send a miracle. I'm certain of it." And so they paddle off to help others.

The rain continues to pour down and the floodwaters rise even higher. The minister finds himself clinging to the steeple of his church, soaking wet from the pelting rain, water lapping at his ankles. A helicopter swoops in and hovers overhead. A rope ladder drops down and the rescue team inside shouts out above the gusting wind, urging the minister to climb the ladder to safety.

He shouts back, "Leave me, I'll be fine. I have perfect faith in God." And so, the helicopter flies away.

A short time later, hands cold and stiff from gripping the steeple, the minister slips into the turbulent floodwaters and drowns. When he reaches the pearly gates of Heaven, he angrily confronts St. Peter.

"I had faith! I waited and waited for God's miracle, but He let me down. Why? Wasn't I worthy? Didn't I preach His Gospel? Why did He fail me?"

St. Peter stares incredulously at the man. "First, we sent your parishioners around to fetch you, but you refused. Next, those guys in the rowboat came for you. Finally, we diverted a helicopter way off course just so they'd spot you and pick you up." St. Peter gives a shrug. "What more were you expecting?"

God does not *always* work in mysterious ways. If we hold out for miracles that will impress our friends over beers, then we've misunderstood their purpose. We've put the ego's desire for specialness above God's will. Miracles are not meant to puff up our egos. They're not intended as spectacles. They're not supposed to make converts of unbelievers. They're intended to help us on our journey by reminding us of our innate connection to Spirit. They demonstrate a radically different way of living in the world, and they make their point in a manner impossible to rationalize away.

We don't get to choose the form that miracles take—and that's a very good thing. Spirit chooses the form, because only it knows what we really need. And Spirit gets it right—every time.

☙

My friend Ryan, a therapist and speaker, decided to offer a workshop. He wanted to share what he'd learned from his many years of spiritual practice without having to dress it all up in psychological jargon. He was ready to go public.

He reserved a room at the local church, distributed flyers, and posted the event on Facebook. He planned to conduct a two-hour program. If that was successful, he'd shoot for a bigger forum, perhaps an all-day workshop.

The night arrived, and Ryan drove to the church very excited. He got there early to set up, expecting about a dozen attendees. But when the start time arrived, the room remained empty. Ryan sat there waiting. As the minutes ticked by, he grew more and more dejected. Didn't Spirit want him to give this workshop? Apparently not. He was just about to call it quits and head home, when a woman hurried in, apologizing for her lateness. Should he tell her he was canceling? Was it worth his time and all that preparation to present to a single person?

Ryan decided he'd at least chat with her for a few minutes. After all, there was no harm in that. Two hours later, as he describes it, he realized, "It was the best conversation of my life." Even though the experience was nothing like what he'd envisioned or what his ego-mind had planned, it was exactly what he needed, and no doubt the woman, too.

This is the wonder of miracles: we think we know what we want and how that should look, and then something or someone comes along to surprise us with an altogether different outcome, which, in retrospect, meets our needs far better than our own design. The miracle confirms that God is with us and that He can take care of us better than we can ourselves.

The Reciprocity of Miracles

Ryan's story points out another important principle of miracles. If a miracle touches more than one person, it will benefit everyone involved. The world of miracles is not a zero-sum game in which one person's gain is another's loss. They never take place at the expense of someone else.

In the fall of 1976, I was a college student in Connecticut living in a big house off campus with nine other students. We were preparing a festive Sunday dinner and had invited our parents to drive up and join us. Judy Skutch, the mother of my best friend and housemate, had promised to bring apple cider as her contribution. It was her son's favorite.

Judy was driving up from Manhattan and assumed she'd have plenty of opportunity to pick up a few gallons along the way. But it was Sunday, and every place she looked, in the city and on the road, was either closed or fresh out of apple cider. Growing increasingly anxious, she stopped at a farmer's roadside stand—only to learn they'd just sold their last bottle. At that point, Judy knew she needed help—not to manifest the cider, though that would be nice—but to release her attachment to it and her fear of disappointing her son. She went inward and asked for help.

As her car exited I-95 only a few miles from our house, she felt a sense of calm. She could let go and accept that there would be no cider. The Sunday dinner would have to proceed without it. Her son might be disappointed, but she could live with that, and so could he. There would be love aplenty, with or without cider.

That's when Judy spotted a solitary man sitting dejectedly in a lawn chair next to an old car parked by the side of the road. Concerned that his car had broken down, she pulled over to ask if he was okay. He was fine, he said, and needed no help. On a whim, she asked if he had any idea where she might find some apple cider at this late hour. His eyes went wide. He stared at her in disbelief, and then said, "Lady, you must be a miracle."

He went on to explain that he had four gallons of cider in the trunk of his car and absolutely had to sell them before he could return home to his wife. He was a local farmer and really needed the cash. If he didn't sell the cider that day, it would likely go bad. He'd sold a few gallons earlier, but had been sitting there in the cold the entire afternoon and not a soul had stopped. He'd just given up and loaded it all back in his trunk, and was trying to figure out what to tell his wife, when Judy appeared.

What was the real miracle here? Was it the sudden appearance of apple cider for our Sunday dinner? Or was it the realization that what helps one helps the other? That, at the deepest level, we are all interconnected—all one in Spirit—and so we partake equally of the miracle. The man selling cider needed cash. Judy needed cider, but far more, she needed peace of mind. By shifting her perception of the situation and releasing her fear of disappointing her son, she received a dramatic demonstration of "I will be with you."

We have many needs in life, and they can look very different at the level of ego. One person needs money, another love, another health, and yet another friendship. As a result, we see ourselves as separate and distinct. *I am not like you. She is not like him.*

At bottom, however, our needs all factor down to the same thing. We need to escape ego's bondage and return home to Spirit, to the Promised Land. Nothing else will do. And so, from the perspective of miracles, we're not at all different. There is but one Moses-mind, and we all share in it. It is our one true Self, descended from God, Who "gave birth" to it. The seeming differences between us are meaningless, because we all travel toward the same destination, holding the same core intention.

Miracles Are for Everyone

If miracles affect us equally, each according to his or her circumstances, then obviously they do not discriminate between us. They're not rewards for good behavior, nor is their absence a sign of sinfulness or a form of punishment. God will always judge us as worthy, because we are His sons and daughters—descended from His lineage. Likewise, He will always judge our egos as unworthy, because they are, from His perspective, unreal.

Many people think that miracles are reserved for only the most exalted of saints and gurus. Indeed, the Catholic Church will not canonize someone as a saint unless he or she has performed a miracle or two in the eyes of the Church. The miracle is a requirement, a proof of holiness—rather like a certificate of authenticity from God. According to this belief, the majority of humans are unworthy of miracles. Saints are a special case. God smiles upon them. The rest of us don't even come close.

Remember, however, that in Exodus the Red Sea did not part for Moses because he was saintly. The miracle was not proof of his worth in God's eyes. That wasn't its purpose. Nor did Moses cross over by himself. *All* the people made the crossing—*that* was its purpose. They were all worthy. And they didn't need to do anything special to prove it.

The Red Sea parts for Moses and the Hebrews not to prove their worthiness, but to help them escape Pharaoh's slavery—a goal which God Himself promised them. The Red Sea parts as an object lesson that, on the spiritual journey, even the seemingly greatest of obstacles can vanish overnight.

As with the Hebrews, miracles come to us, not as proof of saintliness, but as a means of transformation. They carry us to a different perception, a new understanding of who we are and our connection to Spirit. We no longer need to fear for our survival. We no longer need to search for meaning. We've become a conduit for miracles. This is our new purpose. In this sense, once we've committed to the spiritual journey—truly committed—miracles are inevitable.

Miracles: A Better Way to Travel

Miracles work at all times, in all places, and under all circumstances. They cannot be limited by anything of this world. And they're always available. All we need to do is shift from ego-mind to Moses-mind. That's our part. That's what's asked of us—nothing more. Once we change our mind, quite literally, we welcome in the miracle.

But how does this work? From our limited human perspective, we can't know the answer. It's enough to know that it *does* work, that it cannot fail to work. But let me offer an analogy.

Picture a stream. Its waters flow easily and naturally downhill. Now, picture a spot in the stream choked off by a mass of dead leaves and tangled twigs. The water can't flow. It's backed up in a stagnant pool. Now imagine clearing away the debris, gently pushing it aside with your foot. The stream begins to flow again, all on its own, powered by the force of gravity. The water finds its way without any additional help or guidance from you. It follows its own unique path. All that was necessary was to remove the obstacle.

That obstacle is the ego-mind. It keeps us stuck and stagnant. It blocks the flow of miracles that would otherwise be ours. When we remove the blockage by changing our mind, miracles flow forth freely and naturally, like the stream. And there's nothing remarkable about it. It's how things are supposed to work. It's the very nature of miracles. As *A Course in Miracles* states: "Miracles are natural. When they do not occur something has gone wrong."[8]

Once we've experienced miracles, it's impossible to see the world ever again in the same way. We can no longer pretend that we're prisoners of this limited reality, bound by laws of cause and effect and the constraints of linear time. As the *Course* puts it, ". . . miracles violate every law of reality as this world judges it. Every law of time and space, of magnitude and mass is transcended . . ."[9] Miracles can move mountains and split the sea. This is the true meaning of freedom. By liberating us from all earthly constraints, miracles free us from fear. For what is there to fear when we know firsthand the power of Spirit? We become citizens of another world that follows different laws, those of synchronicity and flow. We learn how to be in the world, but not of it.

When we cross the Red Sea and arrive safely on its far bank, this is the world we enter. It's a world where we can receive guidance and miracles directly from Spirit, free of fear. But we must trust and accept these gifts. Unfortunately, as the Hebrews of Exodus will demonstrate, this turns out to be one of the most difficult tasks of the entire journey.

Chapter 12

THE WILDERNESS

Having successfully crossed the Red Sea, the Hebrews are understandably jubilant. They celebrate the triumph of their God
over the Egyptians by singing the Song of the Sea. In most tales,
this would be the end of the story. The Hebrews have, after all,
achieved their goal of freedom. So what remains for them to accomplish? But according to Exodus, a great deal remains. The spiritual journey is not yet finished.

Crossing the Red Sea—as important of a step as it is—does
not bring the Hebrews to the Promised Land. Instead, they enter
a dry, lifeless wilderness where, unbeknownst to them, they will
wander for the next 40 years. If we hope to grasp the challenges of
the different stages of the spiritual journey, it's paramount that we
come to terms with the wilderness and why it proves so daunting.

Up to this point, the central conflict in Exodus has been between Moses and Pharaoh. Moses's drive to free his people collides
with Pharaoh's stubborn resistance. On the opposite bank of the
Red Sea, however, all this changes. Pharaoh is gone, drowned in
the waters that stood aside to let the Hebrews pass into a new life.
What then prevents them from proceeding directly to the Promised Land? With Pharaoh dead, who or what becomes their new

adversary? In the parable of Exodus, once the controlling ego is vanquished, who or what stands in the way of the spiritual journey? What must we still learn before we can achieve an abiding connection with Spirit?

With Pharaoh dead, only three characters remain in Exodus: God, Moses, and the Hebrews. God is obviously not the adversary, and neither is Moses. He continues to serve as leader to his people. All that's left is the Hebrews. If we look closely at their words and their behavior, we'll see that they have indeed become their own worst enemy.

On the opposite bank of the Red Sea, the only thing capable of stopping our progress is our own mind. Only we can stand in the way of our transformation. The loss of the Pharaoh-like ego exposes a primitive, childlike sense of apprehension. *How will we survive?* This is the very fear that drove us into the arms of ego in the first place. For the Hebrews, it proves stronger than God's miracles. It overwhelms all that God has done for them, and it is given full expression by what I call the voice of the Hebrews.

The Voice of the Hebrews

The voice of the Hebrews makes its first appearance when Moses confronts Pharaoh for the first time. Recall how the foremen castigate him: "May the Lord look upon you and judge you, for you have made us odious in Pharaoh's sight and in the sight of his servants, to put a sword in their hand to kill us" (Exod. 5:21). They are afraid that Moses's request for freedom will backfire and the Egyptians will kill them instead. At this point in the story, however, the Hebrews are still slaves. They haven't experienced God's miracles. The plagues, the Passover, and the Red Sea crossing are all still to come.

We next encounter the voice of the Hebrews when they're pinned against the banks of the Red Sea by Pharaoh's armies, the night before the waters part. Again, the voice takes Moses to task.

Is it because there were no graves in Egypt that you have taken us away to die in the wilderness? Why have you dealt with us in this way, bringing us out of Egypt? Is this not the word that we spoke to you in Egypt, saying, 'Leave us alone that we may serve the Egyptians'? For it would have been better for us to serve the Egyptians than to die in the wilderness (Exod. 14:11–12).

The outcome that the foremen feared and gave voice to in Exodus 5 now seems to have come to pass. The Egyptian army will soon sweep down on them, swords in hand, and slaughter them all. But the Hebrews have already witnessed the ten plagues that devastated Egypt yet miraculously left them untouched. They've survived the tenth plague, participated in the Passover rituals, and escaped Egypt. Yet still they do not trust Moses and, by implication, God. Better to serve the Egyptians as slaves than die like this in the wilderness. Like frightened children, they cower at the prospect of danger. They don't understand how completely their circumstances have changed. And indeed, the next morning God comes through and parts the sea for them.

The voice of the Hebrews makes another appearance when Moses leads the people away from the Red Sea into the heart of the lifeless wilderness. They travel for three days without finding any water. They come upon the waters of Marah, but they're bitter. "So the people grumbled at Moses, saying, 'What shall we drink?'" (Exod. 15:24). Soon after, they gripe to him about their hunger.

"Would that we had died by the Lord's hand in the land of Egypt, when we sat by the pots of meat, when we ate bread to the full; for you have brought us out into this wilderness to kill this whole assembly with hunger" (Exod. 16:3).

And not long after, they again complain about lack of water.

Therefore the people quarreled with Moses and said, "Give us water that we may drink." And . . . they grumbled against Moses and said, "Why, now, have you brought us up from Egypt, to kill us and our children and our livestock with thirst?" (Exod. 17:2–3).

The Hebrews continue to distrust Moses and God, despite the amazing miracles they've been given. Such miracles should have proven conclusively that God is with them and so they have nothing to fear. Yet each time their survival appears threatened, they denounce Moses and regret having ever left Egypt. They would rather remain slaves than face the prospect of death from hunger or thirst. Pharaoh may be gone, but his shadow still lingers in the mind-set of the Hebrews. And as long as it does, as long as they retain the mind-set of slavery, they're not ready for the Promised Land. Their fear blocks the way.

The Mind-Set of Slavery

The Hebrews are not condemned to wander the wilderness for 40 years because they've sinned. They're not barred from the Promised Land as punishment. They remain stuck in the wilderness phase of the journey simply because they're not ready to go any farther. A poor student can't be expected to graduate high school without performing some remedial work. Likewise, the Hebrews haven't yet learned what it means to be God's chosen people. They have freedom, but they don't understand it. Wherever they travel, however many miracles they receive, their minds remain shackled to Egypt. Pharaoh may be dead, but their core identity is still that of a slave.

We can see this phenomenon at work in what's known as *lottery-winners' syndrome*. Many of us think that winning some fantastic sum in the lottery would solve all our problems. And yet, a surprising number of people who win manage to squander their newfound fortune in a short period of time. Why?

Consider a man who's worked hard and struggled his whole life to get by. Suddenly he strikes it rich in the lottery. He now has more money than he could ever have imagined. He's ecstatic. His troubles are over. So what does he do? He quits his job and sets about spending his winnings. Anything that he, his friends, or his family have ever dreamed of owning or doing, he can now afford. In fact, he has so much money that he thinks nothing of throwing it at whatever outlandish investment schemes come his way.

As a result, in a few years time—having been duped or reckless, or both—his money's gone and he's back to struggling. He wasn't able to hold onto such a fortune, to integrate it into his self-concept and really own it. The simple fact of all that money did not change his mind-set. Inside, he remained a poor man, and his financial decisions reflect this impoverished sense of self.

To use a computer analogy, he cannot run the "rich man" application on his old "poor man" system software. When he tries, the system crashes. In order to truly make that money his own, he must change his core sense of self. He needs a mental software upgrade.

The Hebrews too need an upgrade. They need to transfer their allegiance from Pharaoh to God, a task that proves more difficult than we might expect. Yet this is the challenge of the wilderness phase of the journey—for us as well as the Hebrews. We've recognized our enslavement to ego. We've seen how everything the ego promised was doomed to failure and death. We've crossed the waters and made the transition to a new sense of self. We've witnessed miracles, we know that they work, and we know they can be ours.

But it's all too new. We don't fully trust it. Without the controlling ego to organize and give shape to our lives, we really are a bit lost. All the usual road markers—the things we strove for and dreamed of—these are gone, drowned with Pharaoh-ego. We no longer know where our lives are headed, what awaits us down the road, and this is terrifying. We don't understand what God asks of us. We know we've changed; we've crossed over. But we don't really know how to live as His chosen people.

We've been enslaved to ego for so long that we can't seem to break the mental habit. Besides, everyone around us continues to chase after those old ego goals as if they still had value. It's easy to envy them. It's easy to relapse and wish that we could somehow return to that state of ignorance when things seemed so clear and obvious.

Longing for the Past

In the film *The Matrix*, the character Cypher, one of a small band who's awakened to the true nature of the matrix world, chooses to betray his comrades. He's grown tired of the desolation of the real world, its hardships and its crappy food—tired of wandering the wilderness, we could say—and he longs to return to the comfortable and familiar illusions of his past in the matrix. After his Judas-like betrayal, he sits down to a sumptuous steak dinner with Agent Smith, the enforcer of the false matrix reality. Cypher relishes every bite of his dinner, even though he knows that none of it—neither the steak nor the place setting on which it's served, nor even the posh restaurant itself—is real. He's chosen to barter his freedom and his knowledge of the truth for a chance to return to the ignorance of the matrix world. He's trying to live in a past that can no longer exist for him.

The voice of the Hebrews longs for the past, too. "Would that we had died by the Lord's hand in the land of Egypt, when we sat by the pots of meat, when we ate bread to the full" (Exod. 16:3). Later, in Numbers, after receiving the Ten Commandments, the voice *still* longs for Egypt. "We remember the fish which we used to eat free in Egypt, the cucumbers and the melons and the leeks and the onions and the garlic . . ." (Num. 11:5).

This portrait of life in Egypt is a bit strange, to say the least. The Hebrews were, after all, slaves. If they ate for free, it was only because they labored all day without compensation. Their suffering was so great that it caused them to cry out to God for help. Yet now they regret leaving Egypt? They miss the pots of meat, all the bread, fish, leeks, cucumbers, and melons they could eat. It sounds so wonderful and sumptuous. But was this really the fare of a slave?

Like Cypher, the Hebrews are indulging in a false recollection of their time in Egypt. The starkness of the wilderness scares them, and they fear for their survival. Because their trust in God is so fragile, they have no remedy for their fear. Instead, they retreat into fantasy. Rather than trusting the miracles of Moses and God, which have not failed them yet, they protest and complain and fantasize about an Egypt that never was—except in their own imaginations.

We are all guilty of such fantasies. For some, childhood was that golden era, when we could play outside until dark, run home to a delicious meal, and curl up in a warm bed with not a care to trouble our sleepy minds. For others, it was high school and the first experience of love, or our first job and the pride of paying our own way, or the early days of marriage when passion still ran high. And who could forget those precious years when the children were babies.

Left out of these fantasies are the fierce insecurities of childhood: the teasing and bullying, the nightmares, the disappointments that left us in tears. When we remember our first love, we overlook the pain of that first breakup and how it felt to see the one we loved in the arms of another. When reminiscing about our first job, we downplay the angry boss, the aloof co-workers, and perhaps the even better job, which we didn't get because we were unqualified. When we recall the passion of the newlywed years, we forget the ugly skirmishes over in-laws and money. And the simple pleasure of cradling our children as babies was negated by the sleepless nights and the strain on our marriages imposed by the demands of parenting a newborn.

The past we long for is an illusion. It never existed. It's a filtered-down version of what really happened. We sift the good from the bad, and from this we concoct a highly selective, idealized version of the past: a golden age when everything was great, exactly the way we wanted it, without hardship or pain. Thus, the Hebrews' slavery becomes a time when meat, bread, and fruits of all varieties were theirs for the taking. In this version, they never went hungry and never suffered. They were happy slaves, stuffing their bellies full under the beneficent gaze of Pharaoh.

But why is there this need to create an idealized fantasy of the past? What purpose does it serve? And why would such a longing come up now, at this stage of the journey, when we've already experienced what God can do for us through His miracles?

※

The Hebrews look to an idealized past in Egypt to counter their fear of the present in the wilderness. They've transitioned to a new identity, but they have no idea how to survive on their own, without Pharaoh. They don't know how to find food or water in such a harsh environment. Back in Egypt as slaves, food and water were provided by their taskmasters. In an unknown land, things are different.

Because the Hebrews have been passive recipients of God's miracles, they don't trust them as a means of survival. They don't feel they can count on Him the way Moses does. Their faith is weak. Imagine their disappointment when they successfully cross the Red Sea to find themselves, not in the Promised Land of milk and honey, but in the wilderness: one of the most desolate and forbidding places on Earth. Naturally, they question their decision to follow Moses. If this is freedom, why bother? What good is freedom to someone dying of thirst?

The Hebrews are understandably scared. In the wilderness, the future looks bleak and uncertain. By contrast, the past in Egypt begins to look good, however difficult and painful its reality. This bountiful Egypt of fantasy becomes a substitute for the Promised Land. It's a false Eden, a safe and easy alternative to the harsh, empty conditions they find themselves in. Of course, the Hebrews can dream all day long of an Egypt with bread and meat in abundance, but it will never fill their bellies.

The longing for Egypt—for an idealized version of the past—is a step backward. It's a regression to the use of fantasy as a means of allaying fear. But fantasy is a defense mechanism. And as we saw with Pharaoh's magicians, the purpose of a defense mechanism is to distract us from the journey.

With our eyes gazing longingly back at the past, it's impossible to move forward. It's impossible not to stumble. Not only do we pursue the wrong goal, we overlook the miracles that *do* sustain us. Our fantasies stand in the way of new learning. They keep us tethered to Egypt and bondage long after Pharaoh-ego is gone.

Gina's Story

Gina came to me devastated. She'd been involved with Pete for over two years. She loved him, he loved her, and both wanted to be together for the rest of their lives. There was only one catch: Pete was married. Consequently, the relationship had been something of a roller-coaster ride—intense highs and giddy hopes plummeting into frequent bouts of disappointment.

When Gina first met Pete, she felt an instant connection that truly left her weak-kneed. But she knew he was married, and so she pushed it aside. But he pursued her. His wife was mentally ill, he told her, and so fragile that he dared not leave her. Not just yet. Could Gina be patient? Although she felt dirty and shameful about being "the other woman," she had no doubt that Pete was the love of her life: the man she'd been waiting for since her teens. Yes, she could be patient. Yes, she could wait for him.

Pete went to great lengths to prove his commitment to her. He rented a condo in an upscale part of the city, furnished it, and moved in, just to prove how serious he was about leaving his wife. Gina would meet him there secretly. Lying in bed together, she'd dream of a time when he was free of his marriage and they could live together openly.

As the months passed, however, the evidence mounted that Pete wasn't being truthful, and that he had no intention of getting a divorce. A friend told her that Pete and his wife took a fancy vacation together. Another confided that he had been seen out and about with yet another woman. And with a little sleuthing,

Gina learned that her secret lover was not in fact living in his new condo. It was a love nest. He remained at home with his wife.

So Gina confronted Pete, broke off the relationship, and came to me for help. She was aching so badly inside that she was sure it would never go away. She still loved him. She still believed that he was the one for her. She hoped and prayed that there was some way to convince him to wake up, get a divorce, and join her. I suggested that, before dealing with Pete, she take a look at herself. How did she get to be the person she was? What forces shaped her?

When Gina was 16, her family suffered a horrible tragedy when a drunk driver killed her older sister. For her family, life came to a halt. Her father, a silent man by nature, withdrew into greater silence, and her mother grew depressed. She'd run the errands, do the chores, make meals, but emotionally she was AWOL. Once night fell, she'd retreat to her room, pop a few pills, and disappear until morning. Gina lost not only a sister, but both her parents. Essentially, she lost her whole family.

How did she cope? She turned to boys—fantasies of boys. Over the decades, she'd had countless crushes, a series of committed long-term relationships, and in between, the occasional lover. On weekend nights, she went to clubs with her girlfriends. They all shared one goal—to find a man. Yet whenever she or her friends did meet someone promising, he seemed to transform overnight, like Cinderella's coachmen, into a rat.

Through therapy, Gina came to see how she'd sought to replace the love and closeness she'd lost at home after her sister's death with a different kind of love and closeness: from a man. Unable to heal her parents' grief, she sought love outside herself. Somewhere out there, someone would love her and make her happy . . . and all would be well again. This created a dependency in her relationships that made her afraid to ask for what she wanted. What if he refused? What if he left her? Could she bear to be alone again? Because deep down, Gina didn't feel worthy of real love. It was better to settle for less than wind up with nothing at all.

But with Pete, Gina realized that she *had* settled for nothing—actually, worse than nothing. She'd embraced a lie. He was her "bottom," her tenth plague. That insecure part of her that made her think that she needed a man to be happy had outlived its usefulness. She could see that it was just old baggage from childhood—an adolescent's attempt to cope with loss and grief—and not some fundamental aspect of her self that could never change. She could choose to let it go. And she did.

I suggested that, instead of pursuing Pete or any man, Gina make a commitment to *herself* by taking a break from *all* men for six months. She readily agreed. On several occasions during that time, she ran into Pete in the strangest of ways. She'd find herself driving right behind him, or rounding a corner to see him getting out of his pickup. These were true synchronicities. But rather than interpreting them as signs that they were meant to be together, Gina saw them as opportunities to reaffirm her commitment to herself and stand on her own.

Without the distraction of men, Gina was forced to face the chasm of grief from her childhood and let it in. As she did, she began to experience, not anxiety, not loss, but a strange sense of inner calm. The obsessions with men stopped. She could enjoy her day just as it was, without a man to distract her or fantasize about.

Gina escaped her Egypt. She left Pete behind and crossed the Red Sea to a new sense of self, freed from the baggage of needing a man. But she still wanted a relationship. Not the addictive kind, but a healthy relationship between equals. How was she going to find it?

With six months of relationship sobriety under her belt, Gina decided that it was safe to venture out to the clubs again with her girlfriends. But to her surprise, the whole scene repulsed her. Where before she'd found intrigue and possibility, she now felt only disgust. That old familiar thrill of anticipation—*Would this be the night? Would he be the one?*—was gone. It offered her nothing.

Gina's girlfriends were hurt; they didn't understand. They felt that she was rejecting them, when in reality she was rejecting their shared fantasy that catching a man was somehow the Promised Land.

Gina tried going out on a few dates engineered by friends, but nothing clicked. She fended off the advances of two co-workers, preferring to spend her weekends alone. She still wanted a relationship, but had no idea how to make it happen. She was in unknown territory.

Gina had entered the wilderness. Her self-concept had changed; her old way of life no longer fit. It could not satisfy her desire for a genuine relationship. Yet she knew no other way to find a man. The very notion that she *had to attract someone,* that she had to do or be something other than herself to charm a man into loving her, felt deeply wrong. But what were her options? She began to feel hopeless and afraid that she might be alone for the rest of her life. But if that were the case, she could accept her fate. She'd rather be alone than enslaved to the likes of Pete.

Instead of idolizing past relationships—longing for an Egypt that never was, like the Hebrews—or looking for a new fantasy, Gina chose to hold out for a healthy, honest, committed relationship, however long it might take to find. She'd wasted two years on Pete; she could certainly afford to wait another two for someone better. Gina discovered trust. She learned how to survive the wilderness.

I hadn't heard from Gina in almost a year when I e-mailed her for permission to use her story. She reported—no surprise to me—that "a great guy walked into my life and I'm not letting him go. . . . Smart, kind, good father, honest, and he's even been through some therapy." Gina had made it out of the wilderness and found a solid, trusting relationship—the very thing she'd wanted all along. It was her version of the Promised Land.

After the Red Sea, the Wilderness

Whenever we make a significant life change—a Red Sea crossing that leads to an entirely new sense of self—we will find ourselves in the wilderness for a time. Without the old ego habits, we wander lost. Wherever we look, we see the burned-out shells of our former life—routines, desires, people, places—all of them achingly familiar, but no longer ours to inhabit. Like returning to a town you lived in years ago, it may be outwardly the same, but no one knows you there anymore. You don't belong.

Alcoholics look out at the world defined by their drinking and see the same bars, clubs, and liquor stores, but they're stripped of their old meaning. They no longer make sense, not to this new, sober self, and this is deeply disturbing. Likewise, sex addicts look out at the world defined by attraction and intrigue. The men and women, the flirtations, the nightclubs, the never-ending games of come-hither and pursuit, none have really changed. However, they're now seen for what they are: empty, without meaning. A desert.

Into this emptiness, fantasies of the past will arise to tempt us. But they offer nothing real. We can and must learn to accept, and even welcome, this emptiness. It's just the space that remains after we've given up the false ego-self or some aspect of it. As long as we don't rush to fill it, it will heal. And with healing will come peace.

The journey to the Promised Land must take us through the wilderness. We must confront the bleakness of our past under Pharaoh-ego with forthrightness and honesty, and not dress it up as something wonderful. We must learn that it is a wasteland and holds nothing for us. Herein lies the challenge of the wilderness phase of the journey.

Entering the Wilderness

The moment the Hebrews cross the Red Sea, they move from a world dominated by water to a stark, rugged landscape where water is nonexistent. It's a complete reversal of imagery, and it signals a new phase of the spiritual journey.

In the opening chapters of Exodus, water was a constant presence, from the first Pharaoh's attempt to drown all male Hebrew infants in the Nile to baby Moses finding salvation on that same river. The first plague transformed these waters from a source of life to blood-red death. The Red Sea blocked the Hebrews' path of escape . . . but then opened for them, allowing them passage to a symbolic rebirth. The same waters then closed upon Pharaoh and the Egyptians, ending forever their oppression. Throughout this first section of Exodus, water is prominent: a symbol of life, of survival, of flow. And suddenly, there is none—only desert wilderness.

What is this wilderness that the Bible describes? It's not what we commonly think of: a dense, dark forest in which we lose our way. The Bible's wilderness is a bleak and forbidding landscape—a dry, barren terrain crisscrossed by steep, craggy ridges that are impossible to traverse. It's a hard land of rock and sand where nothing can take root and grow. Nothing can survive.

The wilderness has never been tamed or cultivated, and it never will be. Unlike Egypt, there are no pyramids or buildings, no farms or fields, no hamlets or cities. The land there has never been divided into parcels and assigned names. In the wilderness, we cannot say, "This land belongs to me and that to you. In this field I grow wheat, and over that hill stand my cousin's fruit trees. On this piece of ground I lay with my wife; on that, I buried my father." The wilderness defies all ego-based categorizations. It's a place unknown to us—a true *terra incognita*.

Symbolically, the wilderness is a mental space untouched by the ego-mind. It has no history, no memories. Whatever happened to us before has no relevance here. The past has been washed away; we're free and clean of it. But that doesn't necessarily feel good.

In the past, under ego's rule, we had beliefs we cherished, roles to play out, and, most of all, a robust self-concept. We knew who we were and where we fit, even if we didn't always like it. In the wilderness, we have none of that. The props of our identity have all been uprooted. Our self-concept is wiped clean, along with the past.

Without the ego to impose structure and definition on our lives, we feel rudderless and adrift. We look out at the world and come to a startling and extremely unsettling realization: the things that seemed to bring us joy while identified with the ego now mean nothing. Romance, fame, sex, wealth, power, longevity, exotic travel, even transcendent spiritual experiences, these hold no allure. Stripped of the ego's investment, they become transparent, and their true nature shows through. They are empty. It's as if someone pulled back the curtain on our world to reveal that it was all just an elaborate stage set—clever and compelling—but unreal. It's a facsimile, an illusion, and we can't live off illusion. Not anymore.

This is a deeply disturbing insight. For some, it's terrifying. Fortunately, the wilderness represents a late stage of the spiritual journey. For were we to encounter it any sooner—without first having experienced God's miracles—we would almost certainly have turned back in despair.

How do we survive the wilderness? How do we come to grips with this emptiness and somehow give it meaning when, by its very nature, *it has no meaning?* The ego-based roles and beliefs learned over a lifetime are useless here. And, unlike the parting of the Red Sea, there is no easy way through.

Purification and Discernment

The stark, forbidding wilderness poses a challenge wholly unlike that of Egypt and slavery. It's not about escaping the clutches of ego; that's already been accomplished. Rather, it's about breaking free from the *habits* of ego: the tendency to fall back into its familiar routines, to pick up and dust off its worldview and try it on for size once more, just as the Hebrews do when they long for Egypt.

The ego may no longer rule over us, but we fall back into its mind-set far too easily. It's a bit like trading in your manual-transmission car for an automatic. Although it's no longer necessary, your foot can't help reaching for that imaginary clutch. Or like moving from a dangerous neighborhood to a safer one and overcoming the habit of always locking your car doors. How do we unlearn such deeply ingrained practices and discover that they're no longer helpful?

We've been ego-addicts for as long as we can remember. We've run its software—its operating system of dos and don'ts—with unquestioning fidelity. But now we've switched over to a new operating system of Spirit and miracles, and it's not so easy to adapt to an entirely new platform, one we don't fully understand. It's natural to revert to the old system with which we're familiar. How do we make the switch and make it stick? Can we really rely on Spirit to provide for us *in every circumstance?* Can we put our entire faith in miracles? This seems like a lot to ask.

This is the main concern of the voice of the Hebrews. They want to know where their food and water are coming from. They're focused on raw survival needs—the very ones that gave rise to the formation of the ego in the first place. Until these are addressed, they're not interested in God or in learning to live as His people.

Survival fears revive the habits of ego. They pose the greatest danger to our journey during this wilderness phase. Yet they also offer a great opportunity: to clearly see these old ego habits and root them out, like Zen master Adyashanti and the training routine that he kept falling back into until it literally made him sick—twice. Hence, the true purpose of the wilderness stage is to purify our minds. They must be purged of every last vestige of ego before we're fit to enter the Promised Land.

We accomplish this through *discernment.* Discernment is the capacity to distinguish what has value from what does not. All that came from ego—everything we relied upon in the past, our most cherished possessions and roles, our assumptions and dreams, our very concept of self—has no value. It brings us nothing real. Only what comes from Spirit has value: miracles, trust, patience, and peace of mind.

How do we tell the difference? How do we cultivate this capacity for discernment? We can apply the test of peace. Does the thought or action we're contemplating bring us to a state of greater peacefulness or not?

We experience this peacefulness in the body as a letting go, a release of tension that occurs without trying to make it happen. We can become aware of it in our minds as well. The turbulent, agitated swirl of thoughts churned up by fear settles into serene silence, like the still surface of a pond undisturbed by wind or debris. If we sense anything other than peace—if our thoughts remain agitated, if we feel angry, hurt, fearful, or self-righteous—then we're chasing after the valueless. We will remain lost, wandering the wilderness, unable to find the Promised Land. We must put every situation—every thought, if possible—to the test of peace. In this way, we build discernment.

✺

Let's review the spiritual journey to this point. We suffered, enslaved under Pharaoh-ego. We cried out for help and God brought the Moses-mind to us. Plagues freed us from the ego's bondage, and a miracle transported us across the Red Sea to a new sense of self. And now we find ourselves in the wilderness. Not exactly what we expected. We thought we wanted freedom—release from bondage. Now we realize we don't know what freedom *is,* much less what it's for. We don't understand it. We can't. The habits of Egypt and ego run too deep.

Freedom is not simply the absence of slavery. It's not about what we're escaping *from,* but what we're moving toward. In the wilderness, where all ego goals are revealed as wasteland, freedom forces us to ask: What do we want? What do we *really* want? What will feed us—not just our bodies, but our souls? What gives us peace? What's our purpose now?

If we think we already know what will make us happy and how to go about getting it, then where does God fit in? Is He merely the agent who makes our prayers come true, like some all-powerful genie in a bottle? Are we asking *Him* to serve *our* will? Or can we recognize that His goals for us, whatever they may turn out to be, *are exactly* what we want? Our greatest happiness lies in following His will. After all, He is leading us to the Promised Land. Why ever would He let us perish along the way?

Therefore, as difficult and challenging as it may be, you must learn to let go of your fears of not having enough. Let go of your schemes and strategies. Stop fretting over the bills and the checkbook balance. Any attempt to meet your needs by your own devices risks reinstating the ego. Why? Because it reinforces the notion that you're separate from God. You *will* survive and even prosper *if you get out of your own way.* Spirit can take care of you. And as we'll see in the next chapter, only Spirit can do so here in the desert wilderness.

God, and Nothing But God

If our survival is guaranteed by God and there is nothing to fear, then we must return to the question: What is it we want? What do we seek? Surely, we must have some purpose in the world beyond mere survival.

The question has only one possible answer: we want God. Wasn't worshipping God in freedom the goal of leaving Egypt in the first place? To know Him directly and personally—that's what we now seek.

But the wilderness teaches us that that's not enough. We must want God, yes. But if we truly want Him, we must want *nothing else.* Why? Because *there is* nothing else! Without God, it's all a desert—empty, worthless, and uninhabitable.

Herein lies the deepest lesson of the wilderness. This bleak landscape is an honest portrayal of our existence when it's scrubbed clean of the ego's illusions, *but not yet aligned with Spirit.* It's a true no-man's-land, a limbo from which we cannot retreat— not into the past, not into fantasy—but from which we may not move forward either, not until we're able to discern what's valuable from what's valueless.

God and His miracles have value. Everything else has none. We cannot cherish *anything* apart from God and still retain the capacity for discernment. The tiniest fantasy of Egypt will blind us to Truth. For Truth is true, and nothing else is true. Bring any piece of falsity into it, and you lose it; it's no longer truth.

Gina cannot make a true commitment to another man if she nurses the faintest hope of a reunion with Pete. We cannot be a little bit ill and claim we're still healthy. The most miniscule particle of pollution renders pure water impure.

The Hebrews cannot simultaneously long for Egypt and enter the Promised Land. Either they want God and only God, or they want nothing. And if they choose nothing in the seductive form of a fantasy, then that's what they'll get: nothing. And as a result, they'll wander lost in this wilderness for as long as it takes to learn the lesson of discernment. Nothingness in the guise of something remains nothing. The choice is literally between the All or nothing.

The experience of the wilderness is shattering but necessary—an unavoidable phase of the spiritual journey. And discernment is the compass that guides us safely through it. Whatever brings us closer to God has value. Everything else has none and isn't worth our slightest attention.

☙ ☙

{ **Chapter 13** }

MANNA AND WATER: OUR DAILY MIRACLES

The process of purification takes place in the wilderness. This is an essential step on the road to the Promised Land, but one perhaps even more difficult than escaping from slavery. In the wilderness, we must learn that miracles are not only possible, but essential. They are never to be taken for granted, of course, but they are never to be doubted either.

The Hebrews must shift from viewing miracles as a way out of slavery to understanding them as the very basis of life itself. The stark, forbidding desert environment provides the perfect classroom in which to learn this lesson. Its miracles are immediate and obvious, because the Hebrews' needs are immediate and obvious: food, water, and survival.

The Lessons of Marah and Elim

After the Hebrews cross the Red Sea, they travel for three days without finding water.

And when they came to Marah, they could not drink the waters of Marah, for they were bitter; therefore it was named Marah. So the people grumbled at Moses, saying, "What shall we drink?" Then he cried out to the Lord, and the Lord showed him a tree; and he threw it into the waters, and the waters became sweet. There . . . He tested them. And He said, "If you will give earnest heed to the voice of the Lord your God, and do what is right in His sight, and give ear to His commandments, and keep all His statutes, I will put none of the diseases on you which I have put on the Egyptians; for I, the Lord, am your healer."

Then they came to Elim where there were twelve springs of water and seventy date palms, and they camped there beside the waters (Exod. 15:23–27).

The meaning of this passage is not subtle. God can turn even bitter waters sweet. He can slake our thirst in the most arid wilderness, where our own efforts at finding water have failed. As long as the Hebrews trust and follow Him, He will lead them to places like Elim, an oasis where fresh water is plentiful and fruit trees abound.

In this one passage, we have a microcosm of the whole spiritual journey. Elim, with its 12 springs (one for each of Israel's 12 tribes), offers a foretaste of the Promised Land itself, a preview of what lies ahead, so long as the Hebrews can pass God's test.

Manna and Water

Unfortunately, the Hebrews do not learn the lessons of Marah and Elim. They continue to complain about a lack of food. They lament ever having left Egypt with its "pots of meat" and unlimited supplies of bread (Exod. 16:3), even though, as we've seen, this is sheer fantasy.

To quell their survival fears and dispel their fantasies, they need something tangible, something they can turn to and rely on day after day. And God gives it to them, in the form of manna.

And the Lord spoke to Moses, saying, "I have heard the grumblings of the sons of Israel; speak to them, saying, 'At twilight you shall eat meat, and in the morning you shall be filled with bread; and you shall know that I am the Lord your God.'"

So it came about at evening that the quails came up and covered the camp, and in the morning there was a layer of dew around the camp. When the layer of dew evaporated, behold, on the surface of the wilderness there was a fine flake-like thing, fine as the frost on the ground. When the sons of Israel saw it, they said to one another, "What is it?" For they did not know what it was. And Moses said to them, "It is the bread which the Lord has given you to eat" (Exod. 16:11–15).

The Hebrews long for "pots of meat." They dream of all the bread they can eat. God brings them both, in the form of quail and manna: "bread from heaven" (Exod. 16:4).

After the Hebrews gather the manna and quail, they make camp at Rephidim, where "there was no water for the people to drink" (Exod. 17:1).

Therefore the people quarreled with Moses and said, "Give us water that we may drink." And Moses said to them, "Why do you quarrel with me? Why do you test the Lord?" But the people thirsted there for water; and they grumbled against Moses and said, "Why, now, have you brought us up from Egypt, to kill us and our children and our livestock with thirst?" So Moses cried out to the Lord, saying, "What shall I do to this people? A little more and they will stone me." Then the Lord said to Moses, ". . . . take in your hand your staff with which you struck the Nile, and go. Behold, I will stand before you there on the rock at Horeb; and you shall strike the rock, and water will come out of it, that the people may drink." And Moses did so in the sight of the elders of Israel (Exod. 17:2–6).

The Hebrews demand water. Again, they accuse Moses of bringing them out of Egypt only to kill them. Despite the miracles of Marah and Elim, despite quail and manna, they still do not trust God. Instead of trying to live up to His testing of them (Ex. 15:25), they flip it around and test Him! No wonder Moses grows so frustrated.

But God is understanding. He instructs Moses to use his staff (the same staff that transformed the life-giving waters of the Nile into blood) to bring forth water from a rock. Although the Bible does not say so directly, Jewish liturgy interprets this passage, along with its doublet in Numbers 20, to infer that the Hebrews carried this rock with them for the entire time they wandered the wilderness. It was known as the Well of Miriam[1] (Moses and Aaron's sister) and it served as their source of water for 40 years.

Up to this point in the story, water has been a symbol for life. In the wilderness, however, it is no mere symbol. Without it, the Hebrews will die. God shows them that, through miracles, water is readily available, and from the most impossible of places: a rock.

Rocks are dense, lifeless, and unmoving. They're the opposite of water in every way—the antithesis of the principle of flow. By causing water to flow from a rock, God demonstrates that He can bring forth the essence of life from that which has never known life.

The twin miracles of manna and water from a rock show that God can meet our needs anywhere we happen to be. We don't need to live by a well or river, because we carry with us a life-giving supply, a bottomless reserve, in the rock that is the Well of Miriam. Never again need we suffer thirst. And wherever we happen to lay our heads at night, we will awaken in the morning to manna, which will feed us. The world will rise up to meet our survival needs, day after day, wherever we find ourselves. Never again must we suffer hunger.

The rock that is the Well of Miriam demonstrates that God accompanies us everywhere we go. We carry Him with us on the journey. Manna shows that wherever we go, to whatever distant lands the journey may lead us, God is already there, waiting to feed us. These are the dual aspects of His caring.

God promised Moses at the burning bush, "I will be with you." Indeed He is, within and without. His Presence will sustain us, guaranteeing our survival through these twin miracles.

A Different Order of Miracle

In the parable of Exodus, manna and receiving water from a rock represent a different kind of miracle. Or, rather, they're a different order of miracle that teaches a different kind of lesson. Their purpose is neither to free the mind from bondage nor help us transition to a new sense of self. They're about survival and sustenance, but equally important, they teach discernment. What truly feeds us, and what does not? What has value, and what does not? What's real, and what's mere fantasy? Without discernment, we cannot know.

❦

When we were slaves to Pharaoh-ego, miracles brought relief from suffering. They did not change us, however. Our fundamental beliefs, roles, and self-concept remained intact. We incorporated the possibility of miracles into our understanding of the world without having to really change that understanding. In the wilderness, this is not enough. When miracles occur every day—when they become the source of our food and water, of our very survival—then our understanding of the world and our place in it requires radical revision.

In this impossible wilderness, we don't know how to survive. Without the ego and its "guidance," we feel lost. Manna and water from rock show us how to make it in this environment. They're God's demonstration that we'll get by just fine without Pharaoh-ego. We *will* survive—through miracles and *only* through miracles. Nothing else will do, because nothing else is real. Nothing else has the ability to sustain us. That is the new purpose of miracles here in the wilderness.

As teaching tools, these twin miracles turn our old ego-based notions about the world upside down. Miracles are no longer the exception to the ego's rule. They're not something wondrous to be called upon only in times of crisis. With ego vanquished, they're the new norm: the warp and woof of daily life. There's nothing special about them. Recall the words of *A Course in Miracles:* "Miracles are natural. When they do *not* occur [my italics] something has gone wrong."[2] Manna—miracles—have become our true source of sustenance, the nourishment of the soul: our daily bread, quite literally. In the words of the Cesár Franck hymn, "Panis Angelicus," *Panis angelicus fit panis hominum*—the bread of angels is become the bread of man.

Manna—Reliable, Everyday Miracles

The parting of the Red Sea is a onetime miracle. Once we cross over and make the transition to a new sense of self, we're free. We never have to do it again. Yes, we can regress; we can forget for a time. But our essential self remains transformed, and it will reassert itself. By contrast, manna is not a onetime phenomenon. It's a miracle we turn to again and again, day in and day out. Each new dawn brings with it new manna. It's as reliable as the rising of the sun.

Because of this constancy, manna doesn't fit into our previous understanding of miracles as synchronistic occurrences: perfectly timed events that leapfrog the normal chain of cause and effect. Manna is *not* a matter of coincidence or good timing (at least not in the way the ego understands time). It's there every morning, and the intention that calls it into being is one we experience on a regular basis: hunger. Manna offers no surprises. It's routine and predictable. In fact, its very predictability is what makes it so important to this phase of the journey.

In Egypt there was predictability, too—that of slavery. We were fed, predictably, in order that we might labor hard, predictably. Days passed, with no hope of change. We needed miracles (in the form of plagues) to break us free from this never-ending stretch of bondage.

In the wilderness, a very different task confronts us. The goal is not to escape ego—we've already accomplished that—but rather to establish trust in God. The two are not the same. The reassuring certainty of manna helps us build this trust.

Although ego no longer dominates, we've seen how easily we fall back into its ways, like the Hebrews and their fantasies of Egypt. We need a *daily* reminder of God's caring, a daily dose of miracles to antidote our habitual fear. In this sense, the constancy of manna is somewhat akin to a methadone maintenance program for newly recovering ego-addicts! It's God's way of weaning our minds from their old dependency on the ego.

Gathering Manna

Thus far in Exodus, God's miracles required little or no effort on the part of the Hebrews. Moses intervened for them. He raised his staff, and plagues rained down on Egypt. He raised his hand over the Red Sea, and it parted. Even during the Passover ritual, the Hebrews' role was essentially passive. Eating the sacrificial lamb and painting its blood on their doorposts and lintels was a significant step, but it played no part in bringing about the miracle of the tenth plague. In truth, the Hebrews have benefited from miracles without ever really having to participate.

In this respect, they behave a bit like infants who cry out but cannot act for themselves. It's up to the parents to meet their survival needs. As children grow older, however, more is expected of them. This holds true for the Hebrews as well.

Manna *does* require their active participation. They must go out each morning and gather it. God provides, but the people must claim what He gives them. Nor does Moses have to raise his staff each morning to invoke the miracle anew. He only has to turn to God once, and manna continues to appear every morning for the next 40 years.

It may seem like a small thing, going out every morning to gather manna, but for the Hebrews it's a big step. Through manna, God engages them in a direct transaction for the first time, without Moses as intermediary. They are growing spiritually. No more can they sit back and remain passive like infants. They must go out and collect their own manna to learn that it's always there for them, day after day, and that it's always sufficient to satisfy their hunger. By actively participating in this miracle, they build trust in God.

Reversing the Curse of Adam

In the book of Genesis, Adam and Eve defy God's command not to eat from the forbidden tree, and He casts them out of Eden. Before He does, He says this to Adam.

> Cursed be the ground because of you;
> By toil shall you eat of it
> All the days of your life:
> Thorns and thistles shall it sprout for you.
> But your food shall be the grasses of the field;
> By the sweat of your brow
> Shall you get bread to eat.
> (Jewish Study Bible, Gen. 3:17–19)

Because of his defiance, Adam and his descendents are condemned to toil for their food. Sustenance will not come easy to them, as it did in the Garden of Eden, but "by the sweat of your brow." And yet now, in the midst of the wilderness, God tells Moses:

> Behold, I will rain bread from heaven for you; and the people shall go out and gather a day's portion every day,

that I may test them, whether or not they will walk in My instruction (Exod. 16:4).

Gathering manna will require some activity on the part of the Hebrews, but it will hardly bring sweat to their brow. Nor does manna come from the ground. It falls like rain from heaven, appearing with the morning dew, which is, after all, a form of water, the element of life. The water found in dew, however, doesn't flow like the Nile; it condenses out of the air itself, to blanket the ground everywhere. Therefore, God's miracle settles upon everything; it touches down in all places at once, without exception, bringing life-giving nurturance.

In providing the Hebrews with manna, God has revoked His curse upon Adam (if only temporarily to test the Hebrews). Having crossed the Red Sea and transitioned to freedom, they are spared the need to plant and harvest. Indeed, here in the wilderness nothing will grow anyway, no matter how hard they toil. Besides, the Hebrews have known toil aplenty. It was the hallmark of their slavery in Egypt. Why would God want His people to continue to labor so hard when He's trying to break them of the habits of Egypt and slavery? Manna—all the bread they can eat—is theirs for the taking. They have only to go out and gather it.

❧

The Hebrews have undergone a profound transformation, from slaves under Pharaoh to a free people under God. Lifting the curse of Adam is proof of this transformation. It suggests that an Eden-like closeness to God is now once again possible. The Promised Land draws near.

When we reach this stage of the journey, we're no longer subject to the same laws. We don't need to toil for our daily bread. Working hard to earn money as a precondition for survival is no longer justified. Our sustenance isn't dependent on the sweat of our brow, the type of work we do, or the number of hours we spend at it. It comes directly from God in the form of miracles—manna—which is readily available to us every day if only we make the effort to claim it.

And how do we do this? By aligning our intention for the day with God. By taking time each morning and asking to receive whatever Spirit intends for us that day—trusting that it will nurture us, body and soul—and asking no more, because we need nothing more. We use our powers of discernment to distinguish the fruits of Spirit, which have value and will nourish us, from the lifeless wilderness, which will not. In this way, we gather our manna.

Manna Is Enough

Might it not have worked better if God had simply given the Hebrews a huge supply of bread and water to carry with them when they left Egypt? Then they would have known for certain that they had enough. They could see it, touch it, and feel secure. They could stop fretting about tomorrow.

And yet, no matter how much we seem to have—whether bread, money, diamonds, or whatever else we deem valuable—no matter how much we manage to stockpile, we still fret that it won't be enough. I've worked with wealthy men and women who lived in ongoing dread of losing their fortunes. All their millions could not keep at bay the fear of growing old and dying in poverty.

The truth is, to the ego, there can never be enough. No matter how much we have, it feels insufficient. We accumulate more and more, in hopes of insulating ourselves from future calamity. But our efforts are doomed, because to the ego-mind, the probability of future disaster will always trump present safety. Nothing can make the ego feel secure.

The idea of scarcity, of going without, is central to the ego's thought system. Why? Because the ego is itself the symbol of lack. By its nature, the ego is "less than." It is not God and can never be. It has no connection to God and no claim on His bounty. It senses its impermanence, its limited range of vision, its inherent uncertainty. It tries to compensate by building bulwarks, real and imagined, against the inevitability of loss and death. But as we saw with the tenth plague, its efforts must end in death. The ultimate fate of the ego is to die.

Manna is God's antidote to the ego's furious need to accumulate and stockpile against the future. When manna first appears, Moses tells the Hebrews, "Gather of it every man as much as he should eat . . ." (Exod. 16:16).

> The sons of Israel did so, and some gathered much and some little. . . . [H]e who had gathered much had no excess, and he who had gathered little had no lack; every man gathered as much as he should eat. And Moses said to them, "Let no man leave any of it until morning." But they did not listen to Moses, and some left part of it until morning, and it bred worms and became foul; and Moses was angry with them. They gathered it morning by morning, every man as much as he should eat . . . (Exod. 16:17–21).

Manna offers the Hebrews perfect sufficiency. They cannot gather more than they can consume in a single day, nor can they gather less. They cannot save it for the next day because it will go bad. But why would they want to save it, when the next morning brings with it more manna, and in just the right proportion for that day's needs? Manna is always exactly enough.

Buddhist monks understand the concept of manna. Each morning they go out into the community to beg for their food. They may only accept as much as they can eat in that single day; they're not permitted to save it. They may not accumulate a surplus, in case the begging goes poorly the next day. Should they grow hungry later in the day, they can't go back out with their bowls and ask for more. Morning (from dawn to noon) is the time designated for gathering food.[3] In this way, the monks gather their manna each morning, and survive only on what's given to them. In the process, they learn to trust their relationship to the Buddha—that is, to Spirit.

189

Manna is antithetical to the ego's belief system. How is it possible that each day could bring with it exactly what's needed, and not a crumb or a penny less or more? The idea of being limited only to what we need in a single day feels frightening. It feels naïve and foolish, deeply wrong and unfair, as if God is intentionally depriving us. No wonder we rebel against it.

The fact that we can only gather what we will use in any 24-hour period, however, is not about God somehow rationing us, distrusting us to handle more, or asking us to make a sacrifice and go without. Rather, it's a simple statement about His nature.

God exists in an eternal present. Notions of past and future are meaningless to Him. In the Mind of God, it's all now—always now. Therefore, He can only provide according to the needs of the present moment—symbolically, the span of a single day—because *that's all there is.*[4] And so, that's all that's needed. Ever. Anything more would be wasted and pointless. But in truth, there can be nothing more; nothing exists beyond the present moment. Spirit touches us only in the now.

Therefore, by gathering up manna every day—by trusting that the miracle will be there for us (reliability) and that it will always be enough (sufficiency)—we break free from the habits of ego and its death grip on the future and enter into God's eternal present. Our bodies may still inhabit a world of finite time and limitation, but not our minds. They are free: to partake in miracles and join with Spirit in the Promised Land.

Manna—"What Is It?"

When this strange substance first appears on the ground with the morning dew, the Hebrews are baffled. "What is it?" they ask Moses. They've never before seen its like. Here is a food different from anything in Egypt—or anywhere else for that matter. They "named it manna, and it was like coriander seed, white; and its taste was like wafers with honey" (Exod. 16:31).

Scholars believe that manna was "the sweet, edible honeydew (still called 'manna' in Arabic)," excreted by certain insects of the Sinai peninsula after they ingest the sap of tamarisk trees.[5] However, it's difficult to believe that this excretion, usually found only during the summer months, could have fed the entire Hebrew populace for 40 years. Once again, manna is best understood symbolically in the context of the parable of Exodus.

The Jewish sages of the Midrash (a continually evolving compendium of biblical exegesis from prominent rabbis over the past 2,000 years) wrote that manna could taste like whatever we wanted it to be. "Manna could assume any flavor that a person wished. If, when eating manna, someone thought, 'I wish I would be able to eat roasted chicken' it immediately tasted like roasted chicken."[6] Just as the quantity of manna gathered each day matches perfectly the needs of the gatherer, so too does its taste conform to the preferences of the person eating it. Clearly, this is no earthly substance.

The etymology of the word *manna* provides a clue to its true nature. In the Hebrew language, it translates as "what is it?" The Hebrews playfully named this bread from heaven to reflect their initial uncertainty about it.[7] Manna is a mystery. It is literally "what is it?"

This linguistic ambiguity takes on a profound significance, however, when we apply it to our understanding of miracles. Manna is the generic form of the miracle. It is whatever we need it to be—and not just a foodstuff. The word itself makes clear that *we don't know what it is* that will nurture and sustain us on any given day. We don't have that ability. Only Spirit knows.

Moses himself makes this point in his address to the Hebrews in Deuteronomy:

> And He [God] humbled you and let you be hungry, and fed you with manna which you did not know, nor did your fathers know, that He might make you understand that man does not live by bread alone, but man lives by everything that proceeds out of the mouth of the Lord (Deut 8:3).

Indeed, we do not live by bread alone. We're sustained by everything that comes to us from Spirit. Herein lies the true meaning of manna. It will take on whatever form we need it to be, understanding that we ourselves are incapable of knowing what that form should look like. Nor do we need to know. We trust that Spirit will provide exactly what's necessary, in exactly the quantity and form best suited to us (to our tastes) for the present moment.

❦

Years before Marie got her job in the bookstore, she worked full-time to put herself through college. The combination of work, classes, and a two-hour commute made for some very long days, and she was often so exhausted on the drive home that she risked falling asleep. One night she stopped at a Starbucks, knowing that without a good shot of caffeine, she wouldn't make it. But when she entered the store, she realized she had no money and no credit card. Desperate, she began searching the parking lot for loose change. She looked everywhere, but found none. That's when she realized that all her frenzied searching had jolted her brain into wakefulness, and she no longer needed the coffee. Her original intention had been fulfilled, just not in the way she'd expected.

We don't know our real needs, but we trust that God does, and that He can and will meet them perfectly. If we symbolically gather our manna and align with Spirit each day (Thy Will be done, not mine), then what comes to us in any given day—the events we experience, the people we meet—will turn out to be perfect for us. Each one will offer a miracle, whether we're consciously aware of it or not.

A Course in Miracles explains it in this way. God "has Thoughts which answer every need. . . . For Love must give, and what is given in His Name takes on the form most useful in a world of form."[8] God is Love. He gives of His Love because it is His nature, the nature of Love, to give Itself. But in this world of form, His Love assumes the shape of whatever we need most *as God deems it.* Such is the essence of miracles. Such is manna.

In summary, manna is God's Love, symbolized in the form of an edible substance that can feed us and see us through the rigors of the wilderness. We must gather it on a daily basis in order to discover that it's perfectly suited to meet our every need. It truly is enough.

Manna and Comparison

There is one final lesson to learn from manna. Given that it comes from God, and that it's perfectly matched to our particular "tastes" and needs, then it follows that we cannot justifiably compare our lots with anyone else's. We receive the manna we need for this day; others receive what they need.

Each of us has a unique purpose in life. Our paths will ultimately all lead to the Promised Land, but they'll traverse some very different terrain in the process. Therefore, we'll have different needs, and the manna we gather will reflect this fact.

Someone called to a life of public service has different needs than a poet. A mother of teens goes through her day very differently than the mother of a newborn. We cannot know the path of another. We cannot know his or her true needs; we don't even know our own. Only Spirit has that knowledge. Therefore, only Spirit is in a position to meet those needs. And so each person's manna will "taste" uniquely delicious to them—perfectly tailored to their purpose and their path.

Even within the span of our own lifetime, our needs change. What suited us ten years ago (or ten days ago) may not work for us today. Our jobs, our relationships, the needs of our physical body, and our understanding of God—all can and do undergo profound shifts. The miracles that helped us escape from bondage in Egypt will not see us through the wilderness. Manna is fresh and unique *each day*. Therefore, its taste can and will change according to our changing circumstances.

Nobody's manna tastes better than our own on the day we gather it. Ours is perfect for us; theirs is perfect for them. When we compare ourselves to others, we're second-guessing Spirit, and no good can come of that.

༺ༀ༻

We most commonly succumb to comparison in the arenas of money, talent, health, and physical appearance. We read about a hedge-fund billionaire and wonder, *What's he got that I don't?* or *What makes her so special?* We envy Hollywood stars and professional athletes for their talent, fame, and astronomical incomes. But we don't know a thing about their real stories. We don't see them through the eyes of Spirit, and so we cannot know how their beauty or athletic prowess factor into their spiritual journeys— whether positively or negatively, as plagues or miracles.

A particularly nasty form of comparison involves spiritual progress. *Who among us,* we wonder, *is the most advanced spiritually? Who's achieved enlightenment? Is the woman singing passionately in the next pew more godly than I am? Or does she just crave attention? Is the bishop living in a state of grace? Is the guru truly enlightened, or faking it?* We don't know. We can't. Nor do we need to know. If we turn the spiritual journey into a game with winners, losers, and a finish line, then we've reinstated the ego-mind, and we indeed lose.

There's also a tendency to deprecate ourselves relative to those whom society has judged to be especially spiritual. We idolize Mother Teresa; Dr. Martin Luther King, Jr.; the Dalai Lama; or Mahatma Gandhi and judge ourselves inferior by comparison. What have we done for humanity lately?

And yet, we cannot all be Mother Teresa, nor does Spirit ask that of us. If we don't know our own worthiness, much less our purpose, how can we possibly judge ourselves, or others who are believed to be more spiritual? Their good deeds may plaster over an aching void. And our smallest act of kindness, seemingly so inadvertent, may play a huge role in changing someone else's life in ways we could never have imagined, and perhaps never will know. Isn't that the whole point of the miracle—that it affects us collectively while assuming the form best suited to us as individuals?

I once worked with a woman who survived physical and sexual torture inflicted by a number of different perpetrators throughout her childhood. Despite her extensive psychological scars, she bravely persevered with treatment, and in time was able to heal. The vivid flashes of cruelty that once flooded in to overwhelm her mind eventually became normal memories with no more power to hurt. One by one, she forgave her abusers, and this was truly a miracle. I would suggest that through her inner work, this woman has done as much to promote peace on Earth as Mother Teresa or the Dalai Lama, and it doesn't matter that no one will ever know her name.

𒀭

Just as we cannot compare positive attributes, we cannot compare suffering. It is singularly unhelpful—in fact, it can be destructive—to look at those who have lost a limb or endured cancer; or had family taken from them by genocide, tsunami, or a drunk driver; and feel that somehow their suffering trivializes our own. And yet, I hear this refrain in my office all the time. "What right do I have to feel bad when so many have it worse?" It's fine to have empathy for the suffering of others. But if I compare my crippling migraine to someone else's brain tumor and belittle my own pain in the process, neither of us benefits.

Viktor Frankl, a psychiatrist who knew about suffering firsthand from the Nazi death camps, wrote that each human being's suffering is maximal. It takes up all of our psychological space, all our bandwidth: "Thus suffering completely fills the human soul and conscious mind, no matter whether the suffering is great or little. Therefore the 'size' of human suffering is absolutely relative."[9] We cannot compare degrees of suffering. Like manna, it is unique to each individual and his or her own journey.

Unfortunately, our brains seem hardwired for comparison. They seek it out. It's the basis for all decision making.[10] And in the arena of material goods, this works out fairly well. I can compare two apartments, two cars, two smartphones, or two hotels in order to decide which offers the most at the best price. But on the spiritual

journey, this practice is worse than useless. Behind every comparison lies inferiority, or its cleverly disguised twin, superiority. Behind every judgment lies insecurity and fear. Comparison shackles
us blindly to another's experience, when we cannot ever know the
path he or she walks. It is infinitely better to focus on our own path,
simply gathering up the manna that awaits us each day.

Manna teaches us to trust Spirit in all circumstances. God will
indeed be with us. He will provide food, water, and whatever else
we may require for the journey. He will not abandon us in the
wilderness, despite our fears and doubts. We will survive. We will
learn to discern what's valuable—the miracle, manna—from the
worthless emptiness that surrounds us. Through discernment, our
minds are purified of the habits of ego, leaving us ready to encounter God at Mount Sinai, and from there travel onward to the
Promised Land.

Unfortunately, the Hebrews of Exodus have not learned the
lessons of the wilderness. They gather manna, and it sustains
them physically, but they do not take in its deeper meaning. They
never truly digest it. They do not learn trust in God. Therefore,
when they arrive at Mount Sinai, they're unprepared.

𝕊𝕊 𝕊𝕊

Chapter 14

MOUNT SINAI AND THE LAW: KEEPING GOD AT A DISTANCE

Three months after leaving Egypt, Moses and the Hebrews arrive at the base of Mount Sinai. This is the same mountain[1] where Moses, pasturing his father-in-law's flocks, first encountered God when he turned aside to investigate the burning bush. It's the place to which God instructed him to lead the Hebrews (see Exod. 3:12).

Mount Sinai is not the Promised Land. It's the mountain of God. It represents an essential step on the journey, but it's not the endpoint—not a place to live and call home. But without this step—without encountering God and forging a direct relationship with Him, as Moses did—the Promised Land will lie forever beyond the Hebrews' reach.

A Kingdom of Priests

God tells Moses to prepare the people, for in three days time he will appear to them on the mountain. "I will come to you in a thick cloud, in order that the people may hear when I speak with you and so trust you ever after" (Jewish Study Bible, Exod. 19:9). God will speak to Moses, as He has in the past. But unlike the past, this time the Hebrews will hear His voice, too. They'll know by their own experience that Moses speaks for God, and they'll trust him always.

In the parable of Exodus, once we realize through our own experience that the Moses-mind receives its guidance directly from Spirit—that it speaks for God—we will trust it forever after. Once we clearly understand the source of our guidance, we'll have no reason to doubt it or look anywhere else for it. We'll finally be willing to embrace the Moses-mind and understand that it is our true identity.

God tells Moses that if the Hebrews "obey My voice and keep My covenant, then . . . you [the Hebrews] shall be to Me a kingdom of priests and a holy nation" (Exod. 19:5–6). These are hugely important words, "a kingdom of priests." But what do they mean?

Priests, unlike laypeople, are empowered to appeal directly to God without an intermediary. They have a direct line to the deity. Because of this, priests are considered special, holier than the average person. And now God offers this same special status to *all* the Hebrews. They can all be like Moses. They can have their own direct and immediate relationship with God.

Standing at a Distance

The appointed day arrives, and Moses gathers his people at the base of Mount Sinai, where God descends to meet them.

> [T]here were thunder and lightning flashes and a thick cloud upon the mountain and a very loud trumpet sound, so that all the people who were in the camp trembled (Exod. 19:16).

> Now Mount Sinai was all in smoke because the Lord descended upon it in fire; and its smoke ascended like the smoke of a furnace, and the whole mountain quaked violently (Exod. 19:18).

Amid this clamor, God speaks the Ten Commandments aloud for all to hear. And how do the Hebrews react? Do they celebrate as they did after crossing the Red Sea? Are they overcome with gratitude? Do they hesitate and hold back, like Moses at the burning bush, asking for further proof? None of the above. In fact, the Hebrews have no reaction to the Ten Commandments. They're too frightened to even listen.

> And all the people perceived the thunder and the lightning flashes and the sound of the trumpet and the mountain smoking; and when the people saw it, they trembled and stood at a distance. Then they said to Moses, "Speak to us yourself and we will listen; but let not God speak to us, or we will die. . . ." So the people stood at a distance, while Moses approached the thick cloud where God was (Exod. 20:18–21).

The Hebrews meet God on the same mountain Moses did, but their perception of Him is strikingly different. Moses saw a bush ablaze with fire but not consumed—a sight that caused him to turn aside from his comfortable domestic routine and return immediately to Egypt to fulfill God's command and free his people. When God called out his name, he made the straightforward reply, "I am here," and in turn God promised, "I will be with you."

The Hebrews, by contrast, behold a terrifying display of smoke and fire, thunder and lightning. They tremble with a fear so overpowering that it stops their ears from hearing anything God says. They stand "at a distance" and ask Moses to speak to them instead.

Why does God appear so much more frightening to the Hebrews than to Moses? Has He changed? Of course not. God is God; He does not change. Why then is the Hebrews' perception of Him so different? Because Moses was ready. He was ripe. The Hebrews are not.

This seems puzzling at first. After all, Moses stumbled upon the burning bush by chance. He wasn't searching for God or for freedom. He was tending his father-in-law's flocks, comfortable in his life of exile. The Hebrews, by contrast, have experienced a series of incredible miracles. How could they *not* be ready? And yet, when their hour comes, they cannot stand in God's Presence as Moses did and proclaim, "We are here." They stand "at a distance" and beg Moses to act as a buffer between them and God. They fail their audition with God, because of their fear.

Experiencing God

A few weeks before my 22nd birthday and the start of medical school, I encountered God. It was during the final day of a weeklong workshop devoted to raising consciousness. I had been seeking such an experience for some time, and yet when it came, I found myself, like the Hebrews, completely unprepared. My ego-mind dissolved in an instant, absorbed into a vast, ever-expanding, infinite field of love: an eternal explosion of the purest light that words will never be capable of expressing. "I" was an infinitesimal point of awareness in this boundless field of love energy—and yet I was simultaneously the All. It seemed to last forever, and yet when I came to on the ground, only seconds had passed. I had no doubt about whether my experience had been real or not. What I touched that day was reality itself. The world I returned to was unreal—a cheap facsimile—not even the palest reflection of God's ultimate reality.

For the next three days, I couldn't look at anyone without crying, because it was so clear that behind the illusion of a body, they were God. We were God—all of us—interconnected seamlessly in the purest love. Physical bodies could not constrain or limit it in any way. They looked so obviously transparent—a thin shell that could never hope to cloak the divine radiance burning through from within.

As transformative as my experience was, it was also shattering. I feared I was going insane. How could I function in a world where the distinction between myself and others didn't exist— where there was only this vast field of light and love, of which we were all a part? How could I continue on to medical school and immerse myself in the study of the body, when the body no longer had meaning for me? It didn't even exist.

My experience (along with that of many mystics) demonstrates that when we encounter God directly, our individual self—the ego-identified self—disappears, consumed in His infinite radiance. For the unprepared, this is terrifying, because we mistake the dissolution of the false ego-self with the act of dying.

I hadn't done the spiritual work necessary to prepare for such an experience. Similar to the Hebrews, my encounter with God left me in awe, but also fearful. On the one hand, I tried desperately through meditation and other spiritual practices to recapture it and merge once again with Him. On the other hand, every time I felt myself getting close, a wave of panic would rush over me, and I was certain that I was about to die. I was too identified with ego, so its loss naturally felt like death. I went back and forth this way for a good ten years, my spiritual journey detoured, before I was finally able to assimilate my encounter with God; or, more accurately, before I could allow the encounter to assimilate me: my ego-self and its worldview.

When we prematurely encounter God, we plunge into fear. In fact, I'd venture to say that the greater the distance between the day-to-day ego-self and God, the more terrifying such an experience will seem. His Being is simply too expansive for the human mind to comprehend. We cannot grasp it, master it, control it, or subjugate it in any way, as the ego-mind seeks to do. We can only *be* it. And this, to the ego, will always inspire terror.

In our fear, we insist on keeping the Moses-mind separate from us. We do not embrace it and become it, recognizing it as our true self. That would bring us too close to God. Instead, we use it as a buffer. Like the Hebrews, we prefer to stand at a distance and hold Him at bay. We approach Him selectively—in church or synagogue, through prayer or meditation—but then we put Him away again and get on with our lives. We do this to preserve a separate sense of self: an ego-based self. But the price we pay is never being able to meet God on His own terms, on His mountain, because He will always seem too fearful.

The mystical encounter with God changes us forever, as Moses can well attest to. But it's *not* the goal of the journey. We do need to know God, but His Presence is so overwhelming that it's incompatible with daily life. The bliss, the rapture, renders us insensate; we cannot function. This is not a state of mind to hold on to. Nor, once experienced, should we strive to recapture it, as I did. Mystical union with God is a vital way station on the journey, but it's not the final destination, not a place in which to dwell. It is not the Promised Land.

❦

The Hebrews' reaction at Mount Sinai proves that they're not yet ready for God. They signed up for the course, but haven't done the homework. They haven't shed the habits of ego. Pharaoh may be gone, but their minds still cling to Egypt. God gives them manna and water, but they don't take it in, not at the deepest level, where it would slake not just their physical hunger and thirst, but their fear. They prefer to fantasize about pots of meat and unlimited bread. The shadow of Pharaoh-ego still looms large over them; therefore, standing in God's Presence necessarily feels like impending death.

The Hebrews are not able to follow Moses's example and enter into a living relationship with God. They can only follow Moses the man, as a child trails along behind his or her parent. Instead of receiving God's guidance and miracles firsthand, they must settle for the next best thing: a set of rules by which to live. The law.

The Next Best Thing

When the Hebrews ask Moses to speak to them in place of God, they fail God's intention for them. They will not become "a kingdom of priests," not on this day. He gave them free will, and they made the choice to keep Him at a distance. He cannot compel them to enter into a relationship they find frightening.

But God, like any good parent, understands their fear. He sees that they're not ready for Him, so He's willing to continue working through Moses. But Moses is human. He can't carry on in this role forever. Clearly, that was never the plan. Moses the man will one day die. And then where will the Hebrews be?

Moses's whole purpose, and that of the Moses-mind, is to lead us out of bondage and into a direct, living relationship with God. Once we arrive at Mount Sinai, the designated meeting place, he has fulfilled his function. To continue to cling to Moses with the purpose of keeping God at a distance is regressive at best. At worst (as we'll see in the next chapter), it's tantamount to idolatry.

The Hebrews must be weaned from their overreliance on Moses. They resemble a child who's learned how to ride a bike with training wheels, but then refuses to give them up. What started as a helpful learning aid is now a hindrance. As long as they need Moses to intercede for them with God, they'll never learn to find Him on their own. They'll never be able to approach Him without fear. Therefore, they need some form of guidance that does not involve Moses or any other authority figure, something they can access on their own that won't frighten them, something that will endure long after Moses is gone.

To help the Hebrews with this problem, God gives them the law—not just the Ten Commandments, but all the laws that follow (613 in total). The law serves as a blueprint by which they can live their lives. Once handed down (first to Moses, then from him to the Hebrews), the law is available to all. Anyone can access it at any time without fear.

With the law in their possession, the Hebrews no longer need Moses to interpret God's Word for them. The law replaces him and relieves him of his function. It becomes the new intermediary between God and the Hebrews. It allows them to wean themselves from their dependency on all authority figures, whether Pharaoh or Moses, and gives them a way to shed the last vestiges of their slave identity.

But let's be clear. Laws are not the same as miracles, nor do they accomplish what miracles can. The Hebrews cannot eat or drink the law. It does not teach discernment; if anything, it precludes the need for true discernment. Why discern the valuable from the valueless when it's all spelled out for you—literally carved in stone? In this regard, the law functions like a crutch. It helps the spiritually immature Hebrews learn how to walk on their own, and yet, as they come to rely on it more and more, it keeps them from ever learning to run.

The law is an attempt to bring God to the people, instead of God's original goal of bringing the people to Him. The law does not make us "a kingdom of priests." It does not bring us into direct relationship with Spirit. It belongs to our world, where it helps us to live *as egos*. It will not take us to the Promised Land, where it's rendered useless. The law is a dim lantern for those who, fearful of the light, choose to continue to live in darkness rather than a shining portal that leads us out of darkness and into the light.

The Map Is Not the Territory

There's a further difficulty with using the law as our primary source of guidance. Whereas miracles are uniquely tailored to the circumstances of each individual in each present moment, the law is not. It's a one-size-fits-all solution for managing life.

When patients come to my office for psychotherapy, I take a detailed history. I try to learn as much as I can about them and their issues. I then offer the treatment plan that I think will be most helpful, taking into account their unique circumstances. I don't hand them a copy of Freud's collected works and tell them that the answer to their problem lies somewhere within. Nor do I assume that what's best for a 20-year-old single woman will work just as well for a 70-year-old retired widower. My treatment is tailored to the individual. How much more so the miracles of Spirit!

𓆩𓆪

The practice of tithing gives a good illustration of the difference between the workings of the law and the miracle. Biblical law requires that we give one-tenth of our earnings to the priesthood (or the church)[2], and this is indisputably a good thing. But if we're receiving guidance directly from Spirit, then who knows where, when, and how much we might be directed to give? And with what unseen benefit? The anonymous woman who sent a check for $20,000 to my friend Pat Hopkins and her co-author to help with their book, *The Feminine Face of God*, was not tithing; she was following guidance. Her gift didn't go through any church or faith community. Nonetheless, it helped make possible a book that touched many thousands of lives.

Think of direct guidance from Spirit as your own internal GPS. Wherever you are, whatever you're doing, however lost you feel, Spirit takes into consideration your exact position in the world—your exact circumstances—and guides you toward what will best serve your journey. The Hebrews refused God's GPS, so instead of direct, immediate, personalized guidance in the form of miracles, they got a map: the law.

Miracles take place in the eternal present. By contrast, the law is frozen in time. It prescribes a set of guidelines intended for the specific era when it was handed down. This is why, when we read the Hebrew Bible today, so much of it seems archaic and irrelevant. Its laws were crafted for the Hebrew tribes of 3,000 years ago. As a result, their relevance has waned with the passing centuries. Rules for the sacrifice of animals (as in Exod. 29:10–22) today seem barbaric. Similarly, rules that govern the disposition of daughters sold by their fathers into slavery (Exod. 21:7–11) strike us as offensive. And what parents today would put their child to death for cursing at them (Exod. 21:17)?

Some denominations of Judaism attempt to deal with this scriptural rigidity by making clear that the law, the Torah, is a living entity—a constantly evolving set of principles. It's not just the Bible as it was originally written, but the entire body of accumulated biblical wisdom and interpretation (midrash) passed down by each successive generation of rabbis and scholars. If the law is to serve as an accurate map, it needs constant updating to keep pace with the times.

Unfortunately, many religions regard the map as if it were the territory itself. They don't do upgrades; in fact, they actively forbid them, going so far as to brand them heresy. The written word—the map—becomes sacred in and of itself, an object to be revered rather than a method of attaining guidance. None dare to challenge it.

In his book *Who Wrote the Bible?*, Richard Elliott Friedman recounts how the Hebrew Bible was stitched together from the narratives of four different writers living in different time periods. The last of these, known as "P" for Priestly, wrote a version that greatly expanded the law (for example, he added the entire book of Leviticus), but eliminated all passages in which God speaks directly to humans. In P's rendition, Adam and Eve do not appear, nor does Jacob's vision of the ladder and his wrestling with the angel, nor Moses and the burning bush. The story of Joseph merits a mere two lines.[3] Imagine such a Bible!

In the self-serving view of the Priestly writer, God does not communicate directly with mortals—ever. To reach Him, one *must* go through the priesthood. This scribe was attempting to consolidate power in this small, elite group of which he was (unsurprisingly) a member. And the priesthood wasn't open to just anyone—only those born into the direct lineage of Aaron need apply.

Fortunately, P's version did not prevail to become "gospel." It was interwoven with the earlier versions so we still have ample evidence in the Bible for direct communication between God and humans. But the trend toward quashing the idea that such communication is possible still persists.

Around the year 90 of the Common Era, the rabbis decreed that the Hebrew Bible was complete. Nothing more could be added to the sacred canon.[4] It was done. Finished. It's as if God had fled the world, leaving behind only these precious words to guide us. The priests and rabbis essentially declared God silent, His book closed. He would speak directly to humans no more.

In Christianity, a similar lockdown took place, as described by Elaine Pagels in *The Gnostic Gospels*. The four canonic gospels of Matthew, Mark, Luke, and John were cherry-picked by the early church fathers from among the many differing accounts of the life of Jesus. The other versions were purged as heresies. "All others [gospels] are false and unreliable, unapostolic, and probably composed by heretics,"[5] or so claimed Irenaeus, an early church father and bishop of Lyon in the 2nd century C.E. Were it not for the lucky discovery of the so-called gnostic gospels in a cave at Nag Hammadi, Egypt, in 1945, we wouldn't have even known that alternate versions existed.

The possibility of direct connection with God obviously threatens the established priestly order. After all, if I can receive God's guidance myself, directly from the Source, then why do I need a priest? The orthodox priesthood reacts to this threat by labeling those who hear His voice or see His visions as heretics or lunatics. They're to be put to death or locked up. Occasionally, they're beatified as saints (after they're dead, of course)—great beings with extraordinary powers and a special connection to God, very different from you or me. Otherwise, the only way to approach God is through the official canon established by the priesthood. So much for God's desire to make us "a kingdom of priests."

In this way, both the Hebrew Bible and the New Testament have become codified bodies of scripture. Neither is open to question; neither can ever be amended or changed. The law—scripture—has replaced the journey. Obey the law and ascend to heaven. Violate it, and hell awaits. Don't trouble yourself about the Promised Land. The road there is closed off. In this way, scripture has become for many people an end in itself and therefore an obstacle to finding God, rather than an aid.

Despite the best attempts of organized religion, however, the map is *not* the territory, and it never will be. The law is necessarily an imperfect vehicle. However helpful it may be, it can never replace the guidance that comes from a direct relationship with God.

Of course, there *is* a way to use scripture in support of the spiritual journey. We must allow it to speak to us directly and personally. We must see in it, not a rigid body of law, but a way to quicken our connection to Spirit. When we read the Bible's words as inspiration rather than literal truth, it can become a wonderful tool for opening our hearts and finding our way back to the Moses-mind.

However, it's not the only way. God isn't choosy or particular. He wants to reach us and will try to do so in any way He can. Anything that opens the mind to Him, He will use. A night sky full of stars, a magnificent piece of music, a poem, a psychedelic experience—even heartfelt lovemaking—can be just as effective as scripture in reminding us who we really are.

Inscribed on Our Hearts

The Hebrews in their fear cannot welcome God on Mount Sinai. Spiritually, they are still children. The voice of the Hebrews remains consistently whiny and juvenile. And children need rules to follow, especially for those times when their parents aren't around. As they grow into maturity, they internalize the rules. They understand when exceptions are called for. They learn when to trust their own judgment and when to ask for help and guidance. But until such time, they will continue to need rules. So it is for the Hebrews and the law.

The words of the prophet Jeremiah anticipate a time when the Hebrews (along with the rest of us) will outgrow their childish fear and embark upon a new covenant with God—one in which they no longer need the written rules—and instead carry His guidance within, inscribed on their hearts.

> See, a time is coming—declares the Lord—when I will make a new covenant with the House of Israel and the House of Judah. It will not be like the covenant I made with their fathers, when I took them by the hand to lead them out of the land of Egypt, a covenant which they broke, though I espoused them—declares the Lord. But such is the covenant I will make with the House of Israel after these days—declares the Lord: I will put My Teaching into their inmost being and inscribe it upon their hearts. Then I will be their God, and they shall be My people. No longer will they need to teach one another and say to one another, "Heed the Lord"; for all of them, from the least of them to the greatest, shall heed Me—declares the Lord[6] (Jewish Study Bible, Jeremiah 31:31–34).

God's ultimate goal is not to enshrine a body of law that will endure forever, promulgated by a special lineage of priests. The goal, God's new covenant, is for each of us to have the law inscribed, not on stone tablets, but upon our hearts, where we will know it intimately for ourselves. It won't need to be spelled out—indeed, it cannot be—because it's uniquely tailored to each of us in each present moment. When this time comes, there will be no further need for priests or the law. We'll relate directly to God. We'll finally have achieved spiritual maturity and become "a kingdom of priests," as God originally intended for us at Mount Sinai.

⚜ ⚜

Chapter 15

THE GOLDEN CALF: THE ROAD TO IDOLATRY

The Road to Idolatry Begins at Mount Sinai

Starting with the birth of Moses and continuing all the way to Mount Sinai, God's goal for the Hebrews has been clear and the path toward it unswerving: to worship Him as a free people in their own land. But when the Hebrews choose to stand "at a distance" from God, their spiritual journey derails. They set in motion a chain of events that leaves them wandering the wilderness, literally and metaphorically, for the next 40 years.

The Hebrews prove they're not ready to hear God's words directly from Him. The law is not inscribed on their hearts. They need it in a tangible form that they can grasp with their hands. They need it written down, so they can turn to it again and again. But this is *their* need, *their* will, not God's. Nowhere does God state that He will lead them out of bondage in Egypt in order to give them the law. That was never the goal, nor is it the function of the Moses-mind.

When we have the chance to encounter God directly and refuse out of fear, the journey stalls. If we insist on standing "at a distance" from Him and receiving His guidance secondhand through the law, then we subvert the function of the Moses-mind. Why? Because we've shown that we don't really believe it to be a part of us. This introduces a split in the mind that says, in effect, "This Moses part is special, different from the rest of me. *It* can approach God safely; *I* cannot." But the Moses-mind doesn't work that way. Its purpose is to join us with Spirit. It's a bridge and can't be split apart. Only the ego would try to maintain such a division.

The wish to replace God with Moses is the first step down the road to idolatry. The moment the Hebrews ask him to speak to them *instead of* God, he no longer represents the Moses-mind. Indeed, to retrieve the law for his people, he must separate from them and, in effect, work against his original purpose. The Moses-mind could never do this. We can never truly separate ourselves from it, any more than we can separate from God. We can, however, lose touch with it by trying to change the goal of the journey.

If you refuse God and embrace the law instead—if you externalize and objectify the Moses-mind in this way, at this stage of the journey—you lose the Moses-mind. It goes missing, absent, away on the mountaintop with God. You can't have it both ways. You can't ask Moses to speak, but not God. You can't ask the Moses-mind to serve a purpose for which it was never intended.

Moses now becomes an intermediary of a different sort. He will go to God and receive the law in written form for his people. But to do so, he must leave his people.

In Moses's Absence

Moses has been with his people ever since he first returned to Egypt from Midian. Now, for the first time, he leaves them. Had they become "a kingdom of priests" as God intended, this would not have been necessary. But if Moses must speak in place of God, as a go-between, then he must go to God on his own and leave them behind in order to receive the law in a form they can use.

Moses meets God at the top of the mountain. He disappears into the cloud that cloaked the "consuming fire" (Exod. 24:17) of God's Presence. There he receives the law inscribed onto stone tablets by God's own Hand. Moses is away from his people for 40 days and 40 nights.[1]

> Now when the people saw that Moses delayed to come down from the mountain, the people assembled about Aaron, and said to him, "Come, make us a god who will go before us; as for this Moses, the man who brought us up from the land of Egypt, we do not know what has become of him." And Aaron said to them, "Tear off the gold rings which are in the ears of your wives, your sons, and your daughters, and bring *them* to me." Then all the people tore off the gold rings which were in their ears, and brought *them* to Aaron. He took *this* from their hand, and fashioned it with a graving tool, and made it into a molten calf; and they said, "This is your god, O Israel, who brought you up from the land of Egypt" (Exod. 32:1–4).

By insisting that Moses speak for God, the Hebrews are forced to part from him and make do without his leadership. This leaves them effectively cut off from God. And what happens when they're left on their own? They lose faith and fashion an idol, a golden calf, in direct violation of God's first commandment:

> "I am the Lord your God, who brought you out of the land of Egypt, out of the house of slavery.
> You shall have no other gods before Me.
> You shall not make for yourself an idol, or any likeness of what is in heaven above or on the earth beneath or in the water under the earth. You shall not worship them or serve them. . ." (Exod. 20:2–5).

This first commandment has barely left God's lips, and the Hebrews are already breaking it. (If we needed any further proof of the law's frailty, here it is.) To compound their transgression, they not only forge an idol, they then proclaim it to be the very god that brought them out of bondage in Egypt. The words they use are a direct parody of God's. How could they so quickly forget all that He and Moses have done for them?

The Transitional Object

When young children are separated from their parents, even for the span of a single night, they can grow frightened and cling to a favorite blanket or teddy bear in order to feel safe and comforted. In psychology, we call this a *transitional object*. The soft, cuddly bear or blanket stands in for the parents and their love. It's a tangible representation of that love, something the child can touch and hold in place of the absent mom or dad.

As children grow older, they no longer need transitional objects to feel safe. They're able to internalize their parents' love and carry it around inside them, inscribed on their hearts, so to speak. Eventually, they grow up and leave the safety of their parents altogether, yet the love still remains within, a constant support.

Moses has been a transitional object for the Hebrews. With him, they feel safe and protected. Through him, they're connected to God. But with him gone, there's nothing to keep their fear at bay. So what do they do? They fashion a new transitional object: a golden calf that stands in for the absent Moses (who himself stands in for God). With the idol, they can once again feel secure.

In the normal course of events, a child grows from dependency to autonomy—that is, to freedom. But the Hebrews are already free. Having passed up the chance for their own direct connection to God, the trajectory of their growth turns sharply retrograde. They replace God with Moses, and then Moses with an idol. They behave rather like an 18-year-old who, refusing to get a job or go to college, prefers only to curl up in bed with his childhood teddy bear. The Hebrews have shifted into reverse gear; their spiritual journey is now moving backward.

The golden calf demonstrates once again that the Hebrews weren't ready for spiritual maturity. In the wilderness, they clung to fantasies of an Egypt that never was. Now they try to replace Moses with a golden calf. But what does it mean to replace Moses and God with an idol such as this?

The Golden Calf

Why would the Hebrews—specifically, Aaron—choose the image of a calf to represent a god? According to James D. Long, in his book *Riddle of the Exodus,* the Egyptian pharaohs were often depicted as bulls. Old Kingdom Egyptian texts referred to Pharaoh as "the bull of the sky."[2] Long believes there's an etymological link at work here as well. In biblical Hebrew, the word for cow is *parah.* This is remarkably similar to the word *pharaoh*[3], especially when we consider that, in biblical Hebrew, words were written without the benefit of any vowel sounds. Thus, both words would be spelled identically, *p-r-h,* with the different vowel sounds implied by the context. If Long is correct, then the golden calf is an attempt to resurrect Pharaoh and reinstate him as their god.

The Hebrews feel abandoned by Moses and God. They need a replacement, and so they forge a golden calf, symbolic of the pharaohs, which they proclaim to be their god—ironically, the god that led them out of Egypt. With Moses away, their confusion is so great that they've remade Pharaoh into the agent of their freedom!

⚘

We find still more evidence for a connection between the golden calf and Egypt when we ask where all that gold came from. The Hebrews strip off their jewelry and give it to Aaron to melt down. But the Hebrews were slaves. How do they happen to possess so much gold?

Before leaving Egypt, God instructs the Hebrews to ask the Egyptians for "articles of silver and articles of gold, and clothing; and the Lord had given the people favor in the sight of the Egyptians, so that they let them have their request. Thus they plundered the Egyptians" (Exod. 12:35–36). The gold from which the idol is forged is Egyptian gold. Originally, it was a sign of the Hebrews' newly won freedom. Their former oppressors showered them with silver and gold: the spoils of a war for independence fought and won on their behalf by Moses and God. Yet now the Hebrews take that gold, proof of their freedom, and melt it down into an idol that symbolizes none other than their former oppressor.

The golden calf, an idol made of Egyptian gold, is an attempt to re-create Pharaoh—that is, to reconstitute the ego-mind—and replace God with its image. It's an attempt to return to the good old days of bondage to ego, when the rules and goals seemed clear.

❧

When the attempt to reach God directly fails, we go about trying to reinvent our old life. We return to chasing after the ego's vision of happiness in its many guises: wealth, acclaim, power, romance, and so on. We get a new job, a new spouse, a new yoga teacher; buy a sleek new car or pay a surgeon to sculpt a new nose. We travel to exotic locales, or better still, move there outright, attempting to craft a new self-concept. Wherever we go, whatever we do, we have created an idol, and the spiritual journey comes to a halt. No wonder God made the prohibition against idolatry the first of His commandments.

This attempt to reinvest in the ego and its priorities has consequences. Our eyes have already been opened. We've crossed the Red Sea. We've been given manna. And so now, when we try to replace the Moses-mind with a reconstituted version of ego, we cannot plead ignorance. Now we defy Spirit knowingly.

As slaves in Egypt, we followed the ego's guidance because we knew no other way. At this stage of the journey, however, what had been bondage to the ego becomes a conscious choice: idolatry. We've decided to value worthless pursuits over Spirit. Discernment has flown out the window. Our Moses-mind is absent, and we willingly pay homage to a worthless facsimile of God.

Of course, we can lose our way at any stage of the spiritual journey. But having come so close to God, the rebound is particularly devastating. It can divert us from the journey for years—in some cases, for a lifetime.

Darlene's Story

Darlene was a thin, frail, white-haired woman in her 70s. She'd been admitted to the hospital by her rheumatologist for evaluation and treatment of severe, generalized joint pain. Darlene hurt all over, all the time. She also had problems with allergies. I was asked to evaluate her and help with any psychological factors that might be contributing to her pain.

I knocked on her door and introduced myself. Darlene was perched on her bed in a hospital gown. She eyed me long and hard, and then greeted me with a note of caution. She'd be happy to talk, but only as a favor to her doctor, whom she trusted and greatly admired. No offense, but she really didn't believe in psychiatry.

Darlene's voice was brittle, her words clipped and precise as she assured me that her pain was real. I told her that I agreed—all pain is real—but since pain can only be experienced by the brain (it truly is "all in your head"), perhaps as a psychiatrist I could help her learn to control it better. She seemed to accept this and motioned for me to sit. She thrust several sheets of paper at me: a handwritten list of over 90 different foods, drugs, and materials to which she was allergic. Looking them over, I thought to myself, *Here is woman who's allergic to life itself.*

Darlene had no close relationships. She was estranged from her only daughter. They'd had no contact for years, but she refused to tell me why. What relevance did her daughter have to her pain, she demanded? Apart from her doctor, Darlene's life was empty. If not for pain, she would have no relationships at all.

Rather than asking more questions that would make her uncomfortable, I thought I'd simply offer Darlene an experience of relaxation, in hopes it might help her. Would she allow me to guide her through an imagery exercise? All she'd have to do is close her eyes and listen to my voice. She agreed it was worth a try.

Darlene didn't care much for beaches or lakes, so I walked her through a beautiful sunlit meadow surrounded by rolling green hills dotted with purple, white, pink, and gold wildflowers. She sat in the shade of a friendly old willow, enjoying a mild breeze. I told her that soon someone would be coming along down the path to pay her a visit. It would be a man or woman of great wisdom, someone who knew her well—far better than she knew herself—and who loved her without reservations, exactly as she was, flaws and all. This person would sit with her, comfort her, and do anything in his or her power to help with the pain.

In the brief silence that followed, I asked if that person had arrived. Darlene nodded. The tautness around her mouth softened and, smiling, her eyes began to brim with tears. She told me to stop talking, so I kept quiet and let her have her experience. When at last Darlene opened her eyes, her look was so warm, so full of joy and gratitude, that it made my own eyes fill with tears. Was this the same woman who, less than an hour before, had greeted me so defensively?

Darlene described her experience in hushed words. She said that the being who came and sat by her side was Jesus. It was amazing. A miracle. Her pain was all gone, for the first time in . . . she couldn't even remember how long. How could she thank me? I told her no thanks were necessary, but that I'd come back the next day and we could do the imagery exercise again. Eventually, she could learn to walk these meadows on her own and meet with Jesus in the shade of the willow any time she liked. Darlene had experienced a true healing. I wanted her to own it, to make it hers, so she could repeat it without me or anyone else having to guide her through it.

The next morning I returned to Darlene's room, eager to continue our work. I entered with a big smile, expecting a warm greeting. Instead, she sat up stiffly and warned me right off that she did *not* want to do any more of that imagery stuff. It was all well and good, and she was glad to have tried it, but her pain was real and there was obviously nothing I could do to help her. She needed a doctor, not a psychiatrist.

But wouldn't she like to sit with Jesus again, I asked. Her eyes moistened. She grew quiet for a few seconds, and then slowly shook her head. Sadly, I understood. She couldn't do it. Darlene couldn't make herself vulnerable like that again. She'd spent years walling herself off from everyone with her allergies and pain. She couldn't risk opening up to that kind of love. She'd touched the hand of Jesus, but instead chosen pain as her god.

Darlene wasn't prepared for the powerful experience that had come her way. She had no way of integrating it into her life. To do so would have demanded too much of her. She'd had a taste of freedom . . . and it led her straight back to Egypt, where she would remain a willing slave to pain. I also suspect that she pushed Jesus away (as she had everyone else who might have cared for her, except her doctor), because she didn't believe she deserved love, for reasons buried deep in her past and known only to her. What she'd felt from Jesus was too much; it threatened her core sense of self. Therefore, she had to reject it, preferring the pain she knew over the love she feared.

In the course of one brief imagery exercise, Darlene had escaped Egypt, made it across the Red Sea, and encountered the love of God. Her rigid ego melted away, leaving her receptive and open—and free of pain to boot. But like the Hebrews, she wasn't ready. She didn't know how to take her experience and make it the foundation for a new sense of self. And so she retreated. Pain was her god, medicine her law, and the rheumatologist her Moses. She wasn't prepared to let *any* of them go, not even for Jesus.

Did Darlene create an idol? Well, it's not obvious. But when she turned away from Jesus and chose to worship at the altar of pain and medicine instead, I believe she did. Before Jesus, her pain was bondage. After, it was idolatry.

Moses Responds to the Golden Calf

When Aaron forges the golden calf, Moses is still off visiting with God atop Mount Sinai. God informs him of what his people are up to and urges him to return to them at once. God is angry. He threatens to destroy this "obstinate" people and start over, fashioning a new race with Moses as the prototype.[4] But Moses reasons with God, asking Him to "turn from Your burning anger" (Exod. 32:12), and God changes His mind.

Moses comes down from the mountaintop to confront his people. He sees the calf and the Hebrews dancing around it, and he becomes enraged.

> . . . Moses' anger burned, and he threw the tablets from his hands and shattered them at the foot of the mountain. He took the calf which they had made and burned *it* with fire, and ground it to powder, and scattered it over the surface of the water and made the sons of Israel drink *it* (Exod. 32:19–20).

Moses's first response to the idolatry of his people is to smash the tablets of the law. This is fitting. Moses breaks the tablets, but the Hebrews broke the law by forging the golden calf. In shattering the tablets, Moses symbolically demonstrates the fallibility and impermanence of the law. Though carved in stone, it's easily fractured. The law is no substitute for God's direct guidance.

Moses's second response is to burn the calf and scatter its powdered remains over water. Of course, there is no water in the wilderness of Sinai. It could only have come from Miriam's Well (the rock). Therefore, Moses negates the toxic effect of the idol with its antidote, a miracle.

But the Hebrews haven't yet appreciated the gravity of their transgression. Moses forces them to drink the mixture, to swallow it down, so they can literally digest the full impact of their deed. Should they vomit it back out, then the idol will serve as its own emetic, flushing the poison from the system. And because it made them sick, they'll be very reluctant to try it again.

We could also say that Moses administers a homeopathic remedy of sorts to his people. By forcing them to ingest a tiny amount of the pathogenic idol in highly diluted form, they'll develop immunity to it. He's inoculating them against idols, treating the Hebrews with the hair of the dog that bit them. But whatever the interpretation, thus far Moses's behavior makes sense. He's trying to cleanse his people of their sin.

Aaron Apart From Moses

Moses next turns to Aaron, whom he left in charge when he went to meet God.

> Then Moses said to Aaron, "What did this people do to you, that you have brought such great sin upon them?" Aaron said, "Do not let the anger of my lord burn; you know the people yourself, that they are prone to evil. For they said to me, 'Make a god for us who will go before us; for this Moses, the man who brought us up from the land of Egypt, we do not know what has become of him.' I said to them, 'Whoever has any gold, let them tear it off.' So they gave it to me, and I threw it into the fire, and out came this calf" (Exod. 32:21–24).

Aaron was appointed chief priest of the Hebrews in Exodus 28:1.[5] But unlike Moses, he is incapable of leading the people. Without the slightest protest, he gives in to their request for an idol and then, like a child, denies all responsibility for his role. The people are "prone to evil," not him. He "threw [the gold] into the fire, and out came this calf." All by itself! Amazing! Aaron played no part in it.

Recall that God recruited Aaron to speak for Moses to Pharaoh. ". . . he [Aaron] will be as a mouth for you and you will be as God to him" (Exod. 4:16). Without Moses to put God's words into his mouth, Aaron is lost. He falls into idolatry as easily as the rest of the Hebrews. Left on his own, he has no connection to

221

God. And without this connection, even though he is officially the chief priest, all his skill with words means nothing. In fact, he uses them dishonestly, to obfuscate and confuse, rather than come clean about what really happened.

The lesson is that those who lack a living connection to God—up to and including the high priest himself—are nothing but empty mouthpieces. Unless their words come from Spirit, they stand in the way of the journey. They cannot lead us to the Promised Land. No priest and no body of law can substitute for the Moses-mind.

Moses Goes Astray

What occurs next is perhaps the most disturbing event in all of Exodus. Even though Moses has broken the tablets of the law and forced his people to drink the idol's charred remains, his anger still burns hotly. He was able to talk God out of His impulse to destroy the Hebrews, but he cannot restrain his own murderous rage. And so he calls out to the camp, "Whoever is for the Lord, come to me!" (Exod. 32:26). So the sons of Levi gather around him.

> He said to them, "Thus says the Lord, the God of Israel, 'Every man of you put his sword upon his thigh, and go back and forth from gate to gate in the camp, and kill every man his brother, and every man his friend, and every man his neighbor.'" So the sons of Levi did as Moses instructed, and about three thousand men of the people fell that day (Exod. 32:27–28).

Moses's function is to speak for God. Ever since the burning bush, whenever he encounters an obstacle, he turns to God and asks how to proceed. He then does exactly what God tells him without protest or interference. Yet now, in his call to take up the sword, he claims to speak for God—"Thus says the Lord, the God of Israel"—when in fact God has told him nothing of the sort. God has already forgiven the Hebrews. No one knows this better than Moses. He was there; he's the one who convinced God to forgive them. So when he gives the order to take up the sword, it's the first time that his words *do not* in fact come from God. Like Aaron, he's being dishonest. He's giving vent to his own rage and justifying it by claiming it's sanctioned by God.

What does Moses command the Levites to do if they are "for the Lord"? They must go through the camp and murder their brethren. Aaron's weakness resulted in the golden calf, a violation of the first commandment's prohibition against idols. But Aaron and the Hebrews had an excuse. Their leader, Moses, was absent, his guidance out of reach. Moses has no such excuse. He brazenly violates the sixth commandment, the prohibition against murder. And perhaps, by falsely claiming that his directive comes from God, he's taking God's Name in vain as well, thus breaking the third commandment. He should know better, but rage overcomes reason, even for Moses.

⊗⊗

Does Moses's behavior have some meaning in the parable of Exodus? How is it possible for the Moses-mind to become disconnected from Spirit? How could it ever sanction murder? The simple answer is: it cannot. By definition, the Moses-mind is *always* connected to God and He does not violate His own laws. But we can push the Moses-mind away, as the Hebrews did, and as Moses himself now does in his fury. And without it there to keep us on track, we're especially vulnerable to raw emotion, in particular anger.

Anger and the Journey

As Moses demonstrates, powerful emotions have the capacity to overwhelm the mind. Under their sway, we can commit all kinds of acts we later regret, from sexual indiscretions to murder. This holds true even at advanced stages of the spiritual journey.

How many sages, saints, and gurus (most often men, not women) tumble from their lofty perches due to scandal? The papers are full of accounts of priests accused of molesting young boys and girls. And every year it seems we learn of another revered spiritual teacher who admits to sexual involvement with a student. One popular Hindu guru was rumored to have used secret underground tunnels at his ashram to pay nightly visits to the women's quarters, where he would sexually fondle prepubescent girls. No one dared challenge his behavior, because, after all, he was the guru; he must have some good reason for his actions.

The higher we climb on the path to Spirit, the farther we risk falling. When driving at high speeds, it takes but a tiny deviation of the wheel, one careless moment, to send us careening off the road. We must pay attention. We must be vigilant—especially regarding our emotions. What situations spark anger? Lust? Greed? Jealousy? Shame? What is it about those situations that triggers us? Is it the lure of great wealth? Sexual hunger? Power over others? Fear of aging? Or is our rage provoked by the injustices of the world and our desire to set them right, like Moses?

When swept up in a tide of powerful emotions, the spiritual journey goes awry. But we need not panic or despair. It's another opportunity to look at ourselves and see where we lost our way—where we're still held hostage by the habits of ego and vulnerable to its plagues. It's another opportunity to free ourselves. We simply need to identify the feeling, trace the path by which it entered our mind, and release it to Spirit. In this way, we negate its power over us. With practice, this process can become almost automatic, leaving us far less susceptible to the influence of strong, negative emotions.

※

Of all the emotions, anger is perhaps the most difficult to master, and certainly the most destructive. This is because anger, unlike other emotions, impels us to action, and actions have consequences. We're determined to *do something* about whatever it was that made us mad. Convinced that we're in the right, we happily take matters into our own hands with no thought for Spirit. Our minds are closed off to guidance in any form. In fact, those who try to divert us from our righteous wrath are likely to become targets themselves!

Whenever we fly into a rage, we've made a judgment of some kind—a comparison between what we *think* should be happening and what actually *is*. We feel as though we're under attack by reality. Whatever it is that's taking place seems to threaten some aspect of our self-concept or worldview. This can only mean that we've re-identified with the ego and its survival fears—fight or flight—rather than with the Moses-mind, which can never be threatened. The moment we give in to anger, our connection to Spirit is severed. Its all-knowing perspective, its flawless guidance, its miracles—all are lost to us. We're flying solo, in bad weather, with no instruments or radio. The results can be disastrous.

This is exactly what Moses teaches us in his rage. He breaks the tablets of the law and incites the Levites to murder. He jumps into action, just as he did when he was young and murdered the Egyptian. He sets himself up as judge and executioner of his people, *whom God has already forgiven*. In this sense, Moses is guilty of idolatry, too. He's put his own judgment above God's. In his fury, Moses has usurped God.

༺༈༻

In his book, *Practical Kabbalah*, Rabbi Laibl Wolf cites *The Tanya* (a work by Rabbi Zalman of Laidi, the founder of Chabad Hassidism) to make the point that "whoever expresses strong anger is practically worshipping idols, because in the very moment of anger his faith has completely departed from him."[6] Anger testifies to a loss of faith in God. It compels us to take action on our own, as if God didn't know how best to respond, or as if He didn't exist. We bow to our anger and make of it an inner idol. Anytime we feel called upon to teach people a lesson, lecture them, or in any way enforce some moral code dear to us that others have transgressed—whether by bombing a building or offering a curt

225

riposte at a dinner party—we are guilty of idolatry, because we've preempted Spirit.

Moses's example helps to explain why anger is regarded as such a dangerous emotion in Jewish thought. "Anger is an exceedingly bad passion," Maimonides wrote in his code of Jewish law, "and one should avoid it to the last extreme. One should train oneself not to be angry even for something that might justify anger."[7] And yet another great Jewish sage, Jesus of Nazareth, said, "But I tell you, do not resist an evil person. If anyone slaps you on the right cheek, turn to them the other cheek also" (Matthew 5:39).

❦

The golden calf is a cautionary tale. It does not tell us how to live; it does not lead us out of bondage or bring us miracles. Rather, it warns of two particularly dangerous pitfalls—two forms of idolatry, outer and inner—that lie in wait at this stage of the journey *if we refuse God*. The Hebrews fall prey to the first when, frightened by the absence of Moses, they try to resurrect Pharaoh by forging a golden calf. Moses is guilty of the second when he lets rage overpower him and usurps the forgiveness of God.

What lessons does this hold for the spiritual journey? Obviously, we must not make anyone or anything a higher priority than God. We must also guard against any narcissistic sense of specialness, particularly when this takes the form of righteous wrath. It's not our place to judge or condemn the actions of others, however wrongful they may seem to us. As we saw in the chapter on manna, we cannot know the nature of their path, their plagues, or their lessons. We can only know our own. Therefore, our judgments of others and the deeds that arise from them are sure to be misguided. Our task is not to correct our neighbor, but to tend to our own relationship with Spirit. Only this will see us safely to the Promised Land.

Idolatry's Aftermath

After Moses murdered the Egyptian, he fled into exile and was of no further help to his people. Are the consequences of his anger any different this time? Well, he's not exiled from the Hebrews, obviously. But he does become increasingly estranged from them. He leads them reluctantly, with an attitude of irritation and frustration. He grows tired of their grumbling. He prefers to keep to himself, isolated in the Tent of Meeting, which he pitched "a good distance from the camp" (Exod. 33:7). When he does address the people, it's from behind a veil that covers his face (to hide its intolerable brightness, the result of having stood in God's Presence). He only removes the veil, like a bride before her bridegroom, when he speaks with God "face to face" (Exod. 33:11). Moses grows closer and closer to God, but ever more remote from his people.

Having failed to embrace God at Mount Sinai, the Hebrews' journey continues to regress. In Numbers 11, they complain again about lack of food. They still long for Egypt, as they did back in Exodus 15 and 16, mere days after having crossed the Red Sea. At that time, Moses was confident God could meet their needs. But at this point, he doubts and questions God's ability to do so (Num. 11:22). When God delivers more quail than anyone could possibly eat, it's as if the lesson of manna had been perverted, giving rise to gluttony and greed instead. As a result, God inflicts a lethal plague on the Hebrews, even as they stuff their mouths full of quail (Num. 11:33). Instead of miracles, they receive plagues like the Egyptians. They fail His test[8] once more, and drift ever farther from their goal.

Sin vs. Error

If Moses himself can lose his bearings and fall prey to the idolatry of anger, what hope is there for his people? Are they doomed to wander forever lost? Will the forging of the golden calf finally, conclusively, shut them off from God's beneficence? Fortunately not.

The ultimate outcome of the Hebrews' idolatry is a renewal of God's original covenant with them. He agrees to give them the Ten Commandments once again (Exod. 34:10). Moses himself will carve the tablets from stone, carry them to God, and inscribe them as He dictates (Ex. 34:28). God gives His people a second chance.

Although the golden calf was a flagrant violation of God's Will and the Hebrews have suffered for it at the hands of both Moses and God (He inflicts a plague on them in Exodus 32:35), they are not condemned to hell. There's nothing irredeemable about their transgression. They've strayed into error, into old ego habits. They have not sinned.

In a world governed by miracles and the Moses-mind, there's no room for the concept of sin. If we follow Spirit's guidance—if our GPS is working properly—we'll get what we need, in the form best suited to our journey. If, on the other hand, we refuse to listen, like Pharaoh, then plagues will escalate, giving us another opportunity to change our minds. Once the law becomes our guide, however, sin becomes real. For if the law comes from God and we choose to disobey it, haven't we committed a crime against God—that is to say, a sin?

The distinction between sin and error is vital to successfully navigating our way to the Promised Land. *A Course in Miracles* makes this point as well.

> It is essential that error not be confused with sin. . . .
> For error can be corrected, and the wrong made right. . . .
> Sin calls for punishment as error for correction . . .[9]

In our own lives, we may lose our way a thousand times—in a single day even! We may find that some overwhelming emotion or circumstance has cut us off from Spirit. We may actively reject the guidance of our Moses-mind and worship again and again at the alter of ego and its idols, in ways both grand and seemingly trivial. But in each moment, we remain free to make a different choice. And when we do, no matter how sinful we believed ourselves to be, Spirit will welcome us back. God has made a covenant with us (for we are all His people), a promise that He will guide our journey and see us safely to the Promised Land. We may choose to turn away from Him in fear or shame and stand at a distance, but He will never turn away from us. He's as close as the next breath. Always.

Alcoholics who fall off the wagon are not sinners. They can restart the journey back to sobriety the instant they finish off the last drop of that wrong-headed drink. No matter how besotted or hopeless their condition appears from the outside, the path to sobriety always remains open. All it takes is a decision.

Isn't this the meaning behind the story of the prodigal son as well?[10] His father makes no distinction between the "good" son who remains at home and behaves as his father wishes, and the "bad" son who rejects his father to wander the world and squander his fortune. A loving father embraces *all* his children in their desire to be with him, no matter the course taken by their life journey. Would God, Father of all, not do the same?

When we at last make the decision to return to God, by whatever path we travel, He will welcome us home. No matter how long it takes, no matter how far afield we wander, no matter how many golden calves we erect and bow down before, the ending is certain: We will return to Him, and He will welcome us home. We will achieve a direct and personal relationship with Him, just as Moses did. We will finish what the Hebrews of Exodus could not. We will complete the journey to the Promised Land.

> Forget not once this journey is begun the end is certain. Doubt along the way will come and go and go to come again. Yet is the ending sure. No one can fail to do what God appointed him to do.[11]

Chapter 16

THE PROMISED LAND

The Hebrews of Exodus never do make it to the Promised Land. After repeatedly griping about how they would have been better off in Egypt, God finally bars the entire generation that left Egypt from entering.

> Surely all the men who have seen My glory and My signs which I performed in Egypt and in the wilderness, yet have put Me to the test these ten times and have not listened to My voice, shall by no means see the land which I swore to their fathers . . . (Num 14:22–23).

To our ears, this sounds like a punishment, but, once again, we're hearing God's words with the ears of ego. It's not punishment. It's the natural consequence of repeated refusals to trust Him. If we consistently choose to engage in harmful behavior, at some point we'll suffer consequences that cannot be reversed. For the smoker with newly diagnosed lung cancer, it's too late to quit. The damage is done.

In later books of the Bible, the Hebrews do indeed enter and live in the land of Canaan, as promised by God. But they do not find there a land flowing with milk and honey. The twin kingdoms of Israel and Judah do not signify the end of the spiritual journey. They're political entities and have no meaning within the parable of Exodus. They are not the Promised Land.

Entering the Promised Land

What, then, does it mean within the parable of Exodus to enter the Promised Land? What state of mind is alluded to with the Pharaoh-like ego vanquished, no fantasies of Egypt left to beguile us, and a full connection to Spirit reestablished?

Entering the Promised Land is not a sudden awakening. It's not a rebirth experience, like crossing the Red Sea. There's no finish line, no fanfare, no sense of triumph—not even relief, really. We do not enter in one great, final leap forward. If you believe that any single event or miracle has decisively brought you to that place, you're deluding yourself. The Promised Land is not won in a day. It takes years of wandering the wilderness and practicing discernment, as Moses and the Hebrews can attest to. Sometimes, we don't even know we've arrived until long after, when we look back and realize that we've been living in a state of peace for some time, uninterrupted by old ego-based fears or desires.

Entering the Promised Land is more akin to going through puberty or menopause. It's a progression—a series of changes and revisions to our self-concept that at last leaves us with no self-concept aside from Spirit. We keep walking, keep growing, until at some point, it fully dawns on us . . . we're there. We proclaim this not with a shout, but a quiet, measured acknowledgment—and not to anyone but ourselves—for who else needs to know? What good will it do them? It's the conclusion of our journey, not theirs. We know, and Spirit knows. That's enough.

Miracles and the Promised Land

The best description of the Promised Land is found not in Exodus, but in Deuteronomy, where Moses delivers his farewell address to his people.

> [It is] a good land, a land of brooks of water, of fountains and springs, flowing forth in valleys and hills; a land of wheat and barley, of vines and fig trees and pomegranates, a land of olive oil and honey; a land where you shall eat food without scarcity, in which you will not lack anything . . ." (Deut. 8:7–9).

Everything and more the Hebrews longed for in their fantasies of Egypt is to be found in the Promised Land. It has food of all varieties in abundance. Water, the symbol of life and birth, flows in profusion from fountains and springs. Survival is never in doubt. Scarcity and lack do not exist, for with God, the Source of All, there can be no lack.

The Promised Land represents a state of abiding receptivity and flow. As with manna, we're set free from the curse of Adam, free from the death grip of Pharaoh-ego. It is a new Eden, where we get exactly what we need without struggle or fear. We're free to experience events fresh, as Spirit brings them to us, unfiltered by the ego and its fears. Spirit is both the music and the dance master; our feet skip lightly to its tune.

In the Promised Land, there are no miracles, at least not as we think of them, because here, they are the norm. They flow forth like the water, to answer every need before we're even aware it exists. In this sense, everything that occurs in the Promised Land is a miracle. There's nothing special, nothing "miraculous," about them. Even when events seem to misfire and go wrong, we trust that they're part of some larger necessity and will ultimately reveal themselves to be a miracle.

Some call this living in a state of grace. Hindus speak of *moksha*—release from the cycle of death and rebirth—while Buddhists refer to it as *nirvana*. *A Course in Miracles* describes it as living in the "real world." By whatever name we call it, this state marks the end of the spiritual journey—and it, too, is nothing special. It's not reserved for the saintly, to be stingily dispensed by God to His select few. Grace, nirvana, the real world—they're available to any and all who earnestly seek them, who want God and nothing else but God. That's all that's required.

Living in the Promised Land

Once we've achieved the state of mind represented by the Promised Land, how do we spend our days? The Bible offers little guidance on this point. Do we still have to go to work? Or is it like one big retirement community? If we lack for nothing, if there's nothing to strive for, nothing to look forward to, then what's the purpose of living? What gives life its meaning?

In a certain respect, these questions are meaningless, because they could only be asked from the limited perspective of a mind still enslaved to ego. The fact is, we don't need to know in advance what the Promised Land will be like; we just need to get there. To try to describe a state that few have achieved, to parse it into words, is like trying to describe flight to a caterpillar. Yet from those who have completed the journey, we do have some sense of what it might be like.

Many of the best descriptions come from the Eastern spiritual traditions and their concept of enlightenment. When we become enlightened, we no longer identify with the physical body and its needs. Nor are we slaves to ego and its goals, nor lost in a wilderness bereft of meaning. To the enlightened mind, concepts of self and personality dissolve away. What remains is perfect, abiding Oneness. There's no "you" and no "I"—no separation. All that's left is pure, eternal consciousness that flows unimpeded beneath and through all phenomena of the physical world.

And so the question, "What do we do in the Promised Land?" reveals itself as tainted by ego. In a state of pure being, there is no "doing." The 8th-century Zen Buddhist Layman P'ang described it this way.

> My days are hardly unusual,
> I'm just naturally in harmony with them.
> Grasping for nothing; pushing nothing away;
> meeting neither obstacles nor conflict.
> My otherworldly powers and miraculous feats:
> drawing water and chopping wood.[1]

Following perhaps from Layman P'ang's poem comes a well-known Buddhist saying that addresses the question of what it's like to live in an enlightened state. "Before enlightenment: chop wood, carry water. After enlightenment: chop wood, carry water." That is to say, outwardly nothing changes with enlightenment. The change is all internal—necessarily so, for the mind is the only true reality.

Outwardly, to the egos of others, we may look no different. We go through the same routines, engage in the same activities. We eat, talk, urinate, sleep. The difference is that, inside, we're at peace. We don't cling to outcomes. We don't identify. We don't get stuck. Like water, we flow across and around all seeming obstacles. We know what we are and what we are not, and in this knowingness lies perfect serenity. As Layman P'ang so beautifully puts it: "Grasping for nothing; pushing nothing away, meeting neither obstacles nor conflict." He's at one with the flow of Being.

But is the Eastern concept of enlightenment really the same thing as living in the Promised Land? I suspect that the two are very close, but perhaps not quite identical. Enlightenment is a state of pure, abiding oneness: no self, no other. In the Promised Land, we do not experience ourselves as one with the All. We continue to have a distinct sense of self, but that self is seamlessly interconnected to Spirit. It's the difference between standing on a mountaintop surrounded by nothing but air and sky, and living in a spacious, comfortable room with big skylights that pour down sunlight and large, open windows that let the breezes blow through.

In the Promised Land, the Moses-mind does not lead us as if we were somehow distinct from it and its ways mysterious. Instead, *we have become* the Moses-mind, and we live and go about our day with that same absolute faith in God that Moses had. We look not to the self, but to Spirit for all our needs and answers. And whatever the day may bring, it will not tarnish the Love of God that glows within us, always in full awareness.

Ego is reduced to its original function: the system software for organizing perception. It allows us to engage with the physical world—a virtual-reality interface of sorts—but nothing more than that. It makes no judgments, undertakes no plans, cares nothing for past or future, and responds to emotions as it might the wind—like gusts that blow and recede without lasting impact.

In the Promised Land, desire—wanting—aligns fully with Spirit. We cannot want apart from God's Will, because there is no other will than His. Therefore, it's not possible to want something that's not on our path and won't come our way easily through miracles. All other desires strike us as ludicrous. Wealth, power, fame, bodily pleasure—these make no sense. It's not that we're somehow forced to sacrifice and renounce them. They simply no longer belong in our world. A 5-year-old treasures her Barbie dolls, but at 25 it's hardly a sacrifice to let them go.

In the Promised Land, we're one tiny step away from the complete dissolution of identity that is enlightenment. We're not yet one with God, but God is with us always.

> God is with me. He is my Source of life, the life within, the air I breathe, the food by which I am sustained, the water which renews and cleanses me. He is my home, wherein I live and move; the Spirit which directs my actions, offers me Its Thoughts, and guarantees my safety from all pain.[2]

Is this not a worthwhile goal? Is it not a compelling reason to undertake the Exodus journey? Who wouldn't want to live in such a state? Why seek anything else?

Moses's Warning

Moses warns the Hebrews that, even in the Promised Land, there is one circumstance against which they must be especially vigilant.

> . . . [W]hen you have eaten and are satisfied, and have built good houses and lived *in them,* and when your herds and your flocks multiply, and your silver and gold multiply, and all that you have multiplies, then your heart will become proud and you will forget the Lord your God who brought you out from the land of Egypt, out of the house of slavery. He led you through the great and terrible wilderness . . . He brought water for you out of the rock of flint. In the wilderness He fed you manna which your fathers did not know, that He might humble you and that He might test you, to do good for you in the end. Otherwise, you may say in your heart, "My power and the strength of my hand made me this wealth." But you shall remember the Lord your God, for it is He who is giving you power to make wealth, that He may confirm His covenant which He swore to your fathers, as it is this day (Deut. 8:12–18).

When everything in our lives exists in flow, when problems seem to melt at our approach, or reveal themselves as part of some greater solution, it is tempting to believe that *we* are somehow the ones responsible and not God—that we're special, gifted, and, of course, far more deeply spiritual than others. But we must never mistake the Source of our beneficence. It does not come from ego and its arrogance. The bounty we receive comes from Spirit.

Moses goes further in his warning: "[I]f you ever forget the Lord your God, and go after other gods and serve them and worship them . . . you will surely perish" (Deut. 8:19). Our egos hear this as a threat, but that's not what it is. It's a statement of fact. We cannot stay in the Promised Land if we're tempted by the ego's false gods. We cannot remain in the state of spontaneous miracles if we mistake their Source. To the extent that we identify with ego

237

and its habits, we will "surely perish," because that's the ego's fate: to die. To the extent that we are one with Spirit and the Moses-mind, we will surely abide in peace in the Promised Land.

Purpose in the Promised Land

Do we still have a purpose in the Promised Land? The Bible says nothing about this, other than to remember God and keep His commandments. Buddhism by contrast offers the concept of the bodhisattva: the enlightened sage who vows to reincarnate lifetime after lifetime until every sentient being is freed from the chains of suffering and illusion. This is the bodhisattva's sole purpose. His or her own journey will remain incomplete so long as any other being remains enslaved. From this perspective, there is no individual spiritual journey. We all travel together. Some appear to arrive sooner than others, but that's just an illusion of time. Until we're all awakened, all enlightened, the journey remains incomplete.

In place of a bodhisattva, the Bible gives us the example of Moses. Like the bodhisattva, he cannot cross into the Promised Land himself because his people aren't ready. He's their leader; their inability is therefore his as well. "The Lord was angry with me also on your account, saying, 'Not even you shall enter there'" (Deut. 1:37).

Moses is our role model for living in connection with Spirit. Did he have a purpose? Yes, he did—to lead his people out of bondage to freedom. This then becomes our purpose, too, our only remaining purpose, once we reach the Promised Land.

On this final leg of the journey, having learned the lessons of the wilderness, we understand that there is no other objective than to teach and lead. We don't *desire* to lead; we're not trying to fulfill some image of being the exalted guru or spiritual master. That's the ego's fantasy. Teaching—leading others—is simply the only purpose that remains in the egoless state. The bodhisattva's vow then implies no sacrifice. It's not noble or praiseworthy. It is a given.

However, from our unenlightened, ego-bound perspective, this purpose can be easily misconstrued. The ego understands purpose in terms of plans to be made and actions to be taken. It proclaims itself willing to sacrifice all for the ultimate goal. It will do anything—climb the highest mountain, swim the widest sea—anything at all . . . except surrender its will to God. That it will never do, for that would be its end.

In the Promised Land, we do not lead by action—not unless we're specifically guided to it. We turn to God, ask, and then listen, as Moses did. We lead not by our deeds, but by our example: by the way we live in flow, free of fear, and by miracles.

We trust that Spirit will bring us to those who will benefit most by our example. Some will be drawn to other teachers better suited to their temperaments and beliefs. Like the taste of manna, we each have our own unique function in this world—a teaching assignment from Spirit that we alone can fulfill. Therefore, our journeys will seem to follow different routes and recruit different traveling companions along the way. But in the end, we will all arrive at the same destination. All roads lead to the Promised Land.

The Exodus Journey Revealed

From the high ground of the Promised Land, we can at last look back over the terrain we've traveled and survey the journey in its entirety. When we do, we come upon an astonishing discovery. We see that there really was no journey. It didn't exist. What we experienced were but the different steps in awakening to the reality of Spirit—like successive veils of illusion lifted from before our eyes until at last we beheld the truth. Described another way, these are like different stage sets in a theater that appear and disappear with the rise and fall of the curtain. Each comes to us when we're ready and, once its lessons are learned, gives way to the next.

The curtain rises. We begin in Egypt, in bondage, suffering under the tyrannical whims of Pharaoh-ego. We'd lost our very identities—that we are God's people, destined to inhabit a land where suffering does not exist. Enter Moses and the Moses-mind, given birth to by the unnamed and unnamable God Whom we'd forgotten. Moses calls down plagues on the ego, forcing it to loosen its hold on our minds and teaching us that we are not the Egyptians. The ego's agenda is not ours. With the tenth plague—death—it finally lets go . . . and at last we're free. *The curtain falls.*

The curtain rises, and instead of Egypt, we find ourselves looking out upon the imposing barrier of the Red Sea. How will we ever make it across? How can we escape the forces of ego that so relentlessly pursue us? Skeptical of Moses and God, we cry out in fear. But a miracle saves us. The waters part and we cross over, making the transition to a new sense of self. We will never be the same again. *The curtain falls.*

The curtain rises, but instead of the much anticipated Promised Land, we look upon the wilderness: a vast emptiness where nothing can survive. This land will surely kill us. In our fear and confusion, we wish we were back in Egypt. We fantasize about how great our lives were as slaves. To help us, God gives us miracles every day—manna and water that flows abundantly from a rock. We accept these gifts, but don't understand their true purpose. We aren't able to learn discernment. We fail to grasp that only through miracles is survival possible in the wilderness. *The curtain falls.*

The curtain rises, and we find ourselves standing at the base of Mount Sinai. God Himself appears: the ultimate revelation. But we aren't prepared. We're too scared to hear His Voice. We choose to cling to Moses instead, to idolize him, as if he were separate from us and could protect us—from God! We lose our connection to the Moses-mind and barter miracles for the law.

The curtain falls and we're back in the wilderness, to wander for as long as it takes to learn discernment and prepare again to meet God. At some point, we'll be ready.

When that time comes, *the curtain will rise for the final act,* and in place of the wilderness . . . behold the Promised Land. Here, there will be nothing more for us to seek or do. Our task will be simply to live in flow—to chop wood and carry water—and serve as a living example for others. We'll gather up manna—only we'll find that it's no longer manna. It's been transformed, just as we have. In the Promised Land, the true nature of manna is revealed. It's become milk and honey. And it will slake our thirst, satisfy our hunger, and meet our every need for as long as we live.

※

Before he dies, Moses explains to the Hebrews that their exodus from Egypt had a greater purpose, that "God was training you as a man trains his child" (Jerusalem Bible, Deut. 8:5). The journey out of Pharaoh's land, across the Red Sea, and through the wilderness was not just an escape to freedom. It was a prolonged learning experience: a training course.

Such is the nature of our journey, too. We're enrolled in a course on spiritual maturity, a course in miracles. Its objectives? To free us from the ego-mind and remind us of our living connection to Spirit; to teach us to trust in God and His miracles, and nothing but these; and to understand that no idols, no other gods, can ever replace Him.

If we accept that Exodus is a parable, a teaching tale, then the Hebrews *cannot* reach the Promised Land, because *we* haven't reached it either. Their story is our story. It's incomplete, and necessarily so. And it can only be completed by each of us making the journey and seeking to live life in full connection with Spirit.

We're in training, learning how to turn aside the voice of ego and rely instead on the voice of the Moses-mind, learning to exchange fear and the ego's false promises of security for miracles. The better we're able to recognize ego and the plagues that travel in its wake—and to escape them through miracles—the closer we come to the Promised Land.

At some point, when we achieve spiritual maturity and pass through the gates of the Promised Land, we'll find that we're no

longer aware of specific needs and the miracles that come to fulfill them. Miracles will arise and subside outside of our conscious
awareness, like the inhalation and exhalation of breath. They'll
become unconscious habits of mind, just as the ego once was. It
will all be flow, all milk and honey. Spirit and the Moses-mind will
be our sole reality—all we know and all we care to know; all we are
and all we'll ever be. For the journey will be over, and with it the
past and its suffering.

༄

In the eternal present of God, there is no journey.
Until we reach God's eternal present, there is only the journey.

༄ ༄

afterword

And so, whether you find yourself still in Egypt suffering under the yoke of Pharaoh-ego; or trembling in fear on the banks of the Red Sea awaiting the miracle that will take you to the other side and transform you forever; or wandering the desert wilderness, gathering manna and learning discernment—the journey calls to you. Trust God. He will be with you. Take the next step.

A Final Wish

In conclusion, I wish for you, reader and fellow journeyer, the felt experience of Spirit in your life. May you learn to know and trust the voice of Moses within you. May all your plagues reveal themselves as miracles. May you win freedom from Pharaoh-ego—freedom that has always been your birthright. May you find yourself prepared to welcome God without fear and fully receive His Love. And may you joyously live out your days on Earth, knowing that you and you alone can make of them the Promised Land.

AMEN

Endnotes

---•◦•---

Introduction

[1] *A Passover Haggadah,* edited by Herbert Bronstein (New York, Central Conference of American Rabbis, 1974, 1994), 34.

[2] Brown, Dan, *The Lost Symbol* (New York, Doubleday, 2009), 499.

Chapter 1

[1] Melzack, Ronald and Patrick D. Wall, *The Challenge of Pain* (New York, Basic Books, 1982), 35.

[2] Tolle, Eckhart, *A New Earth: Awakening to Your Life's Purpose* (New York, Plume/Penguin Group, 2005), 96.

Chapter 2

[1] Seneca, Lucius Annaeus, *Epistles I–LXV, Loeb Classical Library* (Cambridge, MA, Harvard University Press, 1917, 2006), translated by Richard M. Gummere, Epistle XLVII, "On Master and Slave," 311.

Chapter 3

[1] Gaster, Theodor H., *Myth, Legend, and Custom in the Old Testament* (New York, Harper and Row, 1969), 226.

[2] Ibid, 225.

[3] *The Jewish Study Bible, Tanakh Translation* (New York, Oxford University Press, 2004), Footnote to Exodus 2:1–10, 109.

[4] *The Jewish Study Bible, Tanakh Translation,* footnote to Exodus 2:10, 109.

[5] Ibid.

[6] Ibid.

Chapter 4

[1] Skutch, Robert, *Journey Without Distance: The Story Behind A Course in Miracles* (Berkeley, CA, Celestial Arts, 1984), 34.

Chapter 5

[1] Skutch, *Journey Without Distance,* 18.

Chapter 6

[1] Pharaoh's resistance and his changes of heart are mentioned 13 times in all.

[2] *A Course in Miracles, Text* (New York, Foundation for Inner Peace, 1975), "Sharing Perception with the Holy Spirit," 267.

Chapter 7

[1] In this instance, to paraphrase the old 12-step joke, denial really *is* a river in Egypt!

Chapter 8

[1] *A Course in Miracles, Manual for Teachers,* "How Is Judgment Relinquished?" 26.

[2] Adyashanti, *Emptiness Dancing* (Boulder, CO, Sounds True, 2004, 2006), 183-184.

[3] Ibid, 184.

[4] Rumi, Jelaluddin, from *Birdsong,* translated by Coleman Barks (Athens, GA, Maypop, 1993), 13.

Chapter 9

[1] The great cry the Egyptians make when they discover their firstborns dead forms a bookend to the enslaved Hebrews crying out at the end of Chapter 2 of Exodus. The Hebrews cry is heard by God. It marks the beginning of their journey to freedom. When Pharaoh and Egypt cry out, however, there is no solace. It's an exclamation point marking the inevitability of death and sorrow under ego's rule. And it "shall never be again" because we only need to experience ego-death once in order to dedicate ourselves to freedom.

[2] "All commentators agree that *Mitzrayim* [the Hebrew word for Egypt] represents *hardship, distress, oppression, a narrow place,* or *straits.*" See "The Symbolism of the Word 'Mitzrayim' (Egypt)," Etz-Hayim.com, n.d., Web. 24 September 2011.

[3] Ecclesiastes 1:2

[4] The death of Egypt's firstborns is also a fitting rejoinder to the first Pharaoh's decree at the start of Exodus that all male Hebrew infants be drowned in the Nile.

[5] Shantideva, *Guide to the Bodhisattva's Way of Life* (Ulverston, UK, Tharpa Publications, 2002), translated by Neil Elliott and Geshe Kelsang Gyatso, 8:29, 118.

[6] Michel de Montaigne, *Essays*, translated by Charles Cotton, Essay 19, "That To Study Philosophy Is To Learn To Die," *eBooks@Adelaide*, n.d., Web. 24 September, 2011.

[7] Seneca, *Epistles I–LXV, Loeb Classical Library*, Epistle XXVI, "On Old Age and Death," 191.

Chapter 10

[1] Gaster, *Myth, Legend, and Custom in the Old Testament*, 229.

[2] Melville, Herman, *Moby Dick or, The Whale* (Berkley, Arion/ Univ. of California Press, 1979), 490.

Chapter 11

[1] "German Myth 12: The Famous Goethe Quotation," *About.com*, n.d., Web. 24 September, 2011.

[2] *Alcoholics Anonymous* "Big Book," 3rd Edition, (New York, Alcoholics Anonymous World Services, 1976), 59.

[3] Ibid.

[4] Ibid.

[5] *A Course in Miracles, Workbook for Students*, Lesson 359, 474.

[6] Humphreys, Colin J., *The Miracles of Exodus* (New York, HarperCollins, 2003), 249, 253-54.

[7] *A Course in Miracles, Text*, Principles of Miracles, 1.

[8] Ibid.

[9] Ibid, "Looking Within," 214.

Chapter 13

[1] *The Jewish Study Bible, Tanakh Translation*, Footnote to Exodus 17: 5-6, 142.

[2] *A Course in Miracles, Text*, Principles of Miracles, 1.

[3] "Buddhist Studies: Lay Guide to the Monk's Rules," *Buddanet. Net*, n.d., Web. 24 September 2011.

[4] This truth is reflected in 12-step work by the maxim, "One day at a time." Recovery asks that we focus our efforts at sobriety for this one day only. When tomorrow comes, it will be this day. Looking to the future (or the past) is a distraction and risks a relapse back into addiction.

[5] *The Jewish Study Bible, Tanakh Translation*, Footnote to Exodus 16:14, 140.

[6] *Midrash Rabba*, Shemot 25:3.

[7] *The Jewish Study Bible, Tanakh Translation*, Footnote to Exodus 16:31, 141.

[8] *A Course in Miracles, Workbook for Students*, Lesson 186, 344.

[9] Frankl, Viktor, *Man's Search for Meaning* (New York, Washington Square Press, 1984), 64.

[10] For a fascinating discussion of the ways in which we arrive at our purchasing decisions, see Ariely, Dan, *Predictably Irrational*

(New York, HarperCollins, 2008), Chapter 1, "The Truth About Relativity."

Chapter 14

[1] In Exodus 3, the mountain of God is referred to as Mt. Horeb, but scholars agree it is the same mountain as Sinai.

[2] See Leviticus 27:30 and Numbers 18:21.

[3] Friedman, Richard Elliot, *Who Wrote the Bible?* (New York, HarperCollins, 1987), 191, 204.

[4] Kamenetz, Rodger, *The History of Last Night's Dream* (New York, HarperCollins, 2007), 106.

[5] Pagels, Elaine, *The Gnostic Gospels* ((New York, Vintage Books, Random House, 1979), 127.

[6] This passage also appears almost verbatim in the New Testament, in Hebrews 8:8–12.

Chapter 15

[1] The chronology of the story skips from Exodus chapter 20 to 24, and then to 32, in order to accommodate the many laws and detailed instructions for the building of the Tabernacle.

[2] Long, James D., *Riddle of Exodus* (Springdale, AR, Lightcatcher Books, 2006), 21-22.

[3] Ibid, 23.

[4] In the parable of Exodus, this would be equivalent to a new type of mind, one that's never known separation from God and is therefore proof against the ego and its mischief.

[5] Because the chronology of the story is fractured, like the tablets themselves, God instructs Moses to ordain Aaron and his sons as priests while Moses is still away on the mountain with God. So we may presume that Aaron does not yet know he's the chief priest when he agrees to forge the golden calf.

[6] Wolf, Laibl (Rabbi), *Practical Kabbalah* (New York, Three Rivers Press, 1999), 222–223.

[7] Ibid, 222.

[8] See Exodus 15:25 ". . . and there He tested them."

[9] *A Course in Miracles, Text,* "Sin versus Error," 374.

[10] Luke 15:11-32.

[11] *A Course in Miracles, Manual for Teachers,* Clarification of Terms, "Epilogue," 87.

Chapter 16

[1] Adapted by the author from several different internet translations.

[2] *A Course in Miracles, Workbook for Students,* Lesson 222, 392.

ॐ ॐ

bibliography

Adyashanti, *Emptiness Dancing*, Boulder, CO, Sounds True, 2004, 2006

Ariely, Dan, *Predictably Irrational*, New York, HarperCollins, 2008

Brown, Dan, *The Lost Symbol*, New York, Doubleday, 2009

A Course in Miracles: Text, Workbook for Students, Manual for Teachers, New York, Foundation for Inner Peace, 1975

Frankl, Viktor, *Man's Search for Meaning*, New York, Washington Square Press, 1984

Friedman, Richard Elliot, *Who Wrote the Bible?*, New York, HarperCollins, 1987

Gaster, Theodor H., *Myth, Legend, and Custom in the Old Testament*, New York, Harper and Row, 1969

Humphreys, Colin J., *The Miracles of Exodus*, New York, HarperCollins, 2003

The Jerusalem Bible, Garden City, NY, Doubleday & Co., 1966

The Jewish Study Bible, Tanakh Translation, New York, Oxford University Press, 2004

Kamenetz, Rodger, *The History of Last Night's Dream*, New York, HarperCollins, 2007

Long, James D., *Riddle of Exodus*, Springdale, AR, Lightcatcher Books, 2006

Melville, Herman, *Moby Dick or, The Whale*, Berkley, Arion/Univ. of California Press, 1979

Melzack, Ronald and Patrick D. Wall, *The Challenge of Pain*, New York, Basic Books, 1982

Montaigne, Michel de, *Essays*, translated by Charles Cotton

The New American Standard Bible, La Habra, CA, The Lockman Foundation, 1995, (featured on **www.BibleGateway.com**)

Pagels, Elaine, *The Gnostic Gospels*, New York, Vintage Books, Random House, 1979

Rumi, Jelaluddin, *Birdsong,* translated by Coleman Barks, Athens, GA, Maypop, 1993

Seneca, Lucius Annaeus, *Epistles I–LXV, Loeb Classical Library,* Cambridge, MA, Harvard University Press, 1917, 2006

Shantideva, *Guide to the Bodhisattva's Way of Life,* Ulverston, UK, Tharpa Publications, 2002

Skutch, Robert, *Journey Without Distance: The Story Behind A Course in Miracles,* Berkeley, CA, Celestial Arts, 1984

Tolle, Eckhart, *A New Earth: Awakening to Your Life's Purpose,* New York, Plume/Penguin Group, 2005

Wolf, Laibl (Rabbi), *Practical Kabbalah,* New York, Three Rivers Press, 1999

☙ ☙

Acknowledgments

---•◦•---

So many people have contributed to the writing of this book—far too many to acknowledge them all by name. The following individuals, however, deserve my special thanks.

Bill Thetford, Ph.D., co-scribe of *A Course in Miracles*, dear friend and mentor, who modeled the journey for so many of us by the way he lived.

Rachel Harris, Ph.D., who extracted from a rambling first draft the core structure for the current book. Without her help, *From Plagues to Miracles* would be a much inferior work.

Patricia Hopkins, for her thorough, honest, and invaluable feedback.

Bill "Whit" Whitson, for his succinct analysis of the first draft, and for our many wonderful conversations over the years.

Joe Loizzo, M.D., and his wife, Geri, for their enthusiastic encouragement early on, when I most needed it.

Patrick Schretlen and Jill and John Miller, for their unflagging support from the outset.

Rachelle and Wayne Rebarber, for hosting that fateful Seder.

Theodor H. Gaster, Visiting Professor of Religious Studies at Yale my freshman year, whose brilliant understanding of Passover (and just about everything else) planted the first seeds.

Dick Tyre, who taught me how to read—I mean, *really* read.

My literary agent, Bob Silverstein of Quicksilver Books, for recognizing the potential and steering this project to fruition.

My editors, Shannon Littrell and Patrick Gabrysiak, and all the other wonderful folks at Hay House for their help in making this book a reality.

Judy Skutch Whitson, for introducing me to *ACIM* at such a tender age and for her loving support over the decades.

Vivian Greenberg, LCSW, author, therapist, and mother extraordinaire.

Emmanuelle, my wife and companion on the journey, for her fierce and peerless editing, her almost infinite capacity for wisdom . . . and so much more.

My children, Sophia and Avery, for putting up with all the Moses talk.

Al Rosenthal, M.D., my father, a devout atheist who neverthe-less wholeheartedly supported this project. He would have been proud to see it, had he lived.

And most of all, to my psychotherapy patients of the past 30 years, especially those whose stories enrich this book. It's been a rare privilege working with each of you, and I honor and thank you for allowing me to be a part of your journey.

۞ ۞

About the Author

Robert Rosenthal, M.D., is a board-certified psychiatrist and psychotherapist in private practice in the Princeton, New Jersey, area. He is a former Assistant Clinical Professor of Psychiatry at Hahnemann University in Philadelphia (now part of Drexel) and at the University of California San Francisco School of Medicine. He was a close friend of Bill Thetford, Ph.D., one of the scribes of *A Course in Miracles*, and has served on the board of the Foundation for Inner Peace, the publisher of the *Course*, since 1992. He is also a novelist and screenwriter (see **IMDb.com**). *From Plagues to Miracles* is his first work of nonfiction. For more information, see **www.FromPlaguesToMiracles.com**.

NOTES

NOTES